To my darling mum, Judy Lance, who taught me to
cook by her magnificent example, and to Tom, who's
cheerfully eaten the results of those lessons for
28 years.

Sophie

For my husband, the one
and only Perry Westwood.

Katherine

The DINNER LADIES

Sophie Gilliatt
Katherine Westwood

MURDOCH BOOKS

SYDNEY · LONDON

Contents

INTRODUCTION   6

1. Thinner Dinners   12

2. Crowd-pleasers   52

3. Cosy Kitchen Suppers   100

4. Spice AND Fire   138

5. Rib Stickers   178

6. Sweet AND Easy   212

INDEX   250

ACKNOWLEDGEMENTS   255

Introduction

Whenever we're flicking through recipes in a cookbook, newspaper or magazine, we're always drawn to dishes we can make ahead, rather than ones requiring last-minute cooking. One celebrity chef (whom we admire wholeheartedly) has tried to convince the world that we can get dinner on the table in 15 or 30 minutes of frenzied, multi-tasking activity. But even he, with his perfect battery of kitchen equipment, expert knife skills and the energy of a Duracell bunny, doesn't make the job look easy.

The fact is that those of us who are responsible for dinner usually have a lot of other things on our plate as well. After work or the day's chores have been done, children or others ferried around and the shopping quickly grabbed, we've often arrived home to a pile of unsorted laundry, unwalked dogs and scary-looking mail. And then someone – a child, a spouse, a housemate – will, with an air of happy anticipation, ask us what's for dinner, with every expectation that it will be something delicious, creative and catering to their particular whimsical tastes. If they're lucky they get a polite answer, through gritted teeth. If they're very lucky they might even get dinner. It is, however, by no means certain.

It's a tough gig. We know – we live it too, with seven children between us (Sophie with three and Katherine four) and a business to run. But we all still do want to cook for our loved ones, we want to share good times and stories around the dinner table, we want to eat wholesome food that has been cooked with care – it's just we don't want to magic it up in the over-committed half hour between 6 pm and 6.30 pm, when we would rather be meditating, watching bad reality TV or pouring a very large glass of wine (substitute your stress-busting activity of choice here).

Our solution is to cook food that can be prepared ahead of time. It might be on the weekend, it could be late at night or in the morning when the baby's asleep. If you can find half an hour a couple of times a week, you can prepare a few dishes and stick them in the fridge or freezer – then, every time you pull out one of your delicious, home-made dinners you will congratulate yourself on your foresight and wow everyone you know with your efficiency.

If you try to get into the habit of making more than you need and refrigerating or freezing the excess, there are economies of scale both in cost and time. It takes just as long to make one curry as three, it's as quick to measure out a tablespoon of spice as a teaspoon, and a few kilos of meat cooks in the same time as one. As a bonus, if you cook a few extra, these make-ahead dishes are also perfect to take round to an elderly neighbour, sick friend, new parent or, indeed, anyone who could do with a bit of home-made cheer.

Our business, The Dinner Ladies, is a home-delivered dinner service, so a lot of our dinners are completely made ahead – dishes such as curries, pasta sauces and tagines, which are brilliant to stick in the fridge or freezer and only require reheating while you quickly cook some rice, pasta or couscous. Other dishes, such as pies or lasagnes, are completely assembled but need a final cook and usually can go straight into the oven from the freezer.

And then there are seemingly last-minute dishes such as stir-fries or salads, where the hard work of prepping vegetables, marinating meat and mixing up sauces or dressings can actually be done in advance, so that you only have to do a little relaxed, final tossing or wokking and dinner is served.

Food safety

Temperature control is very important when cooking ahead of time. Food is safest when it's very hot (70°C/158°F or above) or very cold (below 5°C/41°F). Anything in the middle is in the danger zone, where pathogens (the little devils responsible for food poisoning) thrive and multiply, more slowly at either end of the spectrum, more quickly in the middle.

So, when you're cooking, make sure food is piping hot (a meat thermometer is a useful tool) before taking it off the heat. To rapidly cool sauces, soups, stews, pie fillings or curries, simply spoon them out of the saucepan into a stainless steel bowl and sit that in a bigger stainless steel bowl two-thirds full of ice slurry (half ice cubes and half water). If you've made a big batch of food, cool it in smaller batches rather than trying to cool the whole quantity at once.

Make sure you stir the food till it has cooled to room temperature, then put it into storage containers, cover and refrigerate. Don't put piping hot food in the fridge – it's not designed to be a blast chiller and its temperature will rise and endanger the food already in the fridge, as well as not chilling your food efficiently.

Storage containers

Bowls are great for mixing but are space hogs in the fridge or freezer. The cheapest and best all-purpose storage containers are the rectangular plastic takeaway containers with lids because they're neat and stackable; if you don't have some already, you can buy them in sets at the supermarket. Not only are they good for storing dishes such as stews, they're excellent for keeping prepped herbs and vegetables or marinated meats for salads or stir-fries. Remember to label and date them with a permanent marker – otherwise, two months down the track you'll be gaily announcing that it's mystery meat for dinner again.

Zip-lock bags, big and small, are handy for storing chopped herbs or marinated meat, too – or, if you're really going to go to town, you could invest in a vacuum-sealing machine (not massively expensive and available at department stores). These extend the refrigerated shelf life of whatever they're sealing but are best for solid food (such as a marinated steak or chicken). Because they suck out most of the oxygen around the food, they're great for the freezer because they don't leave any exposed surfaces, which can be subject to freezer burn.

Cold storage

If you've heated and cooled your food safely, most prepared dishes should be fine in a good fridge for up to three days. We suggest three months as the upper end of freezer life, for the sake of quality rather than safety. If food stays frozen it is pretty much safe to the end of time (woolly mammoth steak, anyone?) but the texture can be impaired by longer storage.

Some people are prejudiced against frozen food, maybe because they associate it with over-processed convenience food. But freezing is a simple, additive-free form of preservation and retains the food's nutritional value as well as being super-convenient – what's not to like?

Defrosting and reheating

Almost any website you see about food safety suggests that you should only defrost in the fridge, which is fine and dandy if you're organised enough to know two days in advance what you want to eat. If, like us, you often need to thaw in a hurry, you can use a microwave or room-temperature running water in a sink. As long as you're going to finish the reheating or cooking process immediately and not leave defrosted food sitting around in the danger zone, it will be fine. What is much more dangerous is bringing out a frozen dinner in the morning and sitting it on a kitchen bench all day. It might have completely defrosted by lunchtime and then sat all afternoon, quietly breeding, without you knowing it, with potentially horrible consequences.

And when you're reheating, make sure that the food reaches 70°C (158°F), which is hot enough to kill most pathogens. If you don't have a thermometer, the food should be steaming hot throughout, not just at the edges; make sure it has been stirred thoroughly during the cooking process.

Finishing dishes

Most pre-prepared dishes require a little love when it's time to serve them. Sometimes the flavours might seem muted and may benefit from a splash of lemon juice or vinegar; other times, the seasoning might have been knocked back. Taste everything (it's the primary rule of cooking anyway, without which all else is redundant) and make whatever adjustments you deem necessary.

Almost all reheated dinners will need a bit of titivating for the table - a flurry of herbs or julienned chillies, a final grating of parmesan cheese, or whatever else might work with the dish - to add a final layer of bright flavour and to make them look as inviting as they are delicious.

Scaling up

For consistency, we've made almost all the recipes in this book to feed four but many lend themselves to scaling upwards, either to feed a crowd or to make future dinners for the freezer. We've become adept at scaling up recipes for The Dinner Ladies, but in the early days we had a few disasters, from which we've learned useful lessons. As people always tell you, you learn more from your mistakes than your achievements (we must be getting really good now). Here are some of our practical tips for scaling up:

* A small quantity needs proportionately more liquid than a larger one. When we first made Daube of Beef (see page 201) for maybe 24 people, multiplying up from a recipe for six, we couldn't work out why it was swimming in miserably thin liquid. The best advice when scaling up a braise or stew is to use just enough liquid to barely cover the meat - which will be much less than a simple multiplication of quantities from the base recipe.

* On a related point, the larger the quantity you're cooking, the harder it is to reduce a sauce at the end of cooking time to the desired consistency or intensity. With smaller quantities, reduction happens through evaporation as you cook, and it's easy to lift out solids and boil down any liquid at the end of cooking time. But in a larger quantity, there is a smaller surface area to dish ratio, so there's less reduction. We get around this by reducing liquids before they go in, so we'll boil down the wine and/or stock first, then add them to the dish.

* This may not make scientific sense, but season more sparingly as you multiply a dish upwards. You might put 1 teaspoon of salt in a dish for four, but if you add 2 teaspoons to the same dish for eight, it may be too salty.

Season conservatively as you go and taste at the end of cooking.

* On the whole, the more you're cooking, the longer cooking times will be. A deep pot will also cook at different rates from the bottom to the top, so give your food a good stir every so often to ensure that it cooks evenly.

Cooking for a crowd

Over the years, we've come up with a few practical tips for cooking for a crowd, which we'd like to share:

* Make sure everything can be prepared ahead of time (hey, that's what this book is for). There's nothing less relaxing than chopping and plucking in front of admiring onlookers.

* Clear out your fridge before you start cooking. All those weird condiments, flat tonic water bottles and bendy carrots – out. You want to have room for all your lovely neat tubs of prepared ingredients. But even so ...

* Put your biggest esky (portable cooler) in the corner of the kitchen and fill it with ice. People always buy ice for drinks for parties but it's the food that puts the most stress on the poor fridge. With a big esky, you can double your cold storage capacity. Before Christmas, we'll often have eskies going for days with brined turkeys and hams in them, just topping up the ice every so often. It makes a big difference.

* Don't be afraid to keep it simple. If you have the Under-10 football team plus their parents descending on you, there's no point in making five different, creative and nutritionally balanced salads – give them pulled pork and coleslaw in a roll with ice cream in a cone afterwards and they'll all be happy. And you won't have any washing-up to do! Which brings us to the next point ...

* Minimise washing-up! If you've chosen food that can't be eaten in the hand, seriously consider disposable plates. This doesn't have to mean tacky placky or sagging paper – there's such great stuff out there now, such as eco-friendly bamboo or woven palm leaf plates. Noodle boxes and wooden chopsticks are always cute and lots of desserts work brilliantly in paper cups. When you dispose of everything in 10 minutes at the end of the night – composting and recycling as you see fit – you will know yourself to be a genius.

* We know this is a seditious observation to make in a cookbook but the success of any gathering rarely rests on your cooking. As long as the food is plentiful, the company in good spirits and the drinks are flowing, everyone's going to have a great time.

THINNER
Dinners

We don't set out to tell people how or what they should eat. We figure there's already a pretty crowded marketplace of fit young things with shiny teeth and blue-white eyes trying to convince us to eat more of the latest wonder food or less of something we've been eating perfectly happily all our lives.

But we are also, shall we say, women of a certain age and we're aware that we can no longer maintain an unbroken diet of lasagne and twice-cooked pork belly. So we also love a Thinner Dinner (one that's low in kilojoules, fat and carbs) at least some of the time, like in the panicky lead-up to summer holidays.

To make the grade with us, a Thinner Dinner has to be a delight rather than a duty to eat, packed with vibrant flavour and contrasting textures. Sit down to a plate of carrot and cucumber sticks and you'll be in no doubt you're on a diet, with the immediate sense of resentment and deprivation that entails. But if you're presented with those same carrot and cucumber sticks, lightly pickled in rice vinegar, with maybe some lean strips of teriyaki beef on the side, well, now you have something to get excited about.

Outside this chapter, a lot of other dishes in this book can still fit the bill as a Thinner Dinner – so much depends on what you make as an accompaniment. Try cauliflower mash puréed with stock instead of mashed potato, zucchini 'spaghetti' instead of pasta, serve meatballs over a big pile of salad or a stir-fry tossed through shirataki noodles. And vast amounts of leafy greens – as a salad or cooked – with everything! By the time you've chomped through them, you'll have forgotten you were ever hungry.

Sesame Prawn Stir-fry
WITH *Asparagus* AND *Broccolini*

SERVES 6   PREP TIME 30 MINUTES   COOKING TIME 20 MINUTES

140 ml (4½ fl oz) soy sauce (gluten-free if desired)

140 ml (4½ fl oz) mirin (rice wine)

1½ tablespoons light brown sugar

1½ tablespoons lemon juice

2 teaspoons sesame oil

1 tablespoon peanut oil or other mild-flavoured oil

1 x 5 cm (2 inch) piece ginger, sliced and cut into very thin matchsticks

3 garlic cloves, thinly sliced

1 kg (2 lb 4 oz) raw prawns (shrimp), peeled and deveined, tails intact

500 g (1 lb 2 oz/2 bunches) broccolini, stalks cut in half lengthways, then across into 5 cm (2 inch) pieces

300 g (10½ oz/2 bunches) asparagus, ends removed and cut into 5 cm (2 inch) pieces

200 g (7 oz) mushrooms (button, fresh shiitake, enoki or whatever looks good), wiped and sliced

8 spring onions (scallions), ends removed, cut into 3 cm (1¼ inch) pieces

2 large handfuls baby English spinach

TO SERVE

1½ tablespoons sesame seeds, toasted

soba noodles or steamed rice

A Japanese-inspired stir-fry of prawns, spring onions, asparagus, mushrooms and broccolini, with a mirin and soy dressing and a lavish sprinkling of toasted sesame seeds. As with other stir-fries, if you do the (not very) hard work earlier, the final flurry of activity seems effortless while making a big impact.

Make ahead: *The finishing sauce can be prepared up to 1 week ahead and kept in an airtight container in the fridge. The vegetables can be fully prepped 1 day ahead of cooking.*

For the finishing sauce, combine the soy, mirin and brown sugar in a saucepan and boil over high heat till the sugar is dissolved and the sauce is lightly reduced (by about 25%) and syrupy. This should take about 5 minutes. Cool before adding the lemon juice and sesame oil and tasting for balance. Set aside.

Heat a wok over high heat until smoking hot, swirl the peanut oil around it and add the ginger, garlic and prawns, in a few batches if necessary to avoid overcrowding. Stir-fry the prawns briskly, scooping and flipping for about 2 minutes till they've just changed colour and have lost their translucency. Quickly remove them to a bowl and reheat the wok, adding more oil if necessary.

When the wok is smoking, add the broccolini pieces and stir-fry them for 1 minute, then add the asparagus. These vegetables will take the longest to cook so keep flipping and tossing till they are still crisp but beginning to be tender, about 4–5 minutes. If they are thick or just taking their time, you can add 2 tablespoons of water to the wok, jam on a lid and steam them for a few minutes, then uncover and boil the water off.

Add the mushrooms and spring onions to the wok and give a quick toss for 1 minute before returning the prawns to the wok and adding the baby spinach. You may need to use two wooden spoons to combine all the vegetables and prawns. As soon as the spinach starts to wilt, pour in the finishing sauce and give everything a last toss.

Sprinkle with toasted sesame seeds and serve with cooked soba noodles or steamed rice.

Spring Pea Soup with Lettuce and Mint

SERVES 4 PREP TIME 10 MINUTES COOKING TIME 30 MINUTES

1 tablespoon salted butter

600 g (1 lb 5 oz) French shallots or onions, diced

1 teaspoon salt

1 iceberg lettuce, outer leaves and core removed, shredded

800 g (1 lb 12 oz) frozen baby peas, defrosted

1 litre (35 fl oz/4 cups) vegetable stock

1 large handful mint, leaves only

TO SERVE

cream or plain yoghurt

toasted sourdough bread or Sourdough Croutons (see page 132)

freshly ground black pepper

This is a delightfully light, fresh, springy sort of soup. You could even serve it cold on a hot summer's day. And don't even contemplate using fresh peas for this dish unless you grow them and have both a glut and an army of unpaid labourers. Frozen are better than fine.

Make ahead: The whole soup may be made ahead and stored in an airtight container either in the fridge for up to 3 days or in the freezer for up to 3 months. Defrost and stir as you reheat to bring the soup back together.

Melt the butter in a large saucepan and gently cook the shallots or onions with the salt over low heat for about 10–15 minutes until sweet, soft and translucent. Add the lettuce, stirring until it is soft and wilted.

Stir in the baby peas, cover with the vegetable stock, turn the temperature up and bring to the boil, then turn down to medium–low and simmer for 10 minutes. Allow to cool slightly, then add two-thirds of the mint leaves to the soup and purée, using a stick blender or food processor. Taste for seasoning.

Serve, scattered with the remaining mint leaves, a swirl of cream or yoghurt, toasted sourdough bread or croutons and plenty of freshly ground black pepper.

Prosciutto-wrapped Chicken
AND *Pistachio Terrine*

SERVES 4   PREP TIME 35 MINUTES, PLUS 4 HOURS CHILLING   COOKING TIME 55 MINUTES

1 tablespoon olive oil

1 large brown onion, diced

2 garlic cloves, crushed

1½ teaspoons salt

500 g (1 lb 2 oz) minced (ground) chicken

2 thyme sprigs, leaves stripped and finely chopped

3 tarragon sprigs, leaves stripped and finely chopped (if unavailable, substitute 1 tablespoon chopped chives)

30 g (1 oz/½ cup) fresh breadcrumbs (substitute gluten-free crumbs if you'd like)

45 g (1½ oz/⅓ cup) pistachio nut kernels

1 egg, beaten

1½ tablespoons wholegrain mustard

freshly ground black pepper

100 g (3½ oz) prosciutto slices

100 g (3½ oz) chicken breast fillet, sliced through lengthways to give long, thin pieces

TO SERVE

mixed green salad

Beetroot and Apple Relish (opposite) or chutney

cornichons (baby gherkins or pickles)

Terrines have an undeserved reputation for being fiddly and fatty but they needn't be so. This one is simple to make, easy on the eye, low in the fat department (especially if you use minced chicken breast) and makes a lovely light lunch or supper with some salad leaves and a chutney or relish.

Make ahead: *The whole terrine should be assembled and cooked 1 day ahead. Once made, it can be kept, covered, in the fridge for up to 5 days, or encased in layers of plastic wrap and frozen for up to 3 months.*

In a small saucepan or frying pan, heat the olive oil over low heat and cook the onion and garlic with 1 teaspoon of the salt for about 10–15 minutes until soft and sweet. Set aside to cool.

In a stainless steel bowl, mix the onion mixture with the minced chicken, herbs, breadcrumbs, pistachios, beaten egg, mustard and a good grind of black pepper.

Preheat the oven to 190°C (375°F).

Make a small patty out of the chicken mixture, about 3 cm (1¼ inches) in diameter, and cook in a small non-stick frying pan over medium heat on both sides until cooked through. This should only take 2 minutes per side. Taste for seasoning – salt especially – and adjust the mixture to your taste.

Take out a small loaf (bar) tin – about 13 x 23 cm (5 x 9 inch)/650 ml (22½ fl oz) capacity – and line it with a large sheet of baking paper, making sure you poke the paper into the four corners. Use the prosciutto slices to line the base and sides of the tin, crossways, so they overhang on each side of the tin, leaving 1–2 slices for the top.

Fill the prosciutto-lined tin with half the chicken mixture, then lay the pieces of chicken breast fillet on top so they fit together in one thin layer only. Sprinkle with the remaining ½ teaspoon of salt, then press the rest of the chicken mixture firmly on top. Fold the overhanging slices of prosciutto over the top so it's a lovely, neat package, then lay the reserved slices lengthways on the terrine, tucking them in at either end.

Put the terrine in a deep ovenproof dish and place in the oven. Use a kettle to fill the dish with hot water up to the level of the terrine's top. After 40 minutes of cooking, check that it's ready by inserting a metal skewer or sharp knife into its centre, then lightly touching it to your lip. It should be piping hot. Alternatively, use a meat thermometer and check that it reads about 75°C (165°F). Pour off the juice that has collected in the tin and cool, in the tin, to room temperature, covered with a tea towel (dish towel). When cool, cover with plastic wrap and place in the fridge for 4 hours or overnight.

To serve, turn the terrine out onto a carving board or platter and, using a sharp knife, cut into neat slices about 2 cm (¾ inch) thick.

Serve with a mixed green salad of baby leaves, cornichons and/or some chutney or relish, such as the beetroot and apple one below.

Beetroot AND Apple Relish

This is a handy chutney to have in the fridge to liven up a basic ploughman's sort of lunch or to do duty in a burger instead of the acrid tinned stuff. Oh, and it makes a lovely accompaniment to the terrine as well. Soften a sliced onion (any colour) in some mildly flavoured oil in a medium saucepan with a pinch of salt, then add 3 grated beetroot (beets), 1 large peeled, cored and diced granny smith apple, 1 teaspoon finely grated ginger, ½ teaspoon ground coriander, 125 ml (4 fl oz/½ cup) red wine vinegar, 55 g (2 oz/¼ cup) sugar and a good grind of black pepper. Cook down for about 25 minutes till the relish is thick and tender. Dish up into hot, sterilised jars if you want to keep it for a long time; otherwise, it will be fine in the fridge for up to 2 weeks.

PROSCIUTTO-WRAPPED CHICKEN
& PISTACHIO TERRINE, *page* 18

SPINACH, RICOTTA & FETA
FILO PIE, *page 22*

Spinach, Ricotta *and* Feta Filo Pie

SERVES 4   PREP TIME 30 MINUTES   COOKING TIME 1 HOUR 5 MINUTES

500 g (1 lb 2 oz) frozen English spinach
2 teaspoons olive oil
1 large brown onion, diced
1 teaspoon salt
1 garlic clove, crushed
1 large handful mint, leaves plucked and chopped
1 large handful parsley, leaves plucked and chopped
1 small handful dill, leaves plucked and chopped
pinch of freshly grated nutmeg
1 large egg, beaten
150 g (5½ oz) good quality feta cheese, diced
150 g (5½ oz) ricotta (low-fat if you prefer)
olive oil spray
150 g (5½ oz/8 sheets) filo pastry

TO SERVE
Greek Salad (opposite) or a tomato salad

This is a low-fat, rustic take on a traditional Greek spanakopita, with ricotta replacing some of the feta and just one spritz of olive oil on the pie's ruffled top instead of the quite unnecessary – though we'd have to admit, quite delicious – melted butter on every layer. Filo itself is pretty healthy as pastry goes, containing only 3% fat as opposed to up to 50% for puff pastry, making it a perfect Thinner Dinner pie.

Make ahead: *The whole pie can be made 1 day ahead, wrapped in plastic wrap and refrigerated, before baking. It can also be frozen successfully – defrost before spraying with oil and baking as below.*

Preheat the oven to 200°C (400°F).

Defrost the spinach in a colander. Squeeze out as much water as you can and set aside.

In a medium frying pan over low heat, heat the oil and cook the onion with the salt gently for about 10–15 minutes, till sweet and soft but not brown. Add the garlic and cook for a further 2 minutes. Remove and set aside to cool.

In a large mixing bowl, stir together the onion, garlic, spinach, herbs, nutmeg, egg, feta and ricotta. Feta's saltiness can vary hugely so taste the mixture for seasoning and adjust it to your taste.

Spray a 20 cm (8 inch) spring-form cake tin with olive oil spray.

Lay 2 filo sheets horizontally across the cake tin, patting them down into the tin. Take another 2 sheets and place them at a 90-degree angle across the first sheets. Turn the cake tin 45 degrees and place another 2 sheets across, horizontally, and another 2 sheets at a 90-degree angle. This all sounds very complicated and mathematical but it's very simple – you should end up with the base of the tin covered by filo, with excess filo draped over the sides of the tin.

Spoon the pie filling into the centre and fold the filo over the top, as messily or as neatly as you choose – messy creates more brown ruffles.

Spritz the top of the pie with olive oil spray and place in the preheated oven for 35–45 minutes. The top may brown earlier than that but don't take it out too soon – filo likes a good long cook to get nice and crisp. Check with a skewer that it's hot through to the centre before removing from the oven.

Allow to cool to room temperature before serving in wedges with a Greek salad – or make a simple tomato salad by combining some thickly sliced tomatoes with salt, oregano leaves and extra virgin olive oil.

Greek Salad

If you haven't made a Greek salad for a while, it's worth reminding yourself what a brilliantly balanced dish it should be, with every element – sweet tomatoes, salty olives, creamy feta, crisp vegetables – providing layers of complementary contrast. Feta varies in quality and taste – see if you can taste a sample before you buy. For a salad for four, mix together 1 telegraph (long) cucumber (chopped or sliced), ¼ red onion (thinly sliced and soaked in cold water, then squeezed dry), 200 g (7 oz/1 punnet) halved grape tomatoes (baby roma/plum tomatoes), 1 handful shiny, plump kalamata olives, 1 handful dill sprigs, 1 handful mint leaves and ½ green capsicum (pepper), chopped or sliced. Dress at the last minute with extra virgin olive oil, lemon juice and white wine vinegar in a ratio of 4:1:1 – we like this dressing on the acidic side – and sprinkle with flakes of salt.

Super Foods Salad

SERVES 4   PREP TIME 25 MINUTES   COOKING TIME 30 MINUTES

450 g (1 lb) sweet potato, diced into 2 cm (¾ inch) cubes
2 teaspoons olive oil
½ teaspoon salt
½ teaspoon sumac
160 g (5½ oz) quinoa
300 g (10½ oz) frozen edamame (green soya beans)
2 spring onions (scallions), ends removed, thinly sliced
1 large handful flat-leaf (Italian) parsley, leaves only, coarsely chopped
1 large handful mint, leaves only, coarsely chopped
100 g (3½ oz) baby English spinach
1 heaped tablespoon slivered almonds, toasted
2 teaspoons sesame seeds, toasted

GINGER-SOY DRESSING
2 tablespoons lemon juice
2 tablespoons gluten-free light soy sauce
1 teaspoon sesame oil
1 x 4 cm (1½ inch) piece ginger, grated
2 teaspoons honey

We came up with this recipe almost as a joke, to see how many 'super foods' we could poke into one salad. What we didn't anticipate was how delicious it would be and how obsessed people would become with it. It makes a perfect jar salad to take to work or school so it's worth making a big batch at a time.

Make ahead: *The dressing can be made up to 1 week ahead and kept in an airtight container in the fridge. All the elements for the salad can be made up to 3 days ahead. The quinoa can be cooked, cooled and mixed with the herbs, edamame and spring onions and kept in an airtight container in the fridge, with the sweet potato in a separate container. The nuts and seeds can be toasted, cooled and kept in a small airtight jar up to 1 week ahead. Allow the sweet potato to come up to room temperature before assembling the salad.*

Preheat the oven to 180°C (350°F).

For the dressing, mix together all the ingredients. Taste for the balance of sweet, sour and salt and make any adjustments you'd like. Set aside in a sealed container in the fridge.

Toss the sweet potato in the olive oil with the salt and sumac in a roasting tin and roast for 30 minutes, or until golden brown and tender. Set aside to cool.

While the sweet potato is roasting, rinse the quinoa well in a sieve and then measure the grain in a measuring cup. Measure 1.5 times that volume of water, pour it into a medium saucepan and bring to the boil over high heat. Add the quinoa, turn the heat right down (use a simmer pad if you have one), cover and simmer for 12 minutes. Turn the heat off and let it stand for another 10 minutes. If the water hasn't yet all been absorbed, rest for another 5 minutes. Uncover the quinoa, fluff it up with a fork and refrigerate, covered, as soon as it has stopped steaming.

Bring well-salted water to the boil in a small saucepan and add the edamame for 30 seconds. Drain under running water to cool, then release the beans by squeezing the pods gently over a bowl.

To assemble the salad, mix the quinoa with the spring onions, parsley, mint and edamame.

Arrange the baby spinach leaves in a bowl, slicked with a little of the dressing. Toss the quinoa with the rest of the dressing and arrange on top of the spinach with the roast sweet potato on top. Scatter with the toasted almonds and sesame seeds and serve.

Teriyaki Beef WITH
Sesame Pickled Vegetables

SERVES 4   PREP TIME 15 MINUTES, PLUS 3 HOURS MARINATING
COOKING TIME 10 MINUTES, PLUS 10 MINUTES RESTING

800 g (1 lb 12 oz) rump (round) steak, trimmed of all fat, cut about 1.5 cm (5/8 inch) thick
3 teaspoons peanut oil or other mild-flavoured oil

PICKLED VEGETABLES
1 telegraph (long) cucumber, peeled, seeded and cut into batons
2 carrots, sliced lengthways and cut into batons
4–5 small radishes, thinly sliced
2 tablespoons mirin (rice wine)
240 ml (8 fl oz) rice vinegar
2 teaspoons salt
2 tablespoons caster (superfine) sugar

TERIYAKI MARINADE
3 tablespoons dark soy sauce (gluten-free if desired)
1½ tablespoons mirin (rice wine)
1½ tablespoons dark brown sugar
½ garlic clove, crushed
1 x 2 cm (¾ inch) piece ginger, grated

TO SERVE
sliced spring onions (scallions)
toasted sesame seeds
steamed rice

Both the main elements in this dish are a moveable feast. You could serve the teriyaki beef with some lightly steamed green vegetables like asparagus, snow peas (mangetout) or broccolini, dressed with soy and mirin, or replace the beef with Teriyaki Salmon (see page 31). The pickled vegetables make an addictive snack straight from the fridge, too.

Make ahead: The meat may be marinated, put in a zip-lock or vacuum-sealer bag and kept in the fridge for up to 3 days or frozen for up to 3 months. The vegetables need to be made 1 day ahead but can be made up to 1 week ahead and stored in an airtight container in the fridge.

For the pickled vegetables, stack the cucumber, carrots and radishes in clean jars or other heatproof containers (this is only a quick pickle and need only last for 1 week so the jars don't have to be sterilised).

In a small saucepan, combine the mirin, rice vinegar, salt, caster sugar and 80 ml (2½ fl oz/⅓ cup) of water, and bring to the boil over medium heat. Turn down to a simmer and stir till the sugar is dissolved.

Pour hot over the vegetables, allow to cool a bit, then cover and refrigerate at least overnight or for up to 1 week.

For the teriyaki marinade, combine all the ingredients in a saucepan over medium–high heat. Bring to the boil, then turn down and simmer till the sugar is dissolved.

Before marinating the steak, cool the marinade to fridge temperature – you can do this quickly in a stainless steel bowl placed inside another one half-filled with ice and water, stirring the marinade frequently until chilled. Place the steaks in the marinade, cover and refrigerate for at least 3 hours or up to 3 days.

When ready to cook, take the steaks out of the marinade, allowing the excess to drain off into a small saucepan.

Preheat a chargrill pan or barbecue hotplate till very hot, rub the hot surface with oil and cook the steaks for 3 minutes each side (for medium-rare) or until done to your liking (cut a little piece to be sure), basting every couple of minutes with the reserved marinade. Rest for 10 minutes.

To serve, scoop the pickled vegetables out of their pickling liquid with a slotted spoon and place on a platter or individual plates.

Slice the beef into 5 mm (¼ inch) thick slices across the grain and arrange next to the vegetables. Scatter with sliced spring onions and toasted sesame seeds and serve with steamed rice on the side.

Tom Yam Goong

SERVES 4   PREP TIME 15 MINUTES   COOKING TIME 25 MINUTES

30 g (1 oz) piece galangal, coarsely chopped
2 lemongrass stems, white parts only, chopped
1 red onion, diced
1 small handful coriander (cilantro), roots and stems separated, leaves plucked
6 bird's eye chillies, seeded (or leave seeds in for extra heat)
1 teaspoon salt
1.25 litres (44 fl oz/5 cups) chicken stock (home-made or low/no salt)
6 kaffir lime leaves, crushed
3 tablespoons fish sauce
2 tablespoons sugar
500 g (1 lb 2 oz) raw tiger prawns (shrimp), peeled and deveined
200 g (7 oz) straw mushrooms, drained
80 ml (2½ fl oz/⅓ cup) lime juice (about 3 limes)

TO SERVE
Shirataki Noodles (below) (optional), drained and rinsed thoroughly

• •

NOTE: Galangal is a rhizome that's often likened to ginger. It's tougher to cut and very perfumed. You can usually find it at supermarkets or Asian grocers.

Hot, sour and spicy, with the clean flavours of lime, lemongrass and galangal, this prawn soup from Thailand is a tonic for anything that ails you, body or soul. It's also low-fat and low-calorie to boot. Now, we understand that there are some people who would rather experience chilli as a tingle than a mucous membrane–shredding out-of-body experience. We get that. But this one's supposed to be spicy – dial it down if you must.

Make ahead: *The whole soup can be prepared up to the time of adding the prawns and refrigerated in an airtight container for 3 days or frozen for up to 3 months. Just defrost it and bring it up to heat before adding the prawns.*

In the bowl of a small food processor or using a stick blender, blitz the galangal, lemongrass, red onion, coriander roots and bird's eye chillies with the salt. Use a bit of water or stock to help if necessary (it doesn't need to be super-fine as it will be strained).

In a 2 litre (70 fl oz/8 cup) saucepan, bring the stock to the boil over high heat, add the galangal/chilli paste and reduce the heat to low. Simmer for 20 minutes, then strain into a clean saucepan.

Bring the soup back to the boil and add the kaffir lime leaves, fish sauce and sugar. Reduce the heat to a simmer. Add the shirataki noodles (if using) before adding the prawns and straw mushrooms. Cook gently for a few minutes or until the prawns are pink and opaque. (The prawns may make the broth cloudy – if a clear broth is important to you, poach them separately in salted water and add to the broth when cooked.)

Add the lime juice and taste for seasoning – it should be fiery, sour and not too sweet but adjust it to your taste.

Scatter with coriander leaves and serve.

Shirataki Noodles

Shirataki noodles are the best friend of the carb-avoider. This Japanese noodle, made from the konjac root, comes in at an amazingly low 40 kJ (9.5 cal) per 100 g (3½ oz), with about 1 g of that being carbohydrate. They taste, well, frankly, of nothing much at all, but they do deliver a pleasing, bouncy, noodle-like slipperiness and they're sold at most supermarkets under names like 'Low Carb noodles'. They always come fresh in a packet of not-very-pleasant-smelling water, which needs to be drained. They're best dry-fried in a non-stick pan before using but they can be added straight to soups or stir-fries after rinsing.

Vietnamese Chicken Salad

<u>SERVES</u> 4–6   <u>PREP TIME</u> 30 MINUTES   <u>COOKING TIME</u> 20 MINUTES

500 g (1 lb 2 oz) chicken breast fillets

1 kg (2 lb 4 oz) Chinese cabbage (wong bok), end removed, quartered lengthways and thinly sliced

300 g (10½ oz) carrots, coarsely grated or cut into very thin matchsticks

6 spring onions (scallions), ends removed, thinly sliced

1 large handful mint, leaves only, coarsely chopped

2 large handfuls coriander (cilantro), leaves only, coarsely chopped

50 g (1¾ oz/⅓ cup) unsalted roasted peanuts, lightly crushed

2½ tablespoons sesame seeds, toasted

VIETNAMESE DRESSING

2 long red chillies, seeded and coarsely chopped

2 garlic cloves, coarsely chopped

100 g (3½ oz/½ cup lightly packed) light brown sugar

2 tablespoons white rice vinegar (or substitute cider vinegar)

100 ml (3½ fl oz) lime juice (about 4 limes)

100 ml (3½ fl oz) fish sauce

TO SERVE

prawn crackers (optional)

For us, this is the definitive Asian salad: healthy, low-fat, low-carb and packed with flavour, crunch and other positive, go-getting qualities. If you poach the chicken breasts and prep the vegetables and dressing earlier, the whole thing comes together in moments – perfect for a midweek summer dinner.

Make ahead: The chicken can be poached up to 2 days ahead and kept in an airtight container in the fridge. Alternatively, poach a few breasts at the same time and, when cool, wrap them tightly in plastic wrap or put them in a zip-lock bag and freeze for up to 3 months – pull one out to defrost whenever you need some for a salad or sandwiches. The dressing may be made up to 1 week ahead and stored in an airtight jar in the fridge. The salad, minus the dressing and the nuts, can be made up to 2 days ahead and kept, refrigerated, in an airtight container.

Trim any visible fat or sinew off the chicken breasts. In a wide saucepan, bring 1.5 litres (52 fl oz/6 cups) of well-salted water to the boil over high heat and then add the chicken breast fillets. Turn the heat down to a low simmer and gently poach the chicken for 10 minutes. Turn the heat off, cover with the saucepan lid and let the chicken continue cooking for a further 10 minutes. Remove with tongs and allow to cool until it's stopped steaming, then cover and refrigerate.

For the Vietnamese dressing, mix all the ingredients in a small food processor bowl or a stick blender container and blitz for a couple of minutes, until well blended. Taste for sweet/sour/salty balance and adjust to your liking.

When ready to serve, shred the chicken breasts with your fingers into rough, bite-sized pieces.

Mix the Chinese cabbage, carrots, spring onions, mint and coriander in a large bowl. Add half the dressing, half the chicken and half the nuts and seeds and toss it all together. Arrange on a platter and scatter with the remaining chicken, nuts and seeds, drizzled with the rest of the dressing.

Serve the salad on its own or with prawn crackers.

Teriyaki Salmon WITH AN Asian Herb Salad

SERVES 4   PREP TIME 30 MINUTES, PLUS 30 MINUTES–3 HOURS MARINATING   COOKING TIME 10 MINUTES

500 g (1 lb 2 oz) boneless, skinless
   salmon fillets, can be 2 x 250 g
   (9 oz) pieces

TERIYAKI MARINADE

2 tablespoons light soy sauce
   (gluten-free if desired)
2 tablespoons mirin (rice wine)
2 teaspoons brown sugar
1 x 2 cm (¾ inch) piece ginger, grated
½ garlic clove, crushed

SALAD DRESSING

1 x 3 cm (1¼ inch) piece ginger, grated
2 teaspoons sesame oil
3 tablespoons honey
3 tablespoons lemon juice
3 tablespoons fish sauce
1½ tablespoons light soy sauce
   (gluten-free if desired)

SALAD

1 red capsicum (pepper), seeded and
   cut lengthways into 5 mm (¼ inch)
   strips
100 g (3½ oz) snow peas (mangetout),
   trimmed, stringed and cut lengthways
   into 5 mm (¼ inch) strips
1 telegraph (long) cucumber, peeled,
   seeded and cut into batons 5 mm
   (¼ inch) x 5 cm (2 inches)
1 large handful tatsoi (substitute baby
   English spinach if it's unavailable)
50 g (1¾ oz) snow pea (mangetout)
   sprouts, stalky ends trimmed off
1 large handful chives, trimmed and
   cut into 2 cm (¾ inch) lengths
1 large handful mint, leaves plucked
1 large handful coriander (cilantro),
   leaves plucked

TO SERVE

2 tablespoons unsalted roasted
   peanuts, lightly crushed
2 heaped tablespoons crisp fried
   shallots

We love this dish as a light lunch, especially in summer, when the combination of crisp, cool vegetables and warm, flaked salmon is particularly welcome. The crisp fried shallots and peanuts are perhaps not strictly Thinner Dinner ingredients – and by all means skip them if you're being tough on yourself – but they're always the bits people scramble for at the bottom of the bowl.

Make ahead: The marinade can be made up to 1 week in advance. The salmon is best marinated up to 3 hours before cooking. All the salad elements can be prepared the day before and kept in a container in the fridge. Leave the shallots and peanuts out until just before serving and keep the dressing in a separate container.

Start by making your teriyaki marinade. In a small, heavy-based saucepan over medium heat, boil the soy sauce, mirin and brown sugar till it is syrupy and reduced by half. Add the ginger and garlic and set aside to cool, then refrigerate. When it is completely cold, add the salmon and marinate for between 30 minutes and 3 hours, then keep covered in the fridge.

Make your salad dressing by whisking together all of the ingredients. It should be tart, gingery, salty and delicious – make any adjustments that you would like.

Assemble all your salad ingredients in a large mixing bowl. If you're assembling ahead of time, layer the wettest and heaviest ingredients (cucumber and red capsicum) first, then the snow peas, sprouts and tatsoi and finally the herbs.

In a heavy-based, non-stick frying pan over medium heat, cook the marinated salmon till it is caramelised on the outside and beginning to become opaque inside. The cooking time will depend on the thickness of your fillets – start to check to see if it is done after 3 minutes each side. You will be flaking it anyway, so it doesn't matter if you make a bit of a mess of the fillets. If your salmon is very thick, you may be better off searing it for 2 minutes a side in an ovenproof pan, then putting the whole pan in a preheated 180°C (350°F) oven for 4 minutes.

When the fish is done, set it aside to cool slightly. Use a fork to flake the flesh.

Toss the salad ingredients with most of the dressing and arrange on a large platter. Strew the flaked salmon artfully on top and sprinkle with one last drizzle of dressing and the nuts and shallots before serving.

Skirt Steak Chimichurri

SERVES 4   PREP TIME 5 MINUTES, PLUS 3 HOURS MARINATING
COOKING TIME 8 MINUTES, PLUS 10 MINUTES RESTING

4 x 200–250 g (7–9 oz) skirt steaks
olive oil

CHIMICHURRI
4 garlic cloves, coarsely chopped
1 French shallot, coarsely chopped
1½ large handfuls flat-leaf (Italian)
   parsley, stalks and leaves, coarsely
   chopped
1 small handful oregano, leaves only,
   coarsely chopped
3 tablespoons red wine vinegar
1½ tablespoons lemon juice
3 tablespoons extra virgin olive oil
1 teaspoon salt

TO SERVE
green salad
Squashed Potatoes (see page 73)

We're big fans of the lesser-known steak cuts, such as skirt, flank and flat iron. For us, they have a more interesting texture and depth of flavour than your average rump or sirloin and they lend themselves to different treatments, such as marinating and slicing after cooking. We'd rarely choose to sit down to a man-size slab of steak on a plate, but a few slices of rare, juicy, marinated beef, strewn across a salad and punched up with a tart green sauce? Now we're talking.

Make ahead: The chimichurri marinade and sauce can be made up to 3 days ahead of time and stored in the fridge in an airtight container. The steak can be marinated up to 1 day ahead. You can freeze the steaks in their marinade but the sauce will lose its colour and look a bit muddy.

Throw all the chimichurri ingredients into the bowl of a food processor and blitz until completely blended into a thick, green sauce.

Remove 3 tablespoons of the sauce and use to marinate the steaks. Set aside in the fridge, covered, for at least 3 hours or overnight.

When ready to cook, preheat a barbecue hotplate or chargrill pan until fiercely hot. Rub the hot surface with a little olive oil, drain the steaks of excess marinade and cook the steaks for 3–4 minutes each side or until done to your liking.

Rest, covered, for 10 minutes before slicing across the grain (see below) into thick fingers. Serve on top of a big pile of salad, drizzled with the remaining chimichurri and (not strictly Thinner Dinners, this, we know) with roasted squashed new potatoes on the side.

Against the Grain

Recipes often go on about slicing against the grain, but is it really necessary? The short answer is yes. If you look at a skirt steak, you can see parallel lines running along the meat. If you cut along one of these lines and then try to eat the strip you've cut, it will be horribly tough. But cut across those lines and the strip will be loosely knit and wonderfully tender. This holds for slicing a chicken breast (always across the breast) and any other flesh where there's a discernible grain. When a cut is made of different muscles, such as a butterflied leg of lamb, it gets trickier. You have to puzzle it out, piece by piece, identifying the grain direction for each muscle. It makes a real difference.

Korean Marinated Skirt Steak with *Ginger Dipping Sauce*

SERVES 4   PREP TIME 10 MINUTES, PLUS 3 HOURS–OVERNIGHT MARINATING
COOKING TIME 8 MINUTES, PLUS 5 MINUTES RESTING

4 x 200 g (7 oz) skirt steaks
2 teaspoons peanut oil or other mild-
    flavoured oil

MARINADE
1½ tablespoons light soy sauce (gluten-
    free if desired)
2 teaspoons white sugar
1 tablespoon mirin (rice wine)
2 garlic cloves, crushed
3 spring onions (scallions), ends
    removed, thinly sliced
1 x 3 cm (1¼ inch) piece ginger, sliced
2 teaspoons sesame oil

DIPPING SAUCE
2 tablespoons sesame seeds, toasted
1 garlic clove, crushed
4 spring onions (scallions), ends
    removed, thinly sliced
2 tablespoons white rice vinegar
1 x 3 cm (1¼ inch) piece ginger, sliced
2 teaspoons caster (superfine) sugar
1 tablespoon (or to taste) Gochujang
    (Korean hot pepper paste)
1 tablespoon water
1 teaspoon salt

TO SERVE
baby cos (romaine) lettuce leaves
steamed rice (optional)

• •

NOTE: Gochujang is available at Asian
grocers and is worth seeking out – it's
delicious and unapologetically spicy.

Skirt is a great cut of meat, lean and deeply flavoured and it sucks up the marinade of garlic, soy, ginger and sesame oil beautifully. We love this steak barbecued, cut into strips, paired with a hot pepper sauce, then wrapped in cool, crisp lettuce leaves.

Make ahead: The marinade and dipping sauces can be made up to 1 week ahead and refrigerated in airtight containers. The steaks may be marinated and placed in a zip-lock or vacuum-sealer bag and refrigerated overnight or frozen for up to 3 months. Defrost before cooking.

For the marinade, blend all the ingredients together thoroughly in a food processor and taste for balance – it should be pretty powerful from the ginger and garlic.

Place the steaks in a glass or ceramic dish or plastic zip-lock bag and coat with the marinade. Refrigerate for at least 3 hours or overnight.

For the dipping sauce, blend all the ingredients together thoroughly in a small food processor or use a stick blender, adding a little more water if necessary for a good sauce consistency and extra Gochujang if you want a more fiery sauce.

Preheat a barbecue hotplate or chargrill pan until very hot. Rub the hot surface with the peanut oil and cook the steaks for 3–4 minutes each side or until done to your liking. Remove, cover with foil and rest for at least 10 minutes.

On a carving board, slice the steaks into 1 cm (½ inch) fingers across the grain (see opposite page). This is essential for making skirt tender but it's a very easy cut to see the grain in – the lines are very defined and fan out from the narrowest part of the steak to the widest.

Serve in baby cos (romaine) lettuce cups, drizzled with the dipping sauce, with steamed rice on the side (if desired).

Bresaola Salad with Shaved Fennel and Cabbage

SERVES 4 FOR LUNCH OR AS AN ACCOMPANIMENT   PREP TIME 10 MINUTES   COOKING TIME NONE

500 g (1 lb 2 oz) Savoy cabbage, outer leaves and core removed, very thinly sliced

400 g (14 oz) fennel bulb, bottom and outermost layer removed, very thinly sliced (use a mandoline if you have one)

1 large handful parsley leaves

125 g (1 oz) bresaola, thinly sliced and torn into rough strips

100 g (3½ oz) parmesan cheese, finely shaved with a vegetable peeler

LEMON AND OLIVE OIL DRESSING

100 ml (3½ fl oz) extra virgin olive oil

juice and zest of 1 lemon, plus extra lemon juice, as needed

freshly ground black pepper

· ·

NOTE: If you can't get your hands on bresaola, you can substitute with prosciutto or a high quality salami, thinly sliced.

This is inspired by a recipe by Karen Martini and is so much more addictively delicious than its simplicity would suggest. Of almost all cured meats, bresaola is the weight watcher's best friend. It's low in kilojoules and fat and packs such a salty, savoury punch that you only need use it very sparingly, shaved into thin slices.

Make ahead: Cabbage and fennel may be sliced and parsley leaves plucked up to 1 day ahead (toss fennel in lemon juice to prevent it from oxidising) and stored in tubs with lids in the fridge. The parmesan cheese and bresaola may be shaved and stored (separately) in airtight containers in the fridge and the dressing made and stored in the fridge up to 3 days ahead.

To make the dressing, combine the olive oil and lemon juice and zest. Season with salt and freshly ground black pepper to taste.

In a large stainless steel mixing bowl, toss together the cabbage, fennel and parsley with two-thirds of the bresaola, parmesan and dressing. Arrange on a platter and scatter with the remaining parmesan and bresaola. Drizzle with a little more dressing and serve. Oh dear, that was a bit simple wasn't it?

Sri Lankan Snapper Curry with *Chickpeas* and *Spinach*

SERVES 4   PREP TIME 20 MINUTES
COOKING TIME 1 HOUR 25 MINUTES (IF USING DRIED CHICKPEAS) OR 40 MINUTES (IF USING TINNED)

50 g (1¾ oz/¼ cup) dried chickpeas,
    or 200 g (7 oz) tinned chickpeas,
    drained and rinsed
600 g (1 lb 5 oz) thick pieces snapper or
    other firm, white-fleshed fish fillets,
    skinned, boned and diced into 4 cm
    (1½ inch) chunks
2 big handfuls baby English spinach

CURRY POWDER
1 teaspoon ground turmeric
2 teaspoons ground coriander, toasted
1 teaspoon ground cumin, toasted
½ teaspoon ground fennel, toasted
½ teaspoon fenugreek seeds
1 teaspoon ground cinnamon
pinch of ground cloves
pinch of ground cardamom
½ teaspoon freshly ground black
    pepper

CURRY SAUCE
1 tablespoon peanut oil or other mild-
    flavoured oil
2 brown onions, thinly sliced
2 garlic cloves, crushed
1½ teaspoons salt
1 stalk fresh curry leaves, leaves
    plucked
2 tablespoons curry powder (above)
2 long red chillies, seeded and cut into
    thin matchsticks
1 piece dried pandanus leaf (optional)
400 g (14 oz) tinned chopped tomatoes
400 ml (14 fl oz) coconut milk
2 teaspoons tamarind purée
1 teaspoon lemon juice

TO SERVE
steamed basmati or Spiced Cauliflower
    Rice (opposite)

This was once a Rick Stein recipe, but we've added chickpeas and spinach and generally messed around with it. We get amazingly fresh snapper from Kevin, our friendly seafood supplier. We make the curry base, drop in the fresh snapper and freeze the lot, so that the fish only ever cooks once, just before serving. Reheating is a sad end for a noble fish. If you can't find good, chunky pieces of snapper, choose another firm, white-fleshed fish. Blue eye would work well, too.

Make ahead: *The curry powder can be made up to 1 week ahead and stored in an airtight jar. The curry sauce can also be made ahead and refrigerated in an airtight container for 1 week or frozen for up to 3 months. When you wish to use it, defrost fully and reheat before adding the raw snapper and vegetables.*

First, make the curry powder by mixing all the spices.

If using dried chickpeas, soak them overnight. Drain and cook them in fresh, unsalted water over low heat until tender (the time will vary depending on the freshness of the chickpeas but start checking after 45 minutes). Drain and set aside. Alternatively, use tinned chickpeas.

To make the curry sauce, heat the peanut oil in a medium saucepan over low heat. Add the onions and garlic with the salt and cook gently, stirring frequently, for about 10–15 minutes until they're soft but not coloured.

Add the curry leaves, curry powder, chillies and pandanus leaf (if using) and continue to cook gently for 2 minutes, stirring constantly, until the spices' fragrance intensifies, then stir in the tomatoes and coconut milk. Turn the heat up to medium and bring the sauce to a simmer, then reduce the heat to low and cook gently for 15 minutes.

Add the tamarind and lemon juice, and add 1 tablespoon of water if necessary to make a good sauce consistency. Season with salt to taste. Remove the pandanus leaf, if used. At this stage, the sauce can be refrigerated or frozen.

Ten minutes before serving, add the chickpeas to the sauce and bring them up to heat, then gently stir in the diced snapper and simmer for 5 minutes or until opaque. Stir in the baby spinach until wilted and serve on a bed of steamed basmati rice or go for the full Thinner Dinner with spiced cauliflower rice (below).

Spiced Cauliflower Rice

We're not totally convinced by cauliflower 'rice' in all its manifestations – cauliflower sushi, anyone? – but it makes a great low-calorie and low-carb base for curries, especially if it has been lightly spiced as well. To make the 'rice', simply pulse the florets from a ½ cauliflower in a food processor until they've broken up into little pieces which, if you squint a bit, look just like rice. You can then pan-fry it, stirring constantly, over medium heat in a dry frying pan till just tender – 5 minutes should be enough. For spiced 'rice', start with 1 teaspoon cumin seeds and toast them over medium heat till they start to darken before adding ½ teaspoon ground turmeric and pan-frying as before. Season with salt. You can also add a handful of frozen baby peas. Serve with any Indian or Sri Lankan curry.

SRI LANKAN SNAPPER CURRY WITH
CHICKPEAS & SPINACH, *page 36*

BEEF & GREEN PAPAPYA STIR-FRY
WITH TAMARIND DRESSING, *page 40*

Beef AND Green Papaya Stir-fry WITH Tamarind Dressing

SERVES 4   PREP TIME 30 MINUTES, PLUS 3 HOURS MARINATING   COOKING TIME 15 MINUTES

600 g (1 lb 5 oz) beef rump (round)
1–2 tablespoons peanut oil or other
    mild-flavoured oil
6 spring onions (scallions), trimmed and
    sliced into 4 cm (1½ inch) lengths
2 large carrots, cut into thin batons
½ green papaya, peeled, seeded and
    cut into thin batons
100 g (3½ oz) tatsoi (substitute baby
    English spinach if it's unavailable)

MARINADE
1 long red chilli, seeded
2 garlic cloves
2 coriander (cilantro) roots, washed
5 kaffir lime leaves, stalks removed
1 lemongrass stem, tough outer layers
    and ends removed, white part only,
    thinly sliced
¼ teaspoon freshly ground black
    pepper
1 teaspoon salt
1 tablespoon peanut oil or other mild-
    flavoured oil
1 tablespoon fish sauce

STIR-FRY SAUCE
1 x 1 cm (½ inch) piece ginger, finely
    chopped
4 tablespoons tamarind purée
2½ tablespoons lime juice (about
    2 limes)
1½ tablespoons light brown sugar
2½ tablespoons fish sauce

This dish makes the most of green papaya's pleasing crispness by pairing it with a lip-smacking tamarind stir-fry sauce and beef strips marinated in a delicious Thai paste of lemongrass, coriander root and kaffir lime leaves.

Make ahead: *Make the marinade and prepare the beef strips up to 2 days ahead. The beef strips may be marinated, sealed in a vacuum-sealer or zip-lock bags, and frozen for up to 3 months, then defrosted on the day of cooking. The sauce may be prepared up to 1 week ahead and refrigerated in an airtight container. The vegetables can be prepared 1 day ahead and refrigerated in an airtight container.*

To make the marinade, finely chop the chilli, garlic, coriander root, kaffir lime leaves and lemongrass, combine in a mixing bowl and add the black pepper, salt, peanut oil and fish sauce. Alternatively, process the whole lot in a small blender.

Cut the rump across the grain into strips about 1 x 5 cm (½ x 2 inches). Place the strips in a glass or ceramic dish, coat with the marinade and refrigerate for at least 3 hours.

For the stir-fry sauce, combine all the ingredients. Taste for seasoning and set aside.

To cook the beef, heat a wok or large frying pan till smoking.

Swirl the peanut oil around the wok and throw half the marinated beef strips into it. Cook the beef, flipping and tossing for approximately 4 minutes or until cooked to your liking. Remove and set aside, then repeat with the remaining beef strips.

Reheat the wok till sizzling hot again, add some more oil if necessary, then add the spring onions and toss. After 1 minute, add the carrots and green papaya, and stir-fry for 3–4 minutes, adding a splash of water if anything is sticking. Finally, add the tatsoi and stir through till just starting to wilt. Put the beef back into the wok along with the stir-fry sauce and toss through quickly till everything is back up to heat and well combined.

Serve with steamed jasmine rice or cooked rice noodles, garnished with crushed peanuts and coriander leaves.

TO SERVE
steamed jasmine rice or cooked rice
    noodles
50 g (1¾ oz/⅓ cup) unsalted peanuts,
    crushed
1 small handful coriander (cilantro)
    leaves

• •

NOTES: Tamarind purée is available
at some larger supermarkets and all
Asian grocers.

Save the rest of the green papaya for
a Green Papaya Salad (see page 153)
another day – it will last in the fridge
for 1 week. If green papaya is not
available, use sliced choy sum, bok
choy or any other Asian green – it will
give a different result but will still be
delicious.

(see page 153)

Tip

Always taste nuts before using. Some are fresh and toasty;
others mealy and even slightly rancid. If you have ended up with
the latter or if you feel your nuts just need a lift, roasting them
for 5 minutes at 200°C (400°F) will boost their flavour.

Green Papaya

Green papaya is a favourite ingredient of ours. In its favour, it
has a pleasing crispness (just this side of chewiness), it's full of
nutrients, is very low in calories and its mild flavour can carry
punchy dressings. On the minus side, it's not always available,
its juice can cause skin irritations (wear rubber gloves if you're
unsure whether you're sensitive) and it's a bit fiddly to prepare.
We cut the whole papaya into manageable quarters, then peel
with a vegetable peeler. With a spoon with a sharp edge, scrape
out the little white seeds in the middle. If the papaya flesh
has begun to turn yellow, taste a piece. There shouldn't be a
pronounced papaya taste and it should be as crisp as a carrot.
If it has begun to soften and ripen, don't use it for this sort of
dish. Green papayas are delicious; ripe papayas are delicious.
Half-ripe papayas are pretty repellent.

Chicken Pho

SERVES 4   PREP TIME 20 MINUTES   COOKING TIME 1 HOUR 5 MINUTES

1 brown onion
1.6 litres (55½ fl oz) chicken stock (home-made or low/no salt)
1 x 6 cm (2½ inch) piece ginger, sliced but not peeled
2 cinnamon sticks
2 star anise
4 cardamom pods, bruised
2 tablespoons crisp fried shallots
600 g (1 lb 5 oz) chicken breast fillets
2 tablespoons fish sauce
2 teaspoons white sugar
500 g (1 lb 2 oz) fresh or dried thick rice noodles
2 spring onions (scallions), ends removed, sliced on the diagonal

TO SERVE
Any or all of the following:
mint, coriander (cilantro), Thai basil and Vietnamese mint leaves
bean sprouts
lime wedges
chilli sauce
chopped fresh chilli

. . . .

NOTE: Substitute the rice noodles with Shirataki Noodles (see page 27) for an extra Thinner Dinner option.

Pho is all about the soup base - a clear, intense broth, deeply flavoured with cinnamon, star anise and cardamom. At its best, it's a magical cure for most of the world's ills. It's worth making or buying the best stock you can for this - watery commercial stock won't give you the result you want.

Make ahead: *The soup base can be entirely made ahead and refrigerated in a sealed container for up to 5 days or frozen for up to 3 months. The herbs for the table salad can be plucked and refrigerated in a sealed container the day before. Because we're using breast fillet here, it's much better to cook the breast once only.*

Preheat the oven to 220°C (425°F).

Cut the onion in half, place the halves on a baking tray and roast in the oven for about 25 minutes till brown and charred.

In a large saucepan over high heat, bring the stock to the boil with the onion halves, ginger, cinnamon sticks, star anise, cardamom pods and fried shallots. Turn the heat down and simmer gently for 30 minutes.

Add the chicken and poach gently for 10 minutes. Remove with tongs and set aside until cool enough to handle. Slice the chicken and set aside.

Line a sieve with muslin (cheesecloth) and strain the broth into a clean saucepan. Discard the spices. Add the fish sauce – only half at first if you've used a commercial chicken stock (which may be salty) – and sugar, then taste. It should have a nice depth of flavour and a balance of gentle sweetness and salt.

Cook the noodles according to the packet instructions, then drain and keep warm.

Bring the soup base back up to a simmer, add the sliced chicken, then poach gently till cooked.

Place a pile of noodles in each of four deep bowls and top with the soup, chicken and sliced spring onions.

Serve, with the table salad of herbs, sprouts, lime wedges, chilli sauce and chopped chilli in the middle, for people to help themselves as they go.

Chickpea AND Coriander Burgers

SERVES 4   PREP TIME 20 MINUTES   COOKING TIME 6–8 MINUTES

800 g (1 lb 12 oz) tinned chickpeas, drained and rinsed – 500 g (1 lb 2 oz) drained weight
1 egg, beaten
1 tablespoon ground cumin, toasted
½ red capsicum (pepper), seeded and diced
1 large handful coriander (cilantro), leaves and stems finely chopped
1 handful mint, leaves only, chopped
4 spring onions (scallions), ends removed, thinly sliced
2 garlic cloves, crushed
zest of 1 lemon
2 tablespoons rice flour
1 teaspoon salt
80 ml (2½ fl oz/⅓ cup) olive oil

TO SERVE
rocket (arugula) leaves
Cucumber-Yoghurt Sauce (below) or spiced tomato chutney
juice of ½ lime (optional)
toasted panini (optional)

· ·

NOTE: For a vegan alternative, replace the egg with chia paste. To make the paste, mix 1 tablespoon chia seeds (crushed) with 1 tablespoon water.

In the name of duty we chomped our way through many different vegetarian burgers – pulsey, nutty, beety, the works – trying to find one that didn't taste either worthy or weird. Then we made one up. It doesn't try to pretend to be a burger – it's just something that is stand-alone yummy.

Make ahead: *The burgers may be made ahead and frozen. They can be defrosted but will be delicate to handle when they defrost. Alternatively, you can cook them straight from frozen, adding 2 minutes each side to the cooking time.*

In a small blender, pulse-chop the chickpeas until some are coarsely chopped and some are puréed.

In a large stainless steel bowl, combine the chickpeas, egg, cumin, capsicum, chopped herbs, spring onions, garlic, lemon zest, rice flour and salt. Form some of the mixture into a little patty about 3 cm (1¼ inches) in diameter and fry in olive oil in a non-stick frying pan over medium heat. This should only take 2 minutes per side. Taste the patty and decide whether you need to adjust the salt or any of the other ingredients.

Roll the mixture into eight evenly sized balls. Flatten them into patties, cover and refrigerate or freeze until using.

When you're ready to cook, heat the olive oil in a large non-stick frying pan over medium heat and carefully add as many patties as will fit in a single layer. Cook until a golden brown crust has formed on one side – about 4 minutes – then gently flip the patties and cook for another 4 minutes on the other side. Remove to one side and drain on paper towel, cover with a tea towel (dish towel) and leave somewhere warm (such as a low-temperature oven) while you repeat with the remaining patties.

Serve with rocket leaves and cucumber-yoghurt sauce or a spiced tomato chutney, and squeeze a little lime juice over the top if desired. If you need bread with your burger, serve with toasted panini.

Cucumber-Yoghurt Sauce

Many cultures share the idea of a cool, cucumber-yoghurt-mint sauce – and we use them interchangeably. If it's to go with Indian food, it's raita; if it's Greekish it's tzatziki. And let's not even get into Turkish cacik or Lebanese laban. They all give freshness and lift to spicy or oily food. A basic recipe to go with everything is 260 g (9¼ oz/1 cup) plain yoghurt, 1 Lebanese (short) cucumber (peeled, grated and the water squeezed out), 1 tablespoon lemon juice, ½ garlic clove, ½ teaspoon salt and 1 tablespoon chopped mint. Mix together well and call it whatever you like.

Spiced Carrot AND Lentil Soup

SERVES 8   PREP TIME 10 MINUTES   COOKING TIME 1 HOUR

1.4 kg (3 lb 2 oz) carrots, cut into 3 cm
   (1¼ inch) chunks
1 tablespoon olive oil
2 teaspoons salt
2 brown onions, diced
1 x 5 cm (2 inch) piece ginger, grated
145 g (5 oz/⅔ cup) red lentils
2 teaspoons ground cumin, toasted
3 teaspoons ground coriander, toasted
1 teaspoon sweet paprika
1 litre (35 fl oz/4 cups) vegetable stock
400 ml (14 fl oz) coconut milk

TO SERVE
plain yoghurt
1 small handful coriander (cilantro),
   leaves only, coarsely chopped
warm Turkish bread (not strictly
   Thinner Dinner, though)

This dish is the love child of two dips we had left over from a charity do in our early days – one a roast carrot, one a spiced lentil. We added a bit of vegie stock, some coconut milk and, like magic, a new soup was born. We made quite a few litres of it. We lived off it for some weeks.

Make ahead: The whole soup can be made ahead and kept in a covered container in the fridge for up to 5 days or frozen for up to 3 months. Defrost and stir while heating to bring it back together if it has separated.

Preheat the oven to 180°C (350°F).

In a deep ovenproof dish, toss the carrots in half the olive oil and 1 teaspoon of the salt and roast in the oven for about 25–30 minutes, or until browning and soft.

Heat the remaining olive oil in a large saucepan over low heat and sauté the onions with the remaining 1 teaspoon of salt for about 10–15 minutes till soft and sweet. Add the ginger and cook for a few minutes more before adding the lentils, cumin, coriander and paprika.

Cover the lentils with vegetable stock and cook over low heat until the lentils have completely collapsed, about 25 minutes. Add the roasted carrots to the saucepan with the coconut milk and allow to cool slightly before puréeing with a stick blender or in a blender until completely smooth. You will probably need to add water or more stock at this stage until the soup is at a consistency that you like. Taste for seasoning.

Serve with a swirl of yoghurt and sprinkled with chopped coriander leaves, and with warm Turkish bread on the side.

Italian Freekeh AND Borlotti Bean Soup

SERVES 4   PREP TIME 10 MINUTES, PLUS OVERNIGHT SOAKING   COOKING TIME 2 HOURS 10 MINUTES (IF USING DRIED BEANS), 40 MINUTES (IF USING TINNED)

150 g (5½ oz/¾ cup) dried borlotti beans (cannellini, lima or other beans would be fine, too)

½ teaspoon bicarbonate of soda (baking soda)

1 bay leaf

2 teaspoons olive oil

1 red onion, sliced

3 garlic cloves, crushed

3 celery stalks, ends and outer stalks removed, thinly sliced

2 leeks, ends removed, thinly sliced

2 large carrots, cut in half lengthways, thinly sliced

2 tablespoons tomato paste (concentrated purée)

150 g (5½ oz) freekeh (roasted green wheat)

200 g (7 oz) frozen baby peas

1–2 teaspoons salt

1 large handful basil, leaves plucked and coarsely chopped

TO SERVE
grated parmesan cheese
freshly ground black pepper

• •

NOTE: Instead of dried borlotti beans, you could use 400 g (14 oz) tinned beans – it's more expensive but more convenient. If you don't have freekeh, substitute with pearl barley, farro or spelt.

For something that weighs in at a puny 1400 kilojoules (335 calories) a serve (a very generous serve, too), this is a seriously hearty soup. Low GI and vegan to boot, it's great for those on the 5:2 diet – you won't feel at all hard done by and the beans and freekeh will make you feel full till tomorrow when you can feast again. Perhaps it's not the prettiest soup around, but it has an honest soul.

Make ahead: We'd almost insist that this soup has to be made ahead of time – it's the only way that these humble ingredients will come together and develop into something altogether more noble. It can be frozen – though beans can go mealy in the freezer – but will be good in the fridge for 5 days. Leave the basil aside and stir it through just before serving.

Cover the borlotti beans with plenty of water, add the bicarbonate of soda and leave to soak overnight. The next day, drain and rinse the beans, then place in a medium saucepan with the bay leaf, cover with plenty of water and bring to the boil over high heat. Skim off the scum that rises to the top, turn the heat down to low and simmer for 45 minutes–1½ hours, or until tender and creamy. Discard the bay leaf, drain the beans and set aside.

Heat the olive oil in a large saucepan over low heat and add the red onion. Cook gently for about 10–15 minutes till beginning to soften, then add the garlic, celery, leeks and carrots and continue to cook until soft.

Add the tomato paste and freekeh (or other grain) and stir to coat in the vegetable mixture. Cover with 1.25 litres (44 fl oz/5 cups) of water (you could also use stock if you have some to hand). Bring to the boil, turn the heat back down and put the beans back in for about 10 minutes – the beans will be on the point of collapse but the freekeh should still have a pleasingly chewy texture. Stir in the peas and salt, and cook for a final few minutes. Just before serving, fold in the chopped basil leaves.

Serve (for the non-vegans) with freshly ground black pepper and plenty of grated parmesan cheese – maybe even the 5:2-ers can knock themselves out and have a teaspoon as well (30 kJ/7 cal – we checked!).

Coriander AND Lemongrass Barramundi Fillets WITH Nahm Jim

SERVES 4   PREP TIME 15 MINUTES   COOKING TIME 10 MINUTES, PLUS 5 MINUTES RESTING

720 g (1 lb 9 oz) barramundi fillets
   (or other white-fleshed fish fillets),
   either 4 x 180 g (6½ oz) fillets or
   8 x 90 g (3¼ oz) strips

*CORIANDER AND LEMONGRASS
MARINADE*
1 large handful coriander (cilantro),
   roots, stalks and all, washed
2 garlic cloves, peeled
1 long green chilli, seeded and coarsely
   chopped
1 x 3 cm (1¼ inch) piece ginger, sliced
2 teaspoons fish sauce
1 teaspoon white sugar
1 lemongrass stem, tough outer layer
   removed, white part only, coarsely
   chopped
1 tablespoon peanut oil or other mild-
   flavoured oil

NAHM JIM
1¼ tablespoons fish sauce
1¼ tablespoons lime juice
1¼ tablespoons caster (superfine)
   sugar
½ garlic clove
1 bird's eye chilli (or to taste), seeded
   and coarsely chopped

TO SERVE
steamed rice
Green Papaya Salad (see page 153)

· ·

NOTE: We've used small farmed barramundi fillets. You could also substitute slender pieces of flathead.

These marinated barra fillets would also be good on the barbecue – just make sure the hotplate is well oiled and the fillets are patted dry before cooking. We've suggested serving them with steamed rice but you could stay totally Thinner Dinner with a green papaya salad on its own or a pile of stir-fried green vegies.

Make ahead: The marinade can be made up to 3 days ahead and the fish marinated overnight. The parcels can be made a few hours before cooking and kept in the fridge. The nahm jim will keep in a sealed container in the fridge almost indefinitely.

For the marinade, throw the coriander, garlic, chilli, ginger, fish sauce, sugar and lemongrass into a food processor and pulse-chop, then purée till you have a fine, vibrantly green paste. Taste for seasoning – the nahm jim will be salty so go easy on the salt in the marinade. Turn the barra fillets gently in the paste till well coated and reserve, covered, in the fridge till you're ready to cook.

For the nahm jim, put all the ingredients in the bowl of a small food processor and blitz. Taste for seasoning and adjust to your liking – make it more fiery, salty, sour or sweet as you prefer. Set aside.

Preheat the oven to 200°C (400°F).

Take four rectangles of baking paper – the width of the roll and 20 cm (8 inches) longer than the fish fillets.

Lay one-quarter of the fish (one or two pieces) with its marinade in the centre of the paper. Fold one side of the paper over into the middle of the fish, then the other, so that they join in the middle, then fold them over in little folds a couple of times to hold, then fold in the two ends. You should have a neat(ish) little parcel.

Repeat for the remaining three fish parcels and place all the parcels on a baking tray.

Put the tray into the oven. The cooking time will depend very much on the thickness of the fillets you use. Thin fillets will only take 10 minutes. Open a parcel and check whether they're ready. Bear in mind that they will continue to cook in the paper once you've taken them out of the oven.

Remove the tray from the oven and rest in a warm place for 5 minutes, then remove each parcel with a spatula and place on a plate, allowing guests to open their own parcels.

Serve with the nahm jim on the side, some green papaya salad and steamed jasmine rice.

Isaan Barbecued Pork
with Chilli Dipping Sauce

SERVES 4   PREP TIME 20 MINUTES, PLUS 2 HOURS MARINATING
COOKING TIME 25 MINUTES, PLUS 5 MINUTES RESTING

2 x 350 g (12 oz) pork fillets
peanut oil or other mild-flavoured oil

MARINADE
1 small handful coriander (cilantro) with
    roots attached, coarsely chopped
2 garlic cloves, chopped
1 lemongrass stem, white part only,
    coarsely chopped
½ teaspoon freshly ground black
    pepper
1 tablespoon brown sugar
1 tablespoon fish sauce
1 tablespoon kecap manis

CHILLI DIPPING SAUCE
2 teaspoons long-grain rice
5 bird's eye chillies, seeds removed and
    chopped
2 long red chillies, seeds removed and
    chopped
1 garlic clove, chopped
3 tablespoons fish sauce
2 tablespoons light brown sugar
1 tablespoon tamarind purée
¼ small red onion (or 1 French shallot),
    chopped

TO SERVE
sliced cucumber
coriander (cilantro) leaves
cos (romaine) lettuce leaves or
    steamed rice

. . . .

NOTE: Kecap manis and tamarind
purée are available at some larger
supermarkets and all Asian grocers.

For those with a predilection for barbecued pork and chilli, this lean and lovely dish from the north-east of Thailand is pretty close to heaven. The kecap manis, fish sauce and lemongrass marinade permeates the meat, and the chilli sauce is super-fiery, salty and delicious.

Make ahead: *The marinade and sauce can be made up to 1 week ahead and stored in the fridge in airtight containers. The pork fillets can be marinated the night before cooking or you can marinate the pork, seal it in zip-lock or vacuum-sealer bags, and freeze for up to 3 months. Defrost before cooking.*

In the bowl of a small food processor or using a stick blender in a tall container (or whatever your chosen blitzer may be), pulse-chop all the marinade ingredients until well amalgamated, then blitz to a paste.

Trim off any visible fat or sinew from the pork fillets. Coat them with the marinade in a stainless steel or non-stick bowl, or in a zip-lock bag, then refrigerate for at least 2 hours or overnight.

To make the sauce, place a small frying pan over medium heat and toast the rice until golden brown and fragrant (watch carefully – this happens quickly). Grind the rice using a mortar and pestle or spice grinder until gritty and powdery.

Blitz the chillies, garlic, fish sauce, sugar, tamarind and red onion until fine. Stir in the ground rice and taste for balance. It should be fiery, salty and sweet, with a bit of a tang. Adjust if necessary and set aside.

When ready to serve, preheat and oil a barbecue hotplate or chargrill pan to medium–low. Take the pork fillets from the marinade, draining any excess marinade. Place them on the hotplate and cover (if you don't have a covered barbecue, improvise with an upturned stainless steel bowl). Keep flipping the fillets 90 degrees every 5 minutes, keeping a careful watch that the marinade doesn't burn, and basting with the excess marinade for a total of about 15–25 minutes. Check after 15 minutes whether the pork is cooked by pressing it with your finger at its fattest part. If it springs back, it's done; if it still feels soft and giving, pop it back on the barbecue.

Rest for 5 minutes before slicing across the fillet at an angle. Arrange the pork on a platter with sliced cucumber, drizzle with some of the sauce and scatter with coriander leaves. Serve with cos lettuce cups or steamed rice on the side.

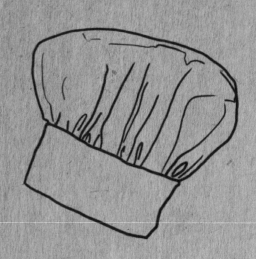

CROWD
Pleasers

In our parents' day, entertaining was often a stressful, formal affair, involving bringing out the wedding silver, polishing crystal glasses and the preparation of four courses culminating in the serving of coffee and after-dinner mints. Nowadays, it's very likely to be a messy crowd of mixed ages, with friends bringing a salad and an unexpected child or two. First courses have mostly been ditched in favour of small bites with drinks and individual, beautifully presented plates have been supplanted by shared platters of cheerful, unpretentious food that can be mixed and matched to suit everyone's individual taste and dietary requirements (not concepts that seemed to exist in our parents' innocent times).

We'd like to think that all our dinners are crowd-pleasers but some are more inherently suited to scaling up to feed a mob. Curries are great, as are tagines. Anything that can be cooked on the barbecue works; even better is barbecue food that can then be wrapped in something (whether that's lettuce, rice paper, pitta bread or a tortilla), dispensing with cutlery altogether. If we've got a crowd coming over, we find it easier to plan if we have a theme at the back of our minds. If you're thinking of a Middle Eastern or Indian or Mexican spread, then you can start building a menu that has some sort of coherence and this stops you from sitting, gulping, notebook in hand, wondering what you're going to cook.

See page 9 for our tips on scaling up recipes and cooking for a crowd.

Mediterranean Chicken with *Fennel* and *Green Olives*

SERVES 4   PREP TIME 10 MINUTES   COOKING TIME 45 MINUTES

4 chicken Marylands (leg quarters),
  each weighing about 250 g (9 oz)
1½ teaspoons salt
3 teaspoons olive oil
2 fennel bulbs, ends removed, bulbs
  sliced lengthways into 5 mm
  (¼ inch) slices
2 brown onions, sliced
2 garlic cloves, crushed
2½ tablespoons white wine
100 ml (3½ fl oz) chicken stock
  (home-made or low/no salt)
100 g (3½ oz) green olives, drained
  and rinsed
zest of 1 lemon, peeled with
  a vegetable peeler
½ teaspoon chilli flakes
2 bay leaves
5 thyme sprigs, leaves stripped

TO SERVE
mashed potato or soft polenta
1 small handful flat-leaf (Italian) parsley,
  leaves plucked, to garnish

Fennel is one of our favourite vegetables, whether it's crisp and thinly sliced in a slaw or cooked till it's melting and sweet as it is here. One of the most delicious dinners for one we know is to brown thick slices of fennel, then braise them with garlic and chicken stock, sprinkle with parmesan and finish in the oven till golden brown. So very good and quietly indulgent. Here, green olives and lemon zest provide a punchy counterpoint to the fennel's mellow sweetness, making a sunny backdrop for the braised chicken.

Make ahead: *The fennel and onion mixture can be made ahead of time and refrigerated for 3 days. The whole dish can be made in the morning, refrigerated, covered, and reheated in the evening.*

Preheat the oven to 225°C (435°F).

Rub the chicken with ½ teaspoon of the salt and brown in the oven in a high-sided – about 4 cm (1½ inch) – ovenproof dish for 20 minutes. Remove the dish, pour off any fat, cover with foil and set aside. Turn the oven down to 130°C (250°F).

Meanwhile, heat the olive oil in a large, heavy-based frying pan and cook the fennel and onion with the remaining teaspoon of salt over medium–low heat, stirring frequently, till both are soft (but not falling apart) and sweet, adding the garlic towards the end. This should take about 10–15 minutes.

Turn the heat up to high, splash on the wine and stock, and allow it to boil off to reduce by about one-third. Take the fennel mixture off the heat and stir in the olives, lemon zest, chilli, bay leaves and thyme.

Arrange the fennel mixture in the baking tray so it nestles around the pieces of chicken.

Place the tray back in the oven at the lower heat for 30 minutes, or until the meat is cooked right through to the bone. As Marylands vary in size and ovens vary in temperature, it's important to check that they're cooked, so give one of them an inquiring poke with a sharp knife right through to the joint.

Serve a Maryland and a pile of fennel and olives to each person, on a bed of mashed potato or soft polenta with a few parsley leaves scattered over the top.

Lamb Koftas

SERVES 4–6 (MAKES ABOUT 10 KOFTAS)   PREP TIME 20 MINUTES
COOKING TIME 10 MINUTES ON BARBECUE OR 15 MINUTES IN OVEN

500 g (1 lb 2 oz) minced (ground) lamb
½ brown onion, diced
3 garlic cloves, crushed
1 teaspoon ground cumin, toasted
1 teaspoon ground coriander, toasted
1 teaspoon ground turmeric
1 handful coriander (cilantro), leaves
    and stems, finely chopped
55 g (2 oz) rice flour or cornflour
    (cornstarch)
1 teaspoon salt
1 egg
1 heaped tablespoon currants

TO SERVE
lemon wedges
pitta bread
Hummus (see page 69)
Cucumber-Yoghurt Sauce (see page 45)
Harissa (see page 69)
Tabouleh (see page 69)

There are three things we love when we have a crowd around: a bit of a theme, a barbecue (there will always be someone who wants to man the fire to look noble and useful while drinking beer so there's the cooking offloaded) and food that doesn't need plates. These lamb koftas fit the bill on all three counts – throw in some pitta breads, a few sauces like hummus, tzatziki (cucumber-yoghurt sauce) and harissa, some tabouleh or a simple salad of chopped tomato and parsley, and you have an easy dinner that feeds the old and the young, the vegos (if they don't include the lamb) and the carnivores. And no washing up.

Make ahead: The koftas can be made ahead and frozen for 3 months or kept in a covered container in the fridge overnight. Defrost before cooking.

In a food processor, pulse all the ingredients except the currants until well combined into a workable paste. Stir through the currants.

Have ready a small bowl of water for wetting your hands and a tray lined with baking paper to receive the finished koftas. Roll the kofta mixture into balls the size of a golf ball and flatten slightly so that they are like plump, oval mini-burgers. Set aside and continue till you've used all the mixture.

Preheat a barbecue plate to hot and oil it lightly. Cook the koftas for 4–5 minutes each side or until cooked right through. You can also cook them in a 200°C (400°F) oven for 10–15 minutes or until brown on the outside and cooked through. (You may have to sacrifice one to check – now you'll have to eat it. Oh dear.)

Serve as part of a spread, with some lemon wedges, pitta bread, hummus, cucumber-yoghurt sauce, harissa, tabouleh or a simple tomato and parsley salad.

Brined AND Roasted Citrus Chicken

SERVES 4–6   PREP TIME 10 MINUTES, PLUS 8 HOURS–OVERNIGHT BRINING
COOKING TIME 1 HOUR, PLUS 10 MINUTES RESTING

125 g (4½ oz/⅔ cup lightly packed)
    light brown sugar
120 g (4¼ oz) salt
½ teaspoon black peppercorns
4 thyme sprigs
4 parsley sprigs
2 garlic cloves, peeled
2 bay leaves
1 orange, quartered
1 lemon, quartered
1 x 1.6 kg (3½ lb) chicken
1 tablespoon olive oil

TO SERVE
Potato Gratin (opposite)
Mixed Leaf Salad (opposite)

Once you get into the habit of brining your chickens, we promise you will never look back. It transforms even an ordinary supermarket chook (free-range, of course!) into a different beast entirely, with silky, sweetly flavoured flesh and a magnificently burnished, crispy skin. The only slight pain is finding a space in the fridge big enough for the chicken in its container of brine – if you're pushed for space, or brining a few chickens at once, you can use a scrupulously clean esky (portable cooler), replace some of the water with ice and do your brining outside the fridge.

Make ahead: *The chicken can be brined overnight, then patted dry, stuffed and left, covered, in the fridge, for up to 48 hours before cooking.*

In a container big enough to fit your chicken snugly, mix the brown sugar, salt, peppercorns and 2 litres (70 fl oz/8 cups) of water, stirring till dissolved. Add the thyme, parsley, garlic and bay leaves, then the orange and lemon, squeezing the juice into the water before you add the pieces to the brining liquid.

Pat-dry your chicken and pull out any excess fat and/or giblets (if there are any) from its cavity, then submerge in the brining liquid, making sure it is completely covered. Place the container in the fridge and leave for 8 hours or overnight.

The following day, remove the chicken from the brining liquid and drain the liquid through a colander, reserving all the flavouring bits. Pat your chicken dry, place a garlic clove, some herbs and a piece each of lemon and orange inside the cavity.

When ready to cook, preheat the oven to 200°C (400°F).

Lightly oil a roasting tin with olive oil, place the chicken in the tin and brush or drizzle a little more olive oil on top. Stick the tray in the oven and roast for about 1 hour, basting occasionally.

By this stage, the chicken should be a deep golden brown and its juices should run clear when it's pierced with a skewer or sharp knife.

Place the chicken, breast side down, on a platter, covered with foil, to rest for 10 minutes. At the end of the resting time, pour off the collected juices (make sure you get the citrusy liquid from the cavity) into a saucepan and reheat while you carve the chicken. Pour the sauce over the carved chicken or serve separately in a jug.

Serve with a wedge of potato gratin and a salad of mixed green leaves.

Potato Gratin

There are few things more irresistible than a golden-topped gratin and they're ideal for making ahead. Preheat the oven to 180°C (350°F). Butter a shallow gratin dish – about 1 litre (35 fl oz/4 cup) capacity. Thinly slice 800 g (1 lb 12 oz) peeled potatoes and arrange in the dish. Mix 1 crushed garlic clove and 1 teaspoon salt with 500 ml (17 fl oz/2 cups) thin (pouring) cream or milk (or half and half) and pour over the potatoes. Dot salted butter and grated parmesan cheese over the surface of the dish. Bake for about 1 hour and finish with a few grinds of black pepper.

Mixed Leaf Salad

We could eat a mixed leaf salad every day, either as the basis for a light lunch or dinner on its own or to accompany other dishes. Mix up your salad leaves – try mache, watercress, baby silverbeet (Swiss chard) and baby cos (romaine) – and, if you can, include some tender herbs, such as chervil and/or dill. For a universal dressing, mix together ¼ crushed garlic clove, 1 teaspoon dijon mustard, 1 tablespoon white wine vinegar, 1 tablespoon lemon juice and 125 ml (4 fl oz/½ cup) extra virgin olive oil – the better your vinegar and olive oil, the better your dressing will be. Season with flakes of salt and freshly ground black pepper and only use as much dressing as you need to lightly coat the leaves. Any remaining dressing will keep for 1 week in an airtight jar in the fridge. Additions to the basic salad could include thinly sliced French shallot pickled in vinegar and thinly sliced fennel, radishes or cucumber.

BRINED AND ROASTED
CITRUS CHICKEN, *page* 58

CHICKEN, CHORIZO & OLIVE
EMPANANDAS, *page 62*

Chicken, Chorizo AND Olive Empanadas

SERVES 4 (3 EMPANADAS EACH)   PREP TIME 30 MINUTES   COOKING TIME 1 HOUR 10 MINUTES

1 tablespoon extra virgin olive oil
1 medium brown onion, chopped
1 large garlic clove, crushed
1 chorizo sausage, quartered
    lengthways, then cut across at 1 cm
    (½ inch) intervals
1 teaspoon smoked paprika
1 tablespoon tomato paste
    (concentrated purée)
500 g (1 lb 2 oz) chicken thigh fillets,
    trimmed and diced into 2 cm
    (¾ inch) cubes
2½ tablespoons chicken stock (home-
    made or low/no salt)
8 green olives, rinsed, pitted and diced
1 small handful coriander (cilantro),
    roots removed, stems and leaves
    finely chopped
plain (all-purpose) flour for dusting
250 g (9 oz) Shortcrust Pastry (see
    page 187 or use store-bought)
1 egg, beaten

TO SERVE
Coriander and Jalapeño Salsa
    (opposite)
Cucumber-Yoghurt Sauce (see page 45)

This is a particularly good combination but you can also fill the empanadas with the Pork Picadillo (see page 86). Hard-boiled eggs are a traditional addition to empanadas – Sophie has a childish abhorrence of them, so we have left them out, but feel free to experiment.

Make ahead: *The empanadas may be completely made ahead of time and refrigerated for up to 1 day (the pastry turns grey if kept for much longer) or frozen for up to 3 months.*

In a large saucepan over medium–low heat, heat the olive oil and cook the onion, garlic and chorizo with a pinch of salt for about 10–15 minutes till soft and sweet.

Add the smoked paprika and tomato paste, then turn up the heat and stir through the chicken. Cook, stirring constantly, until the chicken has all changed colour, then cover with the chicken stock (it shouldn't be too wet). Turn the heat down and simmer until the chicken is fully cooked, stirring occasionally. This should take about 15–20 minutes. When the chicken is ready, stir through the olives and coriander. Taste for the balance of seasoning.

Remove the mixture to a stainless steel bowl and cool, first on a work surface till it has stopped steaming, then covered in plastic wrap in the fridge till properly cold.

Prepare a clear area on your work surface big enough to make your 12 empanadas (if you're making more, make in multiples of 8) and dust with flour. Pour a cup of water and have a pastry brush ready.

Roll out the pastry between two sheets of baking paper to a thickness of 2 mm (1⁄16 inch). Take a large biscuit cutter – 12–14 cm (4½–5½ inches) in diameter – and cut rounds in the pastry (you can also cut around a suitably sized saucer).

Lay your pastry circles on the clear, floured work surface. Working quickly (you need to keep your pastry cold), place 1 heaped tablespoon of filling off-centre on each of the circles. Paint around the edge of one pastry circle with water and fold the top of the pastry over, leaving you with a semi-circle. Repeat, until you have 12 semi-circles. These can then be sealed by pressing with a fork around the edge or, for a more traditional style of empanada crimp, start at one end and fold the edge in on itself at 1 cm (½ inch) intervals.

Refrigerate or freeze until required.

When ready to cook, preheat the oven to 200°C (400°F). Place the empanadas on a baking tray and brush them with the beaten egg. Place in the oven and cook for 20–30 minutes or until they are a lovely glazed golden brown.

Allow to cool slightly before serving with a coriander and jalapeño salsa. A tzatziki (or cucumber-yoghurt sauce) would be cross-cultural but successful.

Coriander and Jalapeño Salsa

Fresh salsas make a disproportionately big impact considering how simple they are to prepare. This zingy little number will jazz up any number of dishes – tacos, chilli, empanadas, enchiladas – and involves about 2 minutes' work. Blitz together 2 coarsely chopped jalapeños, 2 spring onions (scallions), 1 large handful coriander (cilantro) leaves, ½ garlic clove, a good pinch of salt and the juice of 2 limes. If you're pressed for time, 2 tablespoons of this salsa turned through some roughly mashed avocado makes a more than acceptable instant guacamole.

Home-cured Gravlax
WITH Horseradish Dill Cream

SERVES 10–12 ON BLINI OR 6 AS A FIRST COURSE WITH SALAD LEAVES
PREP TIME 15 MINUTES, PLUS 12–18 HOURS CURING   COOKING TIME NONE

GRAVLAX

1 kg (2 lb 4 oz) piece salmon tail fillet, skin on, pin-boned (if you have a bigger or smaller piece, adjust the cure amounts accordingly)

CURE

1 large handful dill, fronds removed and chopped (small stems as well)
60 g (2¼ oz) salt
40 g (1½ oz) white sugar
½ teaspoon freshly ground black pepper

HORSERADISH DILL CREAM

150 g (5½ oz) crème fraîche (or sour cream in a pinch)
2 heaped tablespoons horseradish paste (preferably not horseradish cream, which is often too sweet)
2 tablespoons finely chopped dill leaves
1 tablespoon finely chopped chives
1 teaspoon lemon juice

TO SERVE

lemon slices
blini (buckwheat pikelets) or rye bread; or
2 handfuls baby salad leaves
1 handful mixed soft herbs (any combination of dill, chervil, mint, parsley, basil)
¼ red onion, thinly sliced
1 baby fennel bulb, outer layer removed, thinly shaved
2 tablespoons extra virgin olive oil
juice of ½ lemon

. . . .

NOTE: If you like, you can substitute 1 tablespoon freshly grated horseradish root for the horseradish paste.

Curing a side of salmon is so easy and has an amazingly transformative result. This gravlax recipe is about as simple as you can get but imparts all the essentials – a delicate balance of sweetness, salt and herbiness, while the salmon's flesh becomes firmer and drier, with a texture somewhere between raw and cooked. The horseradish dill cream is heavenly with the salmon, but is also delicious tossed through boiled cocktail potatoes.

Make ahead: *The salmon needs to be cured 1 day ahead of use. It can then be wiped dry, wrapped or vacuum-sealed tightly and stored in the fridge for up to 1 week or in the freezer for up to 3 months. The horseradish cream can be made and kept in a covered container in the fridge for up to 1 week.*

Before you do anything else, clear a space in your fridge big enough to take the salmon on a platter. If you're doubling the recipe and using a 2 kg (4 lb 8 oz) piece, you may need to cure the salmon in an esky (portable cooler) full of ice.

To make the cure, mix together all the ingredients in a medium stainless steel or glass bowl. Lay the salmon fillet, skin side down, on a board lined with a large piece of plastic wrap and pat the curing mixture over the flesh side of the salmon. Wrap the fillet in the plastic wrap. Place on a platter (no matter how tightly you wrap it, there will still be liquid that exudes from the salmon as it cures). Put a chopping board on top of the wrapped salmon and weigh it down with a couple of food tins.

Put the salmon platter in the fridge or an esky and leave for 12–18 hours. Remove the plastic wrap (a messy job – do it near the sink) and gently rinse the excess cure off the salmon – little bits of dill remaining are fine. Thoroughly pat dry and refrigerate, covered, till you're ready to slice it.

For the horseradish dill cream, mix all the ingredients with a pinch of salt and a couple of grinds of black pepper. Taste for seasoning and adjust if necessary.

When you're ready to serve the gravlax, lay it on a tray or chopping board with some lemon slices. Using a very sharp knife, try to slice it as thinly as possible at an angle towards the skin, starting at the tail and working backwards.

Serve the gravlax on blini (buckwheat pikelets) or rye bread with the horseradish dill cream. Alternatively, serve with a salad of baby leaves, herbs, onion and fennel. Dress the salad lightly with a simple olive oil and lemon dressing, and salt and pepper if desired. Dab some of the horseradish cream on the gravlax.

Butterflied Leg of Lamb Shawarma

SERVES 6–8 PREP TIME 10 MINUTES, PLUS 3 HOURS–OVERNIGHT MARINATING
COOKING TIME 30–40 MINUTES, PLUS 10 MINUTES RESTING

1 x 2 kg (4 lb 8 oz) leg of lamb, butterflied
  (ask your butcher to do this)
1 x 4 cm (1½ inch) piece ginger, grated
2 garlic cloves, crushed
1 large handful coriander (cilantro),
  roots and all, chopped
juice of 1 lemon
1 tablespoon olive oil
pinch of ground cloves
pinch of ground cardamom
1 teaspoon ground fennel, toasted
1 teaspoon ground cumin, toasted
pinch of ground star anise
¼ teaspoon ground cinnamon
pinch of ground nutmeg
pinch of ground ginger
1 teaspoon sweet paprika
1 teaspoon sumac
1½ teaspoons salt
½ teaspoon freshly ground black
  pepper

TO SERVE
Tabouleh (see page 69) or chopped
  tomato and cucumber salad
Harissa (see page 69) or chilli sauce
Hummus (see page 69)
pitta bread

. . . .

NOTE: Alternatively, serve with a crisp
salad like Cabbage and Fennel Slaw
(see page 80) and Squashed Potatoes
(see page 73), sprinkled with fennel or
cumin seeds.

This recipe was inspired by Yotam Ottolenghi's Jerusalem. While he uses bone-in leg for a 4½ hour cook, ours is a simpler version, designed for a quick sear on the barbecue. Add a couple of chopped salads, a sauce or two and a pile of pitta breads, and you have an easy crowd-pleaser.

Make ahead: The marinade can be made and the lamb coated in the marinade up to 3 days ahead of time and kept, covered, in the fridge. It's worth considering making double the marinade and keeping half in the freezer for another time – it's just as easy to make and you will feel very smug sometime in the future.

Trim any excess fat off the lamb and make sure it's a nice, flat, even shape for barbecuing.

For the marinade, process the ginger, garlic and coriander in a small food processor or blitz with a stick blender. Add the lemon juice and olive oil and blend until well combined.

In a separate small bowl, mix the remaining ingredients.

Add this spice mix to the ginger, garlic and coriander paste, and stir together well.

Smear the marinade all over the lamb, massaging in well. Set aside, covered, in the fridge, for at least 3 hours or overnight.

➤➤ CONTINUED ON PAGE 68

Butterflied Leg OF Lamb Shawarma

« CONTINUED FROM PAGE 67

When ready to cook, preheat a barbecue hotplate to medium-hot. Place the lamb, fat side down, on the hotplate and cook for 12–15 minutes, covered, then flip to the other side for another 12–15 minutes or until cooked to your liking. (If you don't have a barbecue lid, you can use an upturned stainless steel bowl instead.) Personally, we don't think lamb leg should be served too rare – it requires a certain amount of cooking to be tender. Then again, the great thing with this cut is that it's made up of lots of different muscles that will cook at slightly different times – there should be something to suit everyone.

Place the lamb on a carving board and cover with a double layer of foil for 10 minutes before carving across the grain (see page 32) in 1 cm (½ inch) thick slices. Lift the slices off to a warm platter and pour the collected juices back over the lamb.

Serve with tabouleh or chopped tomato and cucumber salad, harissa or chilli sauce, hummus and pitta bread. Or you could serve with a crisp slaw like fennel and cabbage and squashed roast potatoes sprinkled with fennel or cumin seeds.

Tabouleh

Tabouleh can be made a day in advance – any more and it will become watery. Rinse 60 g (2¼ oz/⅓ cup) fine burghul (bulgur/cracked wheat) in a fine sieve in several changes of running water, then leave on a plate to absorb the water remnants over 30 minutes. Fluff up with a fork and mix with 2 large handfuls chopped parsley, 1 handful chopped mint, 100 g (3½ oz) cherry or grape tomatoes (quartered), 2–3 thinly sliced spring onions (scallions), the juice of 2 lemons and 80 ml (2½ fl oz/⅓ cup) olive oil. Season well with salt flakes and freshly ground black pepper.

Harissa

A tub of harissa in the fridge goes a long way and will give a kick to tagines, barbecued lamb or chicken, and even scrambled eggs. Blitz 1 whole roasted red capsicum (pepper) or equivalent pieces from a jar of roasted capsicum (drained) with 10 dried chillies, 1 tablespoon toasted ground cumin, 2 teaspoons toasted ground coriander, 1 teaspoon salt, 4 garlic cloves and 100 ml (3½ fl oz) olive oil till smooth. Serve as is or swirl through some yoghurt to tame the heat.

Hummus

It doesn't take much longer to make hummus than to open a tub of it, especially if you use tinned chickpeas. To make 330 g (11½ oz/1½ cups) hummus, blitz 400 g (14 oz) tinned chickpeas (drained and rinsed), 1 garlic clove, 2 big tablespoons tahini, 1 heaped teaspoon toasted cumin, the juice of 1½ lemons and 2½ tablespoons olive oil. Season with 1 teaspoon salt and add enough water to make a good spreading consistency, bearing in mind that it will thicken if you refrigerate it.

Duck Ragu

SERVES 4   PREP TIME 20 MINUTES   COOKING TIME 2 HOURS 10 MINUTES

2 large duck Marylands (leg quarters)
1 teaspoon salt
3 teaspoons olive oil
1 brown onion, coarsely chopped
1 large carrot, cut into a few pieces
1 celery stalk, cut into a few pieces
2 garlic cloves, crushed
150 ml (5 fl oz) red wine
400 g (14 oz) tinned chopped tomatoes
2 teaspoons tomato paste
    (concentrated purée)
3 thyme sprigs, leaves stripped
2 bay leaves
250 ml (9 fl oz/1 cup) chicken stock
    (home-made or low/no salt)

TO SERVE
fresh pappardelle, cooked
grated parmesan cheese

. . . .

NOTE: Some supermarkets carry
duck Marylands but check to be sure
or pre-order from your butcher or
chicken shop.

Denise, who has worked with us since the early days, is the proud mother to a pair of amazing twin girl middle-distance runners, whose names you will one day all know if you don't already. For years now, this ragu, with lashings of pasta, has formed a key part of their pre-race strategy. We can think of few happier ways to carb up.

Make ahead: *The whole ragu can be made ahead and kept, covered, in the fridge for 3 days or in the freezer for 3 months.*

Sprinkle the duck Marylands with ½ teaspoon of the salt, then heat the olive oil in a heavy-based saucepan. Pan-fry the duck legs on each side over medium heat till golden brown, about 5 minutes per side. Remove and set aside.

In the bowl of a large food processor, pulse the onion, carrot and celery. Add this soffritto to the oil in the saucepan with the garlic and the remaining ½ teaspoon of salt. Cook over medium–low heat for about 20 minutes, stirring frequently to lift any of the ducky bits from the bottom, till the vegetables are soft and sweet.

Return the duck legs to the pan, turn up the temperature to high, pour in the red wine and bring to the boil. Turn down to a simmer and add the tomatoes and tomato paste, thyme, bay leaves and chicken stock. Cover with a lid left ajar and simmer gently for at least 1½ hours or until the duck is so tender it's almost falling off the bone. Remove the duck pieces with a slotted spoon and allow to cool on a plate while you finish the sauce.

Check the consistency of the sauce – does it have too much liquid? Boil it off a bit. Too thick? Add a bit more stock. Just right? Pat yourself on the back and call in Goldilocks. As soon as the duck is cool enough, shred the meat off the bone (wear clean rubber gloves if you like), being very careful to find the thin spiky bone that runs along the leg. You can discard any bits of skin or fat, or you can smoodge them between your fingers and incorporate them into the sauce. It's up to you – though it does add richness to the sauce's texture. Similarly, you can fish out the bay leaves if you wish – though they add a nicely rustic air to the dish. Stir the duck meat back into the sauce and taste for seasoning.

Serve, stirred through a fresh, cooked ribbon pasta like pappardelle, with freshly ground black pepper and grated parmesan cheese.

Eggplant Parmigiana

SERVES 4–6 AS A SIDE DISH, 2–3 AS A MAIN COURSE   PREP TIME 15 MINUTES   COOKING TIME 1¼ HOURS

2 medium eggplants (aubergines), about
   1.25 kg (2 lb 12 oz)
1 teaspoon salt
2 tablespoons olive oil
1 medium brown onion, diced
1 garlic clove, crushed
400 g (14 oz) tinned chopped tomatoes
3 thyme sprigs, leaves stripped
2 teaspoons balsamic vinegar
1 large handful basil leaves
150 g (5½ oz) fresh mozzarella cheese,
   sliced or torn roughly
50 g (1¾ oz) parmesan cheese, grated

TO SERVE
Mixed Leaf Salad (see page 59)

This is a versatile dish to have on hand as a light vegetarian lunch or supper with a salad, or to serve up on the side of grilled lamb or chicken. Alternatively, you could make it the centrepiece of an easy antipasto, with some slices of salami and prosciutto, a few olives and good bread. Eggplant (aubergine) is a terrible sponge for oil so we always brown it in the oven rather than frying it, which makes for a cleaner, less heavy result.

Make ahead: The whole dish can be assembled up to 3 days ahead and stored, covered, in the fridge. Bake it on the day you mean to serve it and serve warm or allow to cool to room temperature before serving.

Preheat the oven to 180°C (350°F).

   Line two baking trays with baking paper. Cut the eggplants into slices lengthways about 1.5 cm (⅝ inch) thick, sprinkle with the salt, lay in rows on the baking trays and brush with 1 tablespoon of the olive oil. Bake for about 20 minutes or until golden brown and soft. Remove from the oven and set aside to cool. If not making ahead, leave the oven on.

   Meanwhile, in a large saucepan, heat the remaining tablespoon of olive oil over medium–low heat and cook the onion and garlic with a pinch of salt for about 10–15 minutes until soft and sweet, stirring occasionally. When completely soft, add the tomatoes and thyme and continue to cook gently, partially covered, for about 30 minutes. Add the vinegar and taste for seasoning – you may need to add a pinch of salt and/or sugar if the tomatoes are particularly sharp. Set aside to cool.

   Take a medium-size gratin dish and place a layer of eggplant on the bottom. Top with one-third of the tomato sauce, then half the basil and a third of the mozzarella. Repeat until you have three layers of eggplant, finishing with mozzarella and a good sprinkle of parmesan cheese.

   Place the dish in the centre of the oven and bake for 25–30 minutes or until the cheese is melted and bubbling. Serve warm or at room temperature with a mixed leaf salad.

Herb-marinated Butterflied Leg of Lamb

SERVES 10   PREP TIME 10 MINUTES, PLUS AT LEAST 2 HOURS MARINATING
COOKING TIME 30 MINUTES, PLUS 10–15 MINUTES RESTING

4 garlic cloves, crushed
1 large handful rosemary leaves,
    coarsely chopped
1 small handful oregano leaves, coarsely
    chopped
1 large handful parsley leaves
½ teaspoon chilli flakes
2 teaspoons salt
½ teaspoon freshly ground black
    pepper
zest and juice of 1 lemon
3 tablespoons olive oil
1 x 2 kg (4 lb 8 oz) leg of lamb,
    butterflied, skin and most fat
    removed (ask your butcher to do this)

TO SERVE
salt flakes and freshly ground black
    pepper
Any or all of the following:
Squashed Potatoes (below)
Wimmera Grain Salad (see page 93)
Cabbage and Fennel Slaw (see
    page 80)
Eggplant Parmigiana (opposite)
Harissa (see page 69)
Cucumber-Yoghurt Sauce (see page 45)

This recipe was inspired – as so many are – by London's wonderful, long-lived restaurant, The River Café, which reinvented Italian food by paring it back to its simple best. There are few easier cuts to cook for a crowd than a butterflied leg of lamb on the barbie. Because it's composed of different muscles, which all behave a bit differently, there should always be a bit to suit every taste – some rosy pink slices from the middle, knobbly charry end bits and everything in between.

Make ahead: *The lamb may be marinated and covered for up to 3 days in the fridge or 3 months in the freezer. Just defrost and pat dry before cooking.*

Put the garlic, herbs, chilli flakes, salt, pepper, lemon zest and juice, and olive oil in a mortar and use the pestle to pound into a thick green paste. Alternatively, blend in a small food processor. Spread this paste all over the surface of the lamb, cover and refrigerate for 2 hours or up to 3 days.

Preheat the barbecue to medium–hot and place the lamb on the grill, fat side down, for 12–15 minutes, covered (watch that the fat doesn't burn). Flip to the other side and cook for another 12–15 minutes. A total of 24 minutes should give you rare lamb; a total of 30 should be medium. To check if the lamb is done, prod the thickest part with your finger; if it's still soft and giving, it's going to be very rare. If it springs back, it's medium-rare and if it's completely unyielding, it's well done.

Rest for 10–15 minutes, covered with foil, before cutting into slices. Make sure you pour any juices back over the sliced lamb. It may also need a sprinkle of salt flakes and a grind of black pepper.

Serve with squashed potatoes and a selection of salads, such as Wimmera grain salad and cabbage and fennel slaw or eggplant parmigiana. You could also serve a couple of sauces like harissa and tzatziki (cucumber-yoghurt sauce) – it's all a bit cross-cultural but the flavours are all relaxed, sunny and Mediterranean and will work together.

Squashed Potatoes

People go mad for these simple potatoes. First boil 1 kg (2 lb 4 oz) baby potatoes until fully tender. Drizzle a baking tray with olive oil, then spread the potatoes on top. Take a potato masher and squash each potato flat, drizzle with more oil and sprinkle with a few teaspoons of whatever seeds will go best with the dinner – cumin, fennel, sesame, nigella. Scatter with salt flakes and roast in a 180°C (350°F) oven until deep golden brown, with crunchy edges.

Chermoula Chicken

SERVES 4–6 PREP TIME 5 MINUTES, PLUS AT LEAST 3 HOURS MARINATING
COOKING TIME 40 MINUTES, PLUS 10 MINUTES RESTING

1 x 1.6 kg (3 lb 8 oz) chicken, split down the breast and flattened (ask your butcher to do this or use poultry shears to do it yourself)

CHERMOULA PASTE
½ preserved lemon
¼ red onion, coarsely diced
2 garlic cloves, crushed
1 large handful flat-leaf (Italian) parsley, stems and leaves
1 handful coriander (cilantro), stems and leaves
1½ teaspoons ground cumin, toasted
1 teaspoon ground turmeric
pinch of chilli flakes
½ teaspoon sweet paprika
1 teaspoon salt
1 tablespoon extra virgin olive oil

TO SERVE
lemon wedges
coriander (cilantro) leaves
Any or all of the following:
Fattoush (below)
Couscous (see page 159)
Harissa (see page 69)
Cucumber-Yoghurt Sauce (see page 45)

This chermoula marinade can just as happily be slathered on a butterflied leg of lamb or tuna steaks for other, equally crowd-pleasing dinners. We used to find barbecuing chicken a fraught and risky business – liable to end in flaming skin and raw insides – before we started cooking them more slowly and gently, turning every 10 minutes until evenly golden brown. Give it a go and see what you think. This dish goes well as part of a Middle Eastern spread of delicious dips and salads.

Make ahead: *The chermoula can be made up to 5 days ahead and stored in an airtight container in the fridge. The chicken can be coated in its chermoula marinade and stored in a vacuum-sealer or zip-lock bag for up to 3 days in the fridge or 3 months in the freezer. Defrost and pat dry before cooking.*

To make the chermoula paste, pull the inside flesh out of the preserved lemon and discard it. Rinse the preserved lemon peel.

In the bowl of a food processor, blend the preserved lemon peel and the remaining ingredients till it is a smooth, thick paste.

Spread the chermoula all over the chicken, cover with plastic wrap and refrigerate for at least 3 hours.

When ready to cook, preheat an oiled barbecue hotplate to medium–low and place the chicken flat on it, bone side down, for 10 minutes. Flip and cook on the skin side for 10 minutes, then repeat, for a total of 40 minutes cooking time. Check that the juices run clear when the chicken is pierced with a skewer and rest for 10 minutes, covered with foil.

Serve with lemon wedges and scattered with coriander.

Fattoush

The ingredients in a fattoush couldn't be more ordinary but the combination of crisp vegetables, lemony dressing and crunchy pitta lifts this Middle Eastern salad into the realms of the extraordinary. First, preheat the oven to 180°C (350°F). In a mixing bowl, combine sliced or chopped cucumbers, radishes, baby tomatoes, red capsicums (peppers), spring onions (scallions), mint leaves and flat-leaf (Italian) parsley leaves. Meanwhile, brush some pitta bread with olive oil and toast in the oven for 5–10 minutes or until crisp and golden. Allow to cool, break into pieces, then add to the salad. Sprinkle the salad with sumac (skip it if you can't find it) and salt flakes, and toss through a dressing made from equal parts lemon juice and extra virgin olive oil, with a bit of crushed garlic.

Duck Confit

SERVES 4 PREP TIME 10 MINUTES, PLUS OVERNIGHT CURING COOKING TIME 2 HOURS 10 MINUTES

4 duck Marylands (leg quarters)
1 tablespoon salt
1 garlic clove, crushed
1 thyme sprig, leaves stripped
2 tablespoons light brown sugar
2 bay leaves, coarsely chopped
5 black peppercorns, crushed
500 g (1 lb 2 oz) duck fat

TO SERVE
Wimmera Grain Salad (see page 93),
  lentil salad or Roast Duck Fat
  Potatoes (opposite)
Blood Orange Sauce, Pickled Cherries
  or Spiced Cumquats (opposite)
salad of bitter leaves, such as radicchio
  and witlof (chicory)

It's self-evident why duck confits are such a popular restaurant dish – all the work's done ahead of time and they are always a sure-fire hit, with their beautifully seasoned, falling apart meat and crisp skin. They make happy partners with anything sweet, fruity and a bit tart so have a look at the different serving suggestions we've given, see what's in season and work out what goes with the rest of your menu.

Make ahead: The duck legs must be cured and slow-cooked ahead of time. They can be stored in the fridge, covered in a layer of duck fat for 3 months, or placed in a zip-lock bag and stored in the freezer for 6 months. Defrost before cooking. All of the accompanying sauces and preserves can be made up to 5 days in advance and kept, covered, in the fridge.

Trim the duck Marylands of any excess fat and skin (there's often a flap without much meat that can easily go).

In a small bowl, mix the salt, garlic, thyme, sugar, bay leaves and peppercorns. Rub this mixture all over the pieces of duck, cover with plastic wrap and leave in the fridge overnight. The next morning, rub off the cure and discard, along with any collected juices.

Melt the duck fat in a large, heavy-based saucepan over low heat. Place the duck Marylands in the melted fat, ensuring that they are completely covered. If they're not and you have no more duck fat, top it up with a bit of olive oil (the predominant flavour will still be from the duck fat). Adjust the heat so that the fat is very gently simmering – a couple of little bubbles only. Cover with a lid left ajar and leave to cook for 2 hours or until the flesh of the duck is very soft (use a wooden spoon to poke it – not your finger!).

Gently lift the pieces of duck out with a slotted spoon and place in one layer in a container. Strain the fat and separate it from any collected duck juices. This fat can now be poured over the cooling duck pieces for long storage in the fridge or used for roasting potatoes. If you're using the duck in the next few days, you can just store it, covered with plastic wrap or in a vacuum-sealer or zip-lock bag in the fridge. If you've stored the duck in its own fat, you'll need to gently scrape the fat off before use.

When you're ready to cook, heat a heavy-based frying pan over medium heat. Place the duck legs skin side up in the frying pan – no oil is necessary – for 5 minutes, then carefully turn and cook for another 5 minutes or until the skin is brown and crisp. You can also reheat in a 180°C (350°F) oven for 10 minutes and quickly flash under the grill (broiler) if the skin needs further crisping.

Serve with Wimmera grain salad or roast duck fat potatoes, pickled cherries or spiced cumquats, and blood orange sauce. A salad of bitter leaves, such as radicchio and witlof, also works well.

Roast Duck Fat Potatoes

Roasting in duck fat takes potatoes to a whole new level. They're crisper, more golden, more scented, more irresistible. First, preheat the oven to 200°C (400°F). Peel and dice 1 kg (2 lb 4 oz) potatoes into 3 cm (1¼ inch) cubes. Put in a large saucepan and cover with well-salted water. Boil till the potatoes are just starting to soften at the edges (for about 20 minutes), then boil for another 2 minutes. Drain in a colander. Put 2 heaped tablespoons duck fat in a roasting tin – make sure it has sides 4 cm (1½ inches) or so high – and heat the fat for 5 minutes on its own in the oven. Carefully remove the tray from the oven and tumble the potatoes into the hot fat, turning over with a spatula to coat. Return to the oven for 35–45 minutes, turning them over after about 25 minutes. Lift out and drain on paper towel before seasoning well with sea salt flakes.

Cherries, Cumquats AND Blood Orange Sauce

Here are three quick recipes we love, to further jazz up your confit.

Pickled cherries (also great with the Christmas ham)
Put 45 g (1½ oz/¼ cup) light brown sugar in a small saucepan with 100 ml (3½ fl oz) red wine vinegar and any or all of the following: 1 strip lemon zest, 1 star anise, 2 cloves, ½ cinnamon stick, 2 bruised cardamom pods, 1 dried chilli, 3 black peppercorns and 3 juniper berries. You could tie all of these in a piece of muslin (cheesecloth) if you don't want the whole spices in the cherries. Bring to the boil and simmer for 15 minutes, then pour in 200 g (7 oz/1⅓ cups) of beautiful cherries. Pour the lot into a sterilised jar and cover with a lid. Allow to steep for 2 days before use.

Spiced cumquats (amazing with a lentil and watercress salad)
Mix 250 ml (9 fl oz/1 cup) water and 110 g (3¾ oz/½ cup) sugar in a small saucepan. Add 1 star anise, 2 cloves, a sprinkle of cumin and coriander seeds, 2 peppercorns and 1 cinnamon stick, and simmer till lightly syrupy. Cut the cumquats into quarters and pour the syrup over the cumquats. Pour the fruit and syrup into a sterilised jar and cover with a lid. Allow to steep for a few days before use.

Blood orange sauce (use normal oranges if not in season)
Zest 1 large orange and set the zest aside. Combine the juice of the orange and 250 ml (9 fl oz/1 cup) chicken stock in a saucepan and bring to the boil. Reduce until it's glossy and thicker. Add the zest to the sauce and taste-test – you may need to add 1 teaspoon caster (superfine) sugar to achieve the right balance.

DUCK CONFIT, *page* 76

PORCHETTA PANINI WITH CABBAGE &
FENNEL SLAW & APPLE SAUCE, *page* 80

Porchetta Panini with Cabbage and Fennel Slaw and Apple Sauce

<u>SERVES</u> 10–15   <u>PREP TIME</u> 30 MINUTES   <u>COOKING TIME</u> 3 HOURS, PLUS 30 MINUTES RESTING

PORCHETTA

1 large handful rosemary, leaves stripped and finely chopped

1 tablespoon fennel seeds, toasted and coarsely ground

1 teaspoon black peppercorns, ground

5 garlic cloves, crushed

2 teaspoons salt, plus extra for the crackling

1 tablespoon olive oil

2 kg (4 lb 8 oz) piece pork belly or shoulder, skin scored

. . . .

NOTE: Pork belly will give you a neater shape but has more fat; shoulder will be messier but leaner – both will be delicious.

APPLE SAUCE

3 large granny smith apples, peeled, cored and chopped

juice and zest of ½ orange

CABBAGE AND FENNEL SLAW

125 ml (4 fl oz/½ cup) extra virgin olive oil

3 tablespoons lemon juice

pinch of salt flakes

500 g (1 lb 2 oz) Savoy cabbage, outer leaves and core removed, thinly sliced

2 large or 3 smaller fennel bulbs, ends, core and stalks removed, thinly shaved (use a mandoline if possible)

1 handful parsley, leaves plucked

freshly ground black pepper, to taste

TO SERVE

15 panini or other rolls

This is really three recipes in one and we won't compel you to make them all together to stuff the world's most delicious but time-consuming sarnie. We'd like to, but we won't. It may seem like a big faff for a sandwich and you probably wouldn't do it for a family of four but once you're talking about feeding a crowd of 10 or more, this recipe starts to develop economies of scale. The whole thing can be multiplied indefinitely upward, as long as you have an oven big enough for a bigger piece of pork. In any case, the porchetta and apple sauce make a great roast dinner on their own, and the cabbage and fennel are the basis of a delightful salad with shaved parmesan and sliced bresaola.

Make ahead: *The porchetta needs to be prepared ahead of time (ideally the day before) and can be cooked earlier in the day and kept warm for 2 hours (but no longer than 4). The apple sauce can be made up to 5 days ahead and kept, covered, in the fridge. The slaw can be made the day before, undressed but tossed with lemon juice to prevent browning, and kept in a covered container in the fridge. Dress just before use.*

To make the aromatic paste for the porchetta, mix together the rosemary, ground fennel, peppercorns, garlic and salt in a small bowl. Loosen this paste with olive oil and smear it on the flesh side of the pork belly or shoulder.

Take some old-fashioned, ovenproof string and cut it into six pieces about 40 cm (16 inches) long. If you have a clever way of trussing a rolled belly or shoulder, by all means use it instead. Otherwise, lay the pieces of string along your work surface parallel at intervals of about 5–8 cm (2–3¼ inches) – this is not an exact science – then place the pork on top, skin side down. Starting from the side nearest you, roll the pork into a sausage shape and begin to tie it securely along the length of the pork.

When you're ready to cook, preheat your oven as hot as it will go. Dry the pork skin with paper towel, rub with a generous amount of salt and place in a roasting tin in the middle of the oven.

Leave it cooking at the high heat for 30 minutes to puff the crackling but keep an eye on it so the skin doesn't turn black. Once the skin is nicely blistered all over, turn the oven down to 140°C (275°F). Cook at the lower temperature for 1½ hours for the first kilogram, then 1 hour for every kilogram thereafter. So, for a 2 kg piece of pork, cook for 30 minutes to crackle, then an additional 2½ hours at 140°C. For a 5 kg (11 lb 4 oz) piece, it would take 30 minutes in the oven to crackle, plus 5½ hours at the lower temperature.

Meanwhile, to make the apple sauce, combine the apples and the orange zest and juice in a medium saucepan over low heat. Cover the saucepan and cook, lifting the lid and stirring frequently, until the apple is cooked and fluffy. Mash with a fork, or whizz with a stick blender till smooth. Season with a little salt to taste.

For the cabbage and fennel slaw dressing, mix the olive oil, lemon juice and salt flakes in a jug or small bowl. Taste and adjust as you like – it should be very lemony. Add some freshly ground black pepper to taste. Toss through the shredded cabbage, fennel and parsley just before serving.

When the pork is ready (it should be very tender and giving when poked in its fleshy bits), remove it from the oven, wrap it in foil and allow it to rest for 30 minutes. If you are unhappy with your crackling at this point, you can lift it off the joint and return it to a 225°C (435°F) oven to crisp up – keeping a close eye on it, as it will be very easy to burn at this point. You can also stick it under a hot grill (broiler) – again, watch it like a hawk.

Carve or pull apart the pork, smash off shards of crackling, then call the happy hordes to form an orderly queue while you dole out the rolls, stuffed with pork, slaw and apple sauce.

Huli Huli Chicken Wings

SERVES 4   PREP TIME 5 MINUTES, PLUS 3 HOURS–OVERNIGHT MARINATING
COOKING TIME 45 MINUTES, PLUS 1 MINUTE COOLING

1 teaspoon paprika (sweet or smoked –
   they'll have different effects but
   either is good)
1 teaspoon ground cumin, toasted
2 teaspoons crisp fried shallots, ground
   to powder using a mortar and pestle
pinch of freshly ground black pepper
pinch of cayenne pepper (more or less,
   depending on heat tolerance)
2 kg (4 lb 8 oz) chicken wings or
   wingettes (drumsticks would be fine,
   too)
200 ml (7 fl oz) pineapple juice
100 ml (3½ fl oz) tomato sauce
   (ketchup)
75 ml (2½ fl oz) light soy sauce (gluten-
   free if desired)
50 g (1¾ oz) light brown sugar
1 tablespoon red wine vinegar
1 x 3 cm (1¼ inch) piece ginger, grated
2 garlic cloves, crushed
peanut oil or other mild-flavoured oil,
   for the hotplate

TO SERVE
lemon or lime wedges

. . . .

NOTE: Crisp fried shallots can be found
in Asian grocers and the Asian food
section of larger supermarkets.

We love a slightly silly name (apparently huli huli means 'turn turn' in Hawaiian) almost as much as we love a sweet, sticky, spicy chicken wing. These ones are rubbed with dry spices, then marinated and barbecued, and they make excellent beer food.

Make ahead: The wings can be marinated up to 3 days in advance and kept covered in the fridge or they can be stored in zip-lock bags and frozen for up to 3 months. Defrost before cooking.

Combine all the dry spices – paprika, cumin, ground shallots and peppers – in a large mixing bowl and toss the chicken wings in the mixture to coat.

In a medium saucepan over high heat, combine the pineapple juice, tomato sauce, soy sauce, sugar, vinegar, ginger and garlic and bring to the boil. Cook until reduced and syrupy – it should be about half the original volume and will take about 15 minutes. Pour into a jug or bowl and refrigerate, covered, until needed.

Pour half the marinade onto the chicken wings and turn them through it to make sure they're all well coated. Leave for 3 hours or overnight, covered, in the fridge.

When you're ready to cook, preheat a barbecue hotplate to medium-high and spritz or rub with a little oil. Put the chicken wings on the hotplate, well spaced out, and cook for about 30 minutes, turning every 5 minutes and making sure that the marinade doesn't burn.

Alternatively, you can cook them in a preheated 180°C (350°F) oven on a tray lined with baking paper for 30 minutes, basting with the excess marinade and turning a couple of times.

Either way, the end result should be deep red wings with some golden brown and charry spots, with flesh that can easily be pulled away from the bone.

Allow to cool for 1 minute, then serve with lemon or lime wedges.

Pulled Pork IN Barbecue Sauce

SERVES 4   PREP TIME 15 MINUTES   COOKING TIME 5 HOURS, PLUS 30 MINUTES RESTING

1 kg (2 lb 4 oz) pork shoulder in one piece, skin and bone removed (a bit of fat is fine)

RUB
1 teaspoon light brown sugar
2 teaspoons dijon mustard
½ teaspoon smoked paprika
1 teaspoon salt

BARBECUE SAUCE
3 teaspoons olive oil
1 small brown onion, diced
1 garlic clove, crushed
pinch of salt
3 teaspoons cider or white wine vinegar
1½ teaspoons dijon mustard
100 ml (3½ fl oz) tomato sauce (ketchup)
1 heaped tablespoon light brown sugar
pinch of cayenne pepper (more if you like)
½ teaspoon smoked paprika
pinch of ground cloves
pinch of ground cinnamon
pinch of ground star anise
few grinds of black pepper

TO SERVE
crusty rolls
Coleslaw (below)

There's nothing more appealing than juicy shreds of slow-cooked pork shoulder, bathed in a tangy, sweet sauce. Katherine came upon a version of this recipe years ago in an American cookbook. Despite finding the name a bit saucy in a Benny Hill sort of way, we thought we'd give it a go for our more adventurous customers. Now that pulled pork is totally mainstream, the name won't raise an eyebrow, let alone a giggle, but it's still completely delicious. Pile it into a crusty roll with coleslaw and you have an irresistible dinner on the run. It also makes a great filler for tacos.

Make ahead: *The pork can be cooked, shredded, mixed with the sauce and stored, covered, in the fridge for up to 3 days or the freezer for up to 3 months. When you're ready to serve, warm the pork in the microwave or in a covered ovenproof dish in the oven.*

Preheat the oven to 120°C (235°F).

Combine the rub ingredients and rub this mixture over the pork. (This part can be done ahead of time or immediately before cooking.)

Place the pork in a roasting tin and pour 250 ml (9 fl oz/1 cup) of water around it. Cover the tin with a tent of foil and roast in the oven for about 5 hours or until completely cooked and falling apart when prodded. Check it from time to time and add more water if necessary. Take the pork out of the oven and allow it to cool for about 30 minutes until you can shred it with your hands into chunky strips, discarding any excess fat. Set aside, covered, in a warm place, such as a low-temperature oven.

While the pork is roasting, you can make the barbecue sauce. First, heat the olive oil over medium–low heat in a medium, stainless steel or non-stick saucepan and cook the onion and garlic with the salt for about 10–15 minutes, stirring, until the onion is soft and sweet. Add the vinegar, mustard, tomato sauce, brown sugar, cayenne pepper, paprika, cloves, cinnamon, star anise and a grind of black pepper. Simmer this mixture over low heat for 20 minutes, then blitz with a stick blender till a smooth sauce consistency.

When ready to serve, mix the shredded pork with the warm barbecue sauce and pile into crusty white rolls with cold coleslaw.

Coleslaw

For a classic coleslaw, finely shred ¼ Savoy cabbage and mix with 1 grated carrot and 2 thinly sliced spring onions (scallions). Dress with 1 heaped tablespoon each of mayonnaise and crème fraîche (or sour cream), 2 teaspoons each of dijon mustard and cider or white wine vinegar, 1 squeeze lemon juice and some celery salt.

Pork Picadillo

SERVES 4   PREP TIME 10 MINUTES   COOKING TIME 55 MINUTES

1 tablespoon peanut oil or other mild-flavoured oil

1 large brown onion, diced

2 garlic cloves, crushed

1½ teaspoons salt

500 g (1 lb 2 oz) minced (ground) pork, not too lean

pinch of ground chilli (or more, if you like)

2 teaspoons ground cumin, toasted

1½ teaspoons ground cinnamon

1 teaspoon ground allspice

400 g (14 oz) tinned chopped tomatoes

1 tablespoon tomato paste (concentrated purée)

40 g (1½ oz/¼ cup) currants

juice of 1 lime

1 large handful fresh coriander (cilantro), stems and leaves chopped

2 heaped tablespoons slivered almonds, toasted

TO SERVE
lime wedges

There's a stand-off in Sophie's house between chilli con carne and pork picadillo as the taco-stuffer of choice. One teen favours the lighter, more interesting picadillo, with its sweet currants and toasty almonds; the other prefers the classic chilli. The youngest takes himself out of the contest altogether by only eating the side dishes. Odd boy. Like chilli con carne, this can be extended indefinitely to feed any number of people with guacamole, salsas and salads or it can be dished up on its own with a baked potato for an easy Sunday night supper.

Make ahead: *The whole dish can be made ahead without the final additions of coriander, almonds and lime wedges and kept, covered, for up to 3 days in the fridge or 3 months in the freezer. Just defrost before reheating.*

Heat the oil in a large saucepan over medium–low heat and add the onion, garlic and salt. Cook, stirring frequently, for 10–15 minutes until soft and translucent, not coloured.

Turn the heat up to medium–high and add the pork, stirring constantly, moving it about and breaking up lumps until it has all changed colour. Stir in the dry spices, tomatoes and tomato paste and bring to the boil before reducing the heat and simmering gently for 35 minutes or until the pork is tender and the liquid is all but cooked out. Taste for seasoning, then stir in the currants, lime juice and most of the chopped coriander and slivered almonds.

Serve with the remaining coriander and slivered almonds scattered over the picadillo, and lime wedges on the side.

Tandoori Chicken Strips

SERVES 8   PREP TIME 10 MINUTES, PLUS AT LEAST 3 HOURS MARINATING   COOKING TIME 10 MINUTES

1 kg (2 lb 4 oz) chicken breast fillets
1 small brown onion, diced
2 garlic cloves, coarsely chopped
1 x 4 cm (1½ inch) piece ginger, coarsely
   chopped
2 teaspoons ground coriander, toasted
2 teaspoons ground cumin, toasted
1 teaspoon garam masala, toasted
1 teaspoon sweet paprika
1½ teaspoons salt
½ teaspoon ground cinnamon
¼ teaspoon ground nutmeg
¼ teaspoon ground chilli
pinch of ground cloves
2 heaped tablespoons plain yoghurt
juice of ½ lemon
1 tablespoon peanut oil or other mild-
   flavoured oil

TO SERVE
warm pitta bread
Cucumber-Yoghurt Sauce (see page 45)
Fresh Mango Chutney (below)
lime wedges

These chicken strips, marinated in yoghurt and Indian spices, make a great dinner in the hand, wrapped in pitta bread, with some cucumber-yoghurt sauce (or raita) and a chutney. Because we are both lazy beasts, if we have a real crowd coming over, especially if it's mixed adults and children (like a whole football team plus families), we would prefer not to create washing-up. So, no cutlery, no crockery: wraps, kebabs, burgers, pulled pork rolls, porchetta panini ... If you can hold it in one hand and eat the plate as you go, we're all for it.

Make ahead: *The chicken may be prepared and marinated and kept, covered, for up to 3 days in the fridge or 3 months in the freezer. Defrost before barbecuing.*

Take the chicken breasts and slice them into long, thin strips. We cut each breast in half lengthways through the middle, then into three from top to bottom, so each breast should give about 6 strips, plus a tenderloin.

In a food processor, blend the onion, garlic, ginger, spices, yoghurt and lemon juice until they form a smooth paste. Transfer this tandoori paste to a glass or ceramic bowl, add the chicken strips and stir through, making sure that they're well coated in marinade. Leave in the fridge, covered, for at least 3 hours or up to 3 days.

When ready to cook, preheat a barbecue hotplate to medium. Drain the chicken breast fillets of excess marinade if necessary and oil the hotplate. Cook the chicken strips for about 5 minutes each side or until cooked through and a bit charry – the marinade will probably stick a bit but it can't be helped.

Serve in warm pitta bread, with cucumber-yoghurt sauce, mango chutney and a squeeze of lime.

Fresh Mango Chutney

At the height of mango season, when prices plummet, it's worth making a batch of chutney to last you for Indian dinners throughout the year. Boil together till syrupy: 1 teaspoon chilli flakes, 2 chopped garlic cloves, 1 x 5 cm (2 inch) piece ginger (chopped finely), 350 ml (12 fl oz) malt or cider vinegar, 220 g (7¾ oz/1 cup) sugar, a pinch of salt and a good pinch of garam masala. Add the flesh of 5 mangoes (diced) and a handful of sultanas (golden raisins) and cook till pulpy. Store in sterilised jars if you plan to keep it for a few months, or just covered in the fridge for use within a couple of weeks.

Texas Beef Brisket

SERVES 8 WITH ACCOMPANIMENTS   PREP TIME 15 MINUTES   COOKING TIME 5½ HOURS, PLUS 30 MINUTES COOLING

1.25 kg (2 lb 12 oz) piece beef brisket (ask for the thin end, trimmed of most fat)

RUB
1 garlic clove, crushed
pinch of freshly ground black pepper
2 teaspoons light brown sugar
2 teaspoons dijon mustard
½ teaspoon chilli flakes (or more to taste)
1½ teaspoons smoked paprika
1 teaspoon salt

BARBECUE SAUCE
2 teaspoons peanut oil or other mild-flavoured oil
1 small brown onion, diced
1 garlic clove, crushed
1 green capsicum (pepper), seeded and diced
1½ teaspoons smoked paprika
1 teaspoon salt
2 teaspoons light brown sugar
1 teaspoon ground cumin, toasted
140 ml (4½ fl oz) beer (whatever you have on hand will do)
3 tablespoons tomato sauce (ketchup)
2 tablespoons cider vinegar (substitute wine or rice vinegar)
1 tablespoon Worcestershire sauce (check the ingredients to keep the dish gluten free – gluten-free Worcestershire sauce is readily available now)

TO SERVE
tacos or soft rolls
Coleslaw (see page 85) or Rainbow Slaw (see page 95)

This is the sort of beefy, blokey dinner that will go down well with a beer and a football-loving crowd. It's pretty dense and full of flavour so it goes a long way, especially if you accompany the brisket with tacos or rolls and coleslaw. Baked potatoes and salads would be fine, too.

Make ahead: *The rub and the barbecue sauce can be prepared up to 5 days in advance and kept, covered, in the fridge. Alternatively, the whole dish can be made and kept, covered, for up to 3 days in the fridge or 3 months in the freezer. Just defrost and reheat.*

Preheat the oven to 120°C (235°F).

Combine all of the rub ingredients in a small mixing bowl. Rub this mixture all over the brisket and place the meat in a roasting tin. Pour 250 ml (9 fl oz/1 cup) of water around the meat, cover with foil and roast in the oven for about 5 hours or until the meat is so tender it can be pulled apart with a fork. Check on the brisket from time to time and add more water if it's looking dry. Set the meat aside, covered, until it's cool enough to be handled (about 30 minutes).

For the barbecue sauce, heat the oil in a saucepan and cook the onion, garlic and capsicum over low heat for about 10 minutes, stirring occasionally until soft.

Add the remaining ingredients and cook for 20 minutes over medium-low heat, stirring occasionally. Allow to cool slightly and then purée with a stick blender. Taste the sauce for balance and adjust as necessary.

With your hands or two forks, pull the brisket apart into shreds in a large stainless steel bowl. They can be as chunky or as fine as you'd like – both will work. Pour on the barbecue sauce and fold through the meat.

Serve the brisket warm, piled into tacos or soft white rolls with coleslaw or rainbow slaw.

Roast Vegetable Lasagne

SERVES 4   PREP TIME 40 MINUTES   COOKING TIME 1 HOUR 45 MINUTES, PLUS 10 MINUTES RESTING

· ·

Note: This recipe makes one 22 cm (8½ inch) square lasagne. To make a larger lasagne for six, just multiply all the quantities by 1.5 and cook for 15 minutes longer.

2 small eggplants (aubergines), sliced into 1 cm (½ inch) rounds
500 g (1 lb 2 oz) roma (plum) tomatoes, quartered
4 garlic cloves, skins on
1 teaspoon salt, plus a pinch
2 tablespoons olive oil
1 handful baby English spinach
80 g (2¾ oz) red capsicum (pepper), roasted and ripped into strips (by all means make them, but a good jar is fine)
1 small red onion, diced
3 basil sprigs, leaves plucked and roughly torn
4 thyme sprigs, leaves stripped
2 teaspoons baby capers, drained and rinsed
10 kalamata olives, pitted and halved
1½ tablespoons salted butter
1½ tablespoons plain (all-purpose) flour
350 ml (12 fl oz) full-cream (whole) milk
pinch of ground nutmeg
50 g (1¾ oz) parmesan cheese, grated
130 g (4½ oz/1 cup) shredded mozzarella cheese (if using fresh mozzarella, tear roughly into small pieces)
8 instant lasagne sheets

TO SERVE
rocket (arugula) and parmesan salad

A vegetable lasagne can be an insipid, watery, apologetic sort of dish but this is a robustly flavoured, sunny mixture of Mediterranean vegetables punched up with capers and olives with a parmesan-rich bechamel. No apologies necessary.

Make ahead: *The lasagne can be completely assembled, covered and kept for up to 3 days in the fridge or 3 months in the freezer. Defrost before cooking or cook from frozen and add 15 minutes to the cooking time.*

Preheat the oven to 200°C (400°F).

Toss the eggplant pieces, tomatoes and garlic in ½ teaspoon of the salt and 1 tablespoon of the olive oil. Line two baking trays with baking paper and spread the eggplant rounds, tomato quarters and garlic on top. Roast for 30 minutes or until the eggplant is blistered, brown and cooked through.

Transfer the eggplant and tomatoes to a large mixing bowl, squeeze the garlic out of its skins, discarding the skin, and turn the spinach through this mixture to wilt. Rinse the capsicum strips if they have come from a jar and add to the vegetables. Set the mixture aside.

Heat the remaining olive oil in a small frying pan over medium–low heat and cook the onion with the pinch of salt for about 10–15 minutes till soft and sweet. Set aside to cool slightly, then gently fold through the roast vegetables with the basil, thyme, capers and olives.

In a medium saucepan, gently melt the butter over low heat and scatter on the flour, stirring constantly until golden. It should start having an appetising, pastry-ish smell. Still stirring constantly (you can use a whisk for this), pour in the milk slowly, incorporating it into the flour–butter roux. Continue to stir over a gentle heat until the béchamel thickens to the consistency of thin (pouring) cream. If there are any lumps, use a stick blender to blitz them till you have a velvety smooth sauce. Season with the remaining ½ teaspoon of salt (adding more to taste if necessary) and nutmeg, and stir in most of the grated parmesan, reserving a couple of tablespoons for scattering across the top.

To assemble, first divide the vegetable mixture and the mozzarella into thirds. Take a 22 cm (8½ inch) square ovenproof dish and spread a little of the vegetable mixture (stolen from the first third) over the bottom of the dish to prevent the pasta layers sticking to the bottom. Place a single layer of pasta sheets flat over the vegetables, facing lengthways, then cover with the rest of that first third of vegetables. Scatter on a third of the mozzarella, then place another layer of pasta sheets crossways over the cheese. Repeat with another third of the vegetables and mozzarella, then place another layer of pasta sheets lengthways (this helps you keep track of where you are if you get confused, as well as giving the lasagne a firmer structure). Repeat with the final layer of vegetables, mozzarella and pasta, then top with the béchamel. Scatter on the reserved grated parmesan.

When ready to cook, preheat the oven to 200°C (400°F). Place the lasagne tray in the middle of the oven and cook for 45 minutes–1 hour or until the lasagne is speckled with gold and brown across the whole top. Any sunken white patches indicate that the lasagne isn't fully cooked yet.

Remove from the oven and rest for 10 minutes before serving in squares with a rocket and parmesan salad on the side.

Wimmera Grain Salad

SERVES 4   PREP TIME 30 MINUTES   COOKING TIME 45 MINUTES

150 g (5½ oz/¾ cup) pearl barley or other grain

105 g (3½ oz/½ cup) French-style green lentils

4 spring onions (scallions), ends removed, thinly sliced

1 small handful coriander (cilantro), leaves and thin stems plucked and finely chopped

1 small handful parsley, leaves plucked and chopped finely

1 tablespoon finely chopped preserved lemon rind

3 tablespoons dried sour cherries, cranberries or barberries, diced (substitute currants if not available)

2½ tablespoons extra virgin olive oil

juice of 1 lemon

1½ teaspoons salt

2 teaspoons ground cumin, toasted

1 heaped tablespoon flaked almonds, toasted

1 tablespoon sunflower seeds, toasted

1 tablespoon pepitas (pumpkin seeds), toasted

1 tablespoon pomegranate seeds, to garnish (optional)

Make this salad once and we guarantee you'll be making it for every gathering for years. It goes with everything, it's delicious, it's healthy without being worthy and dull – dammit, it's even vegan! The name acknowledges George Calombaris's Cypriot Grain Salad (which inspired this dish), giving a nod to the great grains and pulses being produced in Australia nowadays – notably here the French-style green lentils that used to only be available at chi chi delicatessens but now can be bought at the supermarket. We use pearl barley as the main grain for this version, but feel free to substitute spelt, farro or freekeh – all will supply the requisite bounce and nuttiness. Try to keep the barley and lentils on the conservative side of cooked – if they're overdone, the salad will miss the mark. If you make the salad with cranberries and sprinkle it with pomegranate seeds, it makes a good, festive addition to the Christmas table.

Make ahead: The salad can be made and dressed (minus the nuts and seeds) the day before and kept, covered, in the fridge. Toss through the nuts and seeds just before serving and taste again for seasoning. The grains can suck up salt overnight and it may need a few extra flakes.

Cover the pearl barley with 300 ml (10½ fl oz) of water in a medium saucepan and bring to the boil over high heat. Stir, turn the heat down to a simmer, cover and cook for 35 minutes or until just tender but still with a bit of chew. Drain any unabsorbed water and set the barley aside to cool.

At the same time, cover the lentils with 300 ml (10½ fl oz) of water in a small saucepan over high heat and bring to the boil, before turning down to simmer for 20 minutes or until just tender. Again, drain any unabsorbed water and set aside to cool.

When the barley and lentils are at room temperature, mix them in a large bowl, then add the spring onions, coriander, parsley, preserved lemon, sour cherries, olive oil, lemon juice, salt and cumin.

If you're serving immediately, fold the almonds, sunflower seeds and pepitas through the salad; otherwise, keep them aside till just before you eat and toss through then. Once you've tossed the whole salad, taste it for a good balance of nutty, herby, sweet and salty and make any adjustments you feel are necessary.

Serve, sprinkled with pomegranate seeds, if using.

Twice-cooked Masterstock Pork Belly

SERVES 4–6   PREP TIME 30 MINUTES, PLUS OVERNIGHT FLATTENING
COOKING TIME 3 HOURS 45 MINUTES, PLUS 5 MINUTES RESTING

1 x 5 cm (2 inch) piece ginger, unpeeled
  but thinly sliced

2 coriander (cilantro) roots (save tops
  for another dish)

3 spring onions (scallions), ends
  removed, sliced into 3 cm (1¼ inch)
  pieces

½ teaspoon sichuan peppercorns

1 cinnamon stick

3 star anise

125 ml (4 fl oz/½ cup) dark soy sauce
  (gluten-free if desired)

150 ml (5 fl oz) Chinese rice wine

1 heaped tablespoon light brown sugar

1.5 kg (3 lb 5 oz) pork belly

1 teaspoon salt

TO SERVE

Rainbow Slaw (opposite) or steamed
  rice and Asian stir-fry greens

With this modern take on a Chinese classic, you get the best of both worlds – sweet, tender meat from the long, slow cook in masterstock, and crunchy crackling from the final fierce roast. Does it get any better than that?

Make ahead: *The pork can be braised in the masterstock up to 3 days ahead and can be kept for up to 3 days in the fridge or 3 months in the freezer after weighting overnight (see the method), then wrapping in plastic wrap or sealing in a vacuum-sealer bag. Defrost fully and pat dry before the final roasting.*

Preheat the oven to 140°C (275°F).

In a medium saucepan, place all the ingredients except the pork into 750 ml (26 fl oz/3 cups) of water and bring to the boil over high heat. Turn the heat down to low and simmer for 10 minutes.

Place the pork in a roasting tin large enough to accommodate it snugly. Pour over the masterstock liquid, making sure the pork is completely submerged – you can add a little more water if necessary. Cover with a piece of foil and carefully place in the oven. Cook the pork for 2½–3 hours or until the meat is incredibly soft and giving when you poke it with your finger. Remove the pork from the oven and strain the masterstock into a bowl, discarding the solids. You'll need about half the masterstock to make the sauce for the pork; reserve the other half in the fridge or freezer for another use (remember to boil it before using it again).

Allow the pork to cool. Place it, skin side up, on a flat plate with another plate on top. Weight the top with a couple of 400 g (14 oz) food tins and leave overnight in the fridge. This will give you a nice flat piece for roasting.

When you're ready to start the second cook, preheat the oven to 225°C (435°F).

Pat the pork dry and rub salt into its skin. Place the pork on a wire rack over a roasting tin and put in the oven for about 30 minutes or until the skin is puffed and golden. Keep an eye on it though – it can very quickly go from crackled to carbonised. If the crackling proves recalcitrant, take the skin off and either whack it under a hot grill (broiler) for 5 minutes or turn the oven temperature up to 250°C (500°F) and put it back in the oven. Either way, keep a very close eye on it.

Meanwhile, pour 500 ml (17 fl oz/2 cups) of the strained masterstock into a small saucepan and bring it to the boil over high heat. Reduce until lightly syrupy (keep tasting and stop reducing when it has reached an intensity and taste you like). Keep warm.

Take the pork out of the oven and rest for 5 minutes before cutting into big cubes or fat slices. Serve, Asian style, with rice, mixed Asian stir-fry greens and the reduced masterstock or, for a more modern presentation, serve on a platter of rainbow slaw.

Tip

Leftovers, if there are any, make a delicious filling for sourdough rolls. Spread the rolls with mayo and stuff with slaw and shredded pork belly.

Rainbow Slaw

Rainbow Slaw is a brilliant recipe to have in your repertoire – crisp, fresh and colourful – and, if you serve it alongside the pork, you can convince yourself that it magically transforms pork belly into a healthy dish. Finely shred ¼ red cabbage, ½ Chinese cabbage (wong bok) and 2 carrots, and mix with 1 handful coriander (cilantro) leaves and 4 thinly sliced spring onions (scallions). Chop 1 garlic clove and 1 x 3 cm (1¼ inch) piece ginger, put them in a small saucepan and sweat in olive oil over medium heat for a few minutes. Cool and mix with 2 tablespoons each of mirin (rice wine), rice vinegar and light soy sauce, 2 teaspoons light brown sugar and ½ teaspoon sesame oil. Toss through the slaw and sprinkle with crushed roasted peanuts.

TWICE-COOKED MASTERSTOCK
PORK BELLY, *page 94*

THREE BEAN CHILLI, *page* 98

Three Bean Chilli

SERVES 4 AS A MAIN DISH, MORE AS A SIDE   PREP TIME 15 MINUTES, PLUS OVERNIGHT SOAKING
COOKING TIME 1 HOUR 45 MINUTES

100 g (3½ oz/½ cup) dried black turtle beans, or 400 g (14 oz) tinned black turtle beans, drained and rinsed

100 g (3½ oz/½ cup) dried borlotti beans, or 400 g (14 oz) tinned borlotti beans, drained and rinsed

100 g (3½ oz/½ cup) dried cannellini or other white beans, or 400 g (14 oz) tinned cannellini beans, drained and rinsed

2 teaspoons olive oil

1 small brown onion, chopped

3 garlic cloves, crushed

1 teaspoon salt

1–2 teaspoons chipotle in adobo, puréed

1–2 jalapeño chillies, seeded and finely chopped

170 ml (5½ fl oz/⅔ cup) beer

170 g (6 oz) tinned chopped tomatoes (about ½ tin)

1 tablespoon tomato paste (concentrated purée)

1 heaped teaspoon ground cumin, toasted

1 teaspoon dried oregano

1 large handful coriander (cilantro), leaves plucked

TO SERVE

Soft tortillas, Guacamole and Fresh Chopped Tomato Salad (opposite), Coriander and Jalapeño Salsa (see page 63) and sour cream or shredded cheese for a vegetarian feast
or
add shredded Texas Beef Brisket (see page 89) or Pork Picadillo (see page 86) into the mix
or
serve as a simple supper with a baked potato

This is a good 'meaty' main course to have on the table when you're not sure whether you're providing for vegetarians. We'd always prefer to make sure there's some substantial, protein-rich vegetarian elements in a larger spread of dishes, which may or may not include meat. With a few different elements to choose from, everyone can cater to their own needs, which seems a bit less pointed and awkward than making special dishes just for the vegos.

Make ahead: The whole dish can be made up to 3 days ahead and kept, covered, in the fridge.

If using dried beans, place them in a large saucepan, cover generously with cold water and leave to soak overnight. The next day, drain the beans and cover with fresh water. Bring to the boil and cook until tender – this could take an hour or so, depending on the freshness of the beans. It doesn't matter if they become tender at slightly different rates. Just wait till the last bean is tender – it's a very forgiving dish. If using tinned beans, skip right to the next step.

In another large saucepan, heat the olive oil over medium–low heat and cook the onion and garlic with the salt for 10–15 minutes, stirring frequently, until they're soft.

Add the chipotle in adobo and jalapeño chillies, then pour in the beer, turning up the heat to allow it to come to the boil. Stir in the tomatoes, tomato paste, cumin and oregano, turn down the heat to medium–low and cook till the tomato is reduced and looks cooked and pulpy, stirring occasionally (about 20 minutes).

Stir in the cooked, drained beans and allow to simmer for 5 minutes. Taste for seasoning and adjust as you like. Stir through some of the coriander and scatter the rest over the top of the dish. Serve with any or all of the suggestions given.

Fresh Chopped Tomato Salad

A chopped tomato salad can do triple duty on the side of Mexican, Indian, Middle Eastern or even Italian dishes. Unless we can get very good tomatoes, we always choose the sweet and readily available punnets of grape tomatoes, or baby roma (plum) tomatoes. For about 250 g (9 oz) diced tomatoes, finely chop some red onion or spring onion (scallion) and coriander (cilantro) leaves – or basil or mint, depending on which direction you're going. Finish with a sprinkle of salt and a good squeeze of lime juice or, if you're staying European, bury 1 bruised garlic clove in the tomatoes and dress with a slug of extra virgin olive oil.

Guacamole

The starting point for a good guacamole is good avocados. Don't even bother unless you have beautiful, buttery, ripe ones. Mash or chop the flesh of 4 large avocados with ½ crushed garlic clove, 3 thinly sliced spring onions (scallions), 1 chopped chilli, 1 small handful chopped coriander (cilantro) leaves, 1 teaspoon salt and the juice of 1–2 limes. Serve as a dip with corn chips or to go with any Mexican dish.

COSY
Kitchen
SUPPERS

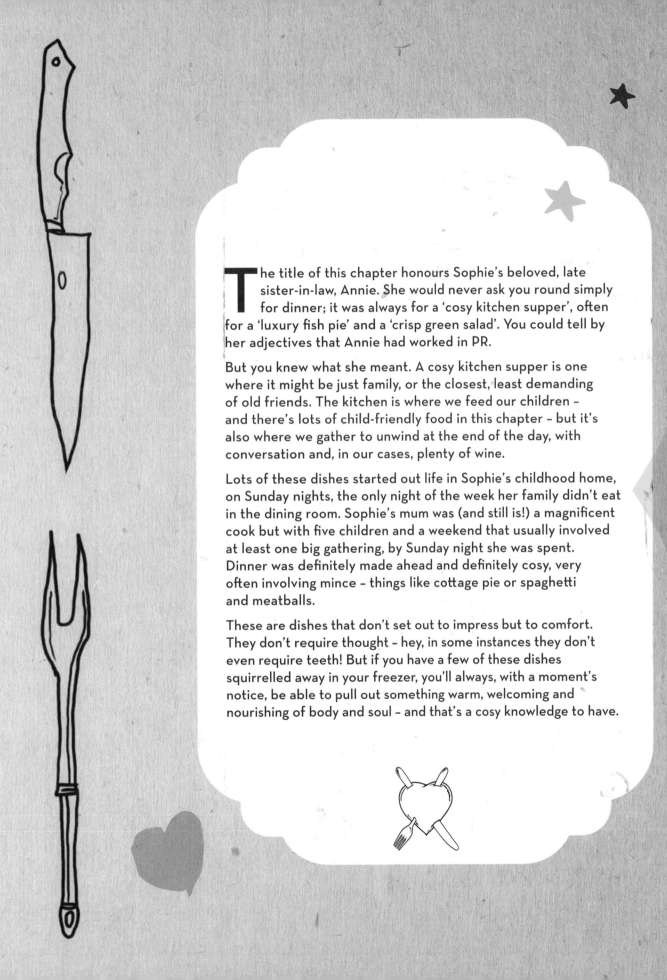

The title of this chapter honours Sophie's beloved, late sister-in-law, Annie. She would never ask you round simply for dinner; it was always for a 'cosy kitchen supper', often for a 'luxury fish pie' and a 'crisp green salad'. You could tell by her adjectives that Annie had worked in PR.

But you knew what she meant. A cosy kitchen supper is one where it might be just family, or the closest, least demanding of old friends. The kitchen is where we feed our children – and there's lots of child-friendly food in this chapter – but it's also where we gather to unwind at the end of the day, with conversation and, in our cases, plenty of wine.

Lots of these dishes started out life in Sophie's childhood home, on Sunday nights, the only night of the week her family didn't eat in the dining room. Sophie's mum was (and still is!) a magnificent cook but with five children and a weekend that usually involved at least one big gathering, by Sunday night she was spent. Dinner was definitely made ahead and definitely cosy, very often involving mince – things like cottage pie or spaghetti and meatballs.

These are dishes that don't set out to impress but to comfort. They don't require thought – hey, in some instances they don't even require teeth! But if you have a few of these dishes squirrelled away in your freezer, you'll always, with a moment's notice, be able to pull out something warm, welcoming and nourishing of body and soul – and that's a cosy knowledge to have.

Cottage Pie

<u>SERVES</u> 4   <u>PREP TIME</u> 20 MINUTES   <u>COOKING TIME</u> 1 HOUR 35 MINUTES, PLUS 5 MINUTES RESTING

2 tablespoons olive oil

650 g (1 lb 7 oz) minced (ground) beef

1 teaspoon salt, plus a pinch

1 large brown onion, diced

1 plump garlic clove, crushed

1 large carrot, finely diced

150 ml (5 fl oz) red wine

1½ tablespoons tomato paste
    (concentrated purée)

3 thyme sprigs, leaves stripped

2 tablespoons Worcestershire sauce

750 g (1 lb 10 oz) potatoes, peeled and
    diced into 5 cm (2 inch) cubes

2 tablespoons salted butter, cubed

100 ml (3½ fl oz) milk

175 g (6 oz) baby peas (frozen are fine)

So many of the recipes in this chapter started out life as Sunday night suppers from childhood, eaten on our knees in front of Countdown or Sixty Minutes. This is one of those family classics, comforting, complete and so very easy when it comes to preparation and clean-up. Just the way to end the weekend.

Make ahead: The whole dish can be made, assembled and stored, covered, in the fridge for up to 3 days or the freezer for up to 3 months. You can defrost it before cooking or cook straight from frozen, adding 15 minutes to the cooking time and making sure that the pie is heated right through to the middle.

Preheat the oven to 180°C (350°F).

In a large, heavy-based saucepan, heat 1 tablespoon of the oil over medium–high heat and add the minced beef with the 1 teaspoon of salt. Brown the beef, breaking up any lumps with a wooden spoon or potato masher. Remove with a slotted spoon, leaving any oil behind.

To the same pan, add the onion, garlic and carrot with the pinch of salt and the remaining oil and cook over low heat for about 10–15 minutes, stirring frequently until soft and sweet but not coloured. Return the beef to the pan and splash in the red wine, turning the heat up to high for about 5 minutes to allow some of the wine to reduce.

Turn the heat down to low again and add the tomato paste, thyme and Worcestershire sauce. Simmer, stirring occasionally, until the meat is tender and the mixture has reduced and is looking a bit shiny (about 20 minutes or so). Taste for seasoning and adjust if you like. Set aside, keeping warm if you're using within an hour, or chilling for later use.

While the beef is cooking, put the potatoes in a large saucepan of cold, well-salted water. Bring to the boil, then turn the heat down to medium–low and simmer for 20–25 minutes. When the potatoes are tender, remove from the heat and drain. Put the potatoes back in the dry saucepan and shake over medium heat for a moment to dry out any excess moisture. Mash with a potato ricer or masher, add the butter, allowing it to melt, then the milk and whisk till smooth. Taste for seasoning.

When you're ready to cook, take a 1.5 litre (52 fl oz/6 cup) ovenproof dish with sides at least 5 cm (2 inches) high and spoon the beef into the bottom of the dish. Add a layer of baby peas, then blobs of mashed potato, smoothing them together to form a continuous crust to the edges. Use a fork to rough up the potato if you'd like some nice brown ruffles as it cooks.

Put the dish in the oven and cook for 30–45 minutes. Ensure that it's heated right through to the centre either by checking the heat with a sharp knife or skewer inserted into the middle then lightly touched to your lip, or testing with a meat thermometer – at least 70°C (158°F) is safe.

Allow to rest for 5 minutes or so before dishing up.

Char Siu Pork

SERVES 4–6, DEPENDING ON THE FINISHED DISH   PREP TIME 5 MINUTES, PLUS 3 HOURS–3 DAYS MARINATING
COOKING TIME 30 MINUTES, PLUS 10 MINUTES RESTING

2 garlic cloves
60 g (2¼ oz) fermented red bean curd
    (plus 1 tablespoon or so of its liquid)
1 teaspoon Chinese five-spice
1½ tablespoons gluten-free light soy
    sauce
2 tablespoons miso paste
1½ tablespoons white rice vinegar
1½ tablespoons Chinese rice wine
120 g (4¼ oz) honey
1 kg (2 lb 4 oz) pork neck fillets, cut into
    4 long strips (use tenderloins for a
    leaner option)

TO SERVE
steamed rice
stir-fried Asian greens

· ·

NOTE: Larger supermarkets now stock miso paste and Chinese rice wine, but you can source these as well as the fermented red bean curd from Asian grocers.

So many quick, easy (and cheap!) dinners can be made with this sweet, red-rimmed pork, which stars in small quantities in fried rice, noodles, rice paper rolls, Chinese omelettes ... We came up with this recipe because of an unwholesome addiction to the char siu marinade in jars, which is delicious but contains a few additives we'd rather do without. This version is also gluten free.

Make ahead: *The pork can be marinated and stored, covered, in the fridge for up to 3 days or in the freezer for up to 3 months. Once cooked, the pork can be kept in the fridge, covered, for up to 5 days and used for a variety of dishes.*

In the bowl of a food processor, combine the garlic, fermented red bean curd, Chinese five-spice, soy sauce, miso paste, rice vinegar, Chinese rice wine and honey, and blitz till smooth. Taste for seasoning – it should be powerfully salty, sweet and rich.

Put the pork fillets in a large glass or ceramic bowl and coat well with the marinade. Refrigerate for at least 3 hours or up to 3 days.

Preheat the oven to 200°C (400°F) and have ready a roasting tin with a wire rack positioned over the top.

Take the fillets out of the marinade, reserving the marinade. Place the fillets on the rack and put into the oven to roast. Meanwhile, boil the reserved marinade in a small saucepan over high heat for 5 minutes to reduce slightly as well as to pasteurise it before basting the pork.

Cook the pork for 30 minutes, basting with marinade every 10 minutes, until the pork is red-gold and smelling delicious.

Rest for 10 minutes on a board to collect the juices before carving in thin slices across the pieces of pork. Serve immediately with steamed rice, the pork juices and stir-fried Asian greens. Any leftovers can be used in lots of different ways (see below).

A Few Ways WITH Leftover Char Siu Pork

Because char siu packs such a big flavour punch, a little leftover pork can go a long way. We love to make an omelette of eggs beaten with some soy sauce and then fill it with chopped char siu pork, spring onions (scallions) and snow pea (mangetout) sprouts, drizzled with a bit of oyster sauce. Another favourite dinner is shredded char siu pork rice paper rolls with carrot, cucumber and spring onion (all cut into thin matchsticks), sprigs of mint and coriander (cilantro), chopped chillies, crushed roasted peanuts, cooked rice vermicelli, hoisin sauce and nuoc mam cham.

Bucatini all'Amatriciana

SERVES 4   PREP TIME 5 MINUTES   COOKING TIME 55 MINUTES

1 tablespoon olive oil

350 g (12 oz) thickly cut pancetta, diced into 1.5 cm (⅝ inch) cubes

1 medium brown onion, diced

2 garlic cloves, crushed

2 teaspoons salt, plus pinch

200 ml (7 fl oz) dry white wine

1 small dried chilli, crumbled

800 g (1 lb 12 oz) tinned chopped tomatoes

500 g (1 lb 2 oz) bucatini (tubular spaghetti)

1 large handful basil, leaves plucked and roughly torn

TO SERVE

grated parmesan or pecorino cheese

. . . .

NOTE: Substitutes for the pancetta include guanciale (a delicious alternative) or bacon (at a pinch).

This is the fall-back dinner in Sophie's house, the one that is quick to prepare, uses ingredients that are often already hanging around in the fridge and pantry, and is greeted with universally happy cries. Make a vat of it and freeze in 1 litre (35 fl oz/4 cup) tubs. You will congratulate yourself for months.

Make ahead: *The sauce can be made ahead and stored, covered, in the fridge for 3 days or in the freezer for 3 months. Defrost before reheating and add the basil at the end.*

Heat the olive oil over medium–high heat in a large, heavy-based frying pan and fry the pancetta, stirring frequently, until the fat is beginning to render and the pancetta just beginning to get crisp at the edges. Scoop the pancetta out with a slotted spoon, leaving the oil in the pan. Put the pancetta on a plate, cover and set aside.

In the same oil (add more oil if necessary), cook the onion and garlic over medium–low heat with the pinch of salt, stirring frequently, until they are soft and sweet but not browned – this will take 10–15 minutes.

Turn the heat up to high and splash in the white wine, allowing it to come to the boil and bubble for a few minutes. Crumble in the dried chilli and stir in the tomatoes.

Turn the heat back to medium–low and simmer for about 30 minutes or until the sauce tastes more intense and looks shiny rather than watery. You can blitz it with a stick blender at this stage if you'd like a smoother sauce. Return the cooked pancetta to the pan and keep warm while you cook the pasta.

Bring 2 litres (70 fl oz/8 cups) of water to a vigorous boil over high heat in a large saucepan and add 2 teaspoons of salt, then boil the pasta according to the packet instructions.

Drain through a colander and return to the saucepan, along with the sauce and most of the basil. Toss the sauce, pasta and basil together with tongs and serve, scattered with extra basil and grated parmesan or pecorino cheese.

Classic Fish Pie

SERVES 4   <u>PREP TIME</u> 30 MINUTES, PLUS 4 HOURS–OVERNIGHT CHILLING   <u>COOKING TIME</u> 1 HOUR 10 MINUTES

1 fennel bulb, bottom and outermost
   layer removed, diced into 1.5 cm
   (5/8 inch) cubes
1 large brown onion, sliced
2 teaspoons olive oil
1 teaspoon salt
60 g (2¼ oz) salted butter
1½ tablespoons plain (all-purpose)
   flour
300 ml (10½ fl oz) milk
zest of 1 lemon, finely grated
2 teaspoons wholegrain mustard
3 thyme sprigs, leaves stripped
1 small handful parsley, leaves and top
   stems finely chopped
600 g (1 lb 5 oz) firm white-fleshed fish,
   skinned, boned and cut into 3 cm
   (1¼ inch) chunks
2 tablespoons coarse, fresh
   breadcrumbs

MASHED POTATO
700 g (1 lb 9 oz) potatoes, peeled and
   diced into 4 cm (1½ inch) cubes
2 teaspoons salt
2 tablespoons salted butter
2 tablespoons milk

TO SERVE
sliced fennel and rocket (arugula) salad
   or
steamed English spinach with garlic,
   lemon and olive oil

. . . .

NOTE: We use snapper in this dish, but
any fish or a combination of fish and
even raw, peeled prawns (shrimp) could
be used.

An old-fashioned mashed potato–topped fish pie, with chunks of spanking fresh fish in a herb and lemon-flavoured béchamel. We've been disturbed by fish pies in the past where the fish and seafood have been cooked twice, once in the sauce, and then again in the oven. The texture has been chalky (the fish) and/or rubbery (the seafood). Feeling that chalk and rubbers are best kept in pencil cases, we've come up with a different method.

Make ahead: The best (and safest) way to make this dish is to have all the elements – the sauce, the mash, the fish – ready and chilled, then to assemble it cold, with the fish raw, so that it only cooks once. This way you can assemble the dish any time on the day you plan to cook it – or freeze it for up to 3 months (don't defrost before cooking – just add 15–20 minutes to the cooking time). If you're not making the dish ahead, have the sauce and potatoes at the same temperature (room temperature or warm) and cook the pie as soon as it's assembled. Avoid putting cold fish in warm sauce and letting it sit around before cooking.

In a large saucepan over medium heat, cook the fennel and onion in the olive oil with the salt until completely soft and sweet but not browned. This should take 10–15 minutes. Reserve, warm, until needed.

In a separate small saucepan, melt 2 tablespoons of the butter over low heat and sprinkle in the flour, stirring vigorously. Cook until the flour smells toasty and no longer raw, then add the milk gradually, whisking constantly until it's all incorporated. Keep stirring over a gentle heat until the béchamel is thick like cream. If there are any lumps, blitz with a stick blender. Stir through the lemon zest, mustard and herbs, then pour the sauce over the reserved vegetables. Taste for seasoning and adjust if necessary. Chill, covered, in the fridge anywhere from 4 hours to overnight.

Meanwhile, cover the potatoes with cold water, add the salt and bring to the boil over high heat. Turn down to medium and boil for 20–25 minutes until completely tender. Drain, then mash with a masher or ricer. Add the butter and milk and whisk till smooth. Chill, covered, in the fridge.

When you're ready to cook the pie, preheat the oven to 180°C (350°F).

Mix the diced raw fish with the cold sauce. Fill a 1.5 litre (52 fl oz/6 cup) capacity pie dish with the fish mixture, dollop the mashed potato on top and smooth with a spatula. Use a fork to create ridges in the mash and sprinkle with the breadcrumbs. Dot with butter and put the pie in the oven.

Cook for 45 minutes or until golden brown on top and a skewer inserted into the middle feels good and hot when you touch it lightly to your lip – you can also check with a meat thermometer that reads 60°C (140°F).

Serve with a fresh green salad, such as thinly sliced fennel and rocket, or steamed English spinach with garlic, lemon and olive oil.

Chicken Noodle Soup

SERVES 4   PREP TIME 30 MINUTES   COOKING TIME 1 HOUR 20 MINUTES

1 x 1.3 kg (3 lb) chicken
1½ teaspoons salt
2 garlic cloves, 1 whole, 1 crushed
1 large handful parsley, stems removed and reserved, leaves coarsely chopped
3 celery stalks, thinly sliced
3 carrots, diced
2 brown onions, diced
1 tablespoon olive oil
2 leeks, white parts only, thinly sliced
60 g (2¼ oz) risoni or other small soup pasta
50 g (1¾ oz) baby English spinach

TO SERVE
freshly ground black pepper
crusty bread

Sophie found some of this stashed in the freezer recently when she was at home with the flu and cried with happy relief. Admittedly, she was at a particularly low ebb, but this soup is the essence of comfort and we would be most surprised if it doesn't have magical healing powers.

Make ahead: The whole soup can be made ahead and stored, covered, in the fridge for up to 3 days or in the freezer for up to 3 months. The pasta continues to suck up liquid after it's cooked and when it's reheated, so add some water if necessary when you reheat the soup.

Put the chicken in a large saucepan with 1 teaspoon of the salt and cover with water – 1.25–1.5 litres (44–52 fl oz/5–6 cups) should do it. In with the chicken, place the whole garlic clove, the parsley stems, half the celery, half the carrots and half the onions. Bring to the boil over high heat, skim, then turn down to low and simmer for 1 hour or until the chicken is able to be pulled off the bone and the broth is flavoursome.

Remove the chicken and allow to cool until able to be handled. Strain and skim any fat from the broth. You can reduce it over high heat at this stage if you want to intensify the flavour. When the chicken is cool, shred the meat off the bones into bite-sized pieces – the bones have given up all their goodness now and can be discarded. Cover the shredded chicken till needed. (This will give you more chicken than is strictly necessary for this dish. Either go to town and have your soup chock-full of chicken or save some of the breast for sandwiches or salads.)

In another large saucepan, heat the olive oil over medium–low heat and cook the remaining celery, carrot, onion and garlic with the sliced leeks and the remaining ½ teaspoon of salt for about 10–15 minutes until soft and sweet. Pour in the reserved chicken broth and turn the heat up to medium to bring it back to temperature. Add the risoni or other pasta and cook according to the instructions on the packet, until al dente.

Stir through the shredded chicken, baby spinach and parsley leaves and taste for seasoning.

Serve hot, with freshly ground black pepper, crusty bread and a nice warm blanket.

The Dinner Ladies Lasagne

SERVES 4–5   PREP TIME 30 MINUTES   COOKING TIME 2 HOURS 10 MINUTES, PLUS 10 MINUTES RESTING

2 tablespoons olive oil
1 brown onion, chopped
1 celery stalk, diced
1 carrot, diced
1 garlic clove, chopped
1½ teaspoons salt
600 g (1 lb 5 oz) minced (ground) pork
    and veal
75 ml (2½ fl oz) red wine
400 g (14 oz) tinned chopped tomatoes
1 tablespoon tomato paste
    (concentrated purée)
2 thyme sprigs, leaves chopped
2 bay leaves
2 tablespoons salted butter
35 g (1¼ oz/¼ cup) plain (all-purpose)
    flour
400 ml (14 fl oz) full-cream (whole) milk
50 g (1¾ oz) parmesan cheese, grated
pinch of ground nutmeg
9 instant lasagne sheets
100 g (3½ oz) mozzarella cheese,
    shredded

TO SERVE
Mixed Leaf Salad (see page 59)

There's an argument to be made that lasagne is the cosiest of all kitchen suppers. The whole thing has to be made in advance and takes at least 45 minutes to cook, leaving you with nothing more to do than sit chatting with your friends and family over a glass of wine. Feel free to substitute beef if you don't eat pork. This makes one 20 x 30 cm (8 x 12 inch) rectangular lasagne, and feeds the average family. It can easily be multiplied upwards to feed more in a larger baking dish – just add 15–20 minutes to the cooking time as well and make sure the whole surface of the lasagne is speckled with golden brown to ensure that it's cooked. If you want a recipe for bolognese sauce, just make the ragu without the lasagne sheets and béchamel – this amount will feed about six with pasta, but obviously the recipe can be multiplied ad infinitum.

Make ahead: The whole, uncooked lasagne can be made ahead, wrapped in plastic wrap and stored, covered, for up to 3 days or frozen for up to 3 months. Cook from frozen, adding 15 minutes to the cooking time.

In a medium saucepan, heat the olive oil over medium–low heat and gently cook the onion, celery, carrot and garlic with 1 teaspoon of the salt till very soft and sweet. Don't rush this step – it should take 10–15 minutes.

Raise the heat to high, add the pork and veal, and cook until it has all changed in colour, breaking up lumps as you go. A potato masher works well as a lump-smasher.

Add the red wine and bring to the boil, then stir in the tomatoes, tomato paste and herbs. Turn the heat down very low, partially cover with a lid and simmer gently for 45 minutes–1 hour or until the sauce is thick and rich and the meat is tender. Taste for seasoning.

While the ragu is cooking, melt the butter very gently over low heat in another medium saucepan. Add the flour and stir constantly with a wooden spoon, until the flour–butter mix is cooked out and no longer raw-tasting. This should take about 3–4 minutes. Pour in the milk, stirring constantly with a whisk to stop lumps forming and cook gently until the béchamel has thickened to the consistency of cream. (If there are any lumps, blitz it with a stick blender.) Add half the parmesan, the nutmeg and the remaining ½ teaspoon of salt. Taste for seasoning.

Preheat the oven to 200°C (400°F).

To assemble, spoon one-third of the ragu into the base of a 20 x 30 cm (8 x 12 inch) rectangular ovenproof dish and then place 3 lasagne sheets side by side over the sauce. Spread half of the remaining ragu over the lasagne sheets, then sprinkle with half the mozzarella. Add 3 more lasagne sheets, then the final portion of ragu and the second half of the mozzarella. Finally, place on 3 more lasagne sheets and top with the béchamel.

Sprinkle with the remaining grated parmesan and put in the oven for 45 minutes or until golden all the way across the top. Any sunken white patches suggest that the lasagne is still uncooked.

Remove from the oven and rest for 10 minutes to come together, then serve with a green salad.

THE DINNER LADIES
LASAGNE, *page* 110

SAUSAGE ROLLS
WITH SNEAKY VEG, *page* 114

Sausage Rolls WITH Sneaky Veg

MAKES 12 LUNCH-TIME SAUSAGE ROLLS OR 24 PARTY-SIZED ROLLS   PREP TIME 30 MINUTES
COOKING TIME 50 MINUTES

1 tablespoon olive oil
½ large brown onion, diced
1 garlic clove, crushed
¼ red capsicum (pepper), seeded and diced
1 small zucchini (courgette), diced
1 small carrot, diced
½ teaspoon ground fennel, toasted
200 g (7 oz) tinned chickpeas, drained and mashed or puréed with a stick blender
2 thyme sprigs, leaves stripped
1 small handful parsley, leaves and stems chopped
1 teaspoon salt
250 g (9 oz) minced (ground) pork (not too lean) or beef
500 g (1 lb 2 oz) puff pastry (store-bought is absolutely fine – we like butter puff)
1 egg, beaten, to brush

TO SERVE
tomato sauce (ketchup), for dunking

Between us, we have the full, delightfully varied range of vegetable-eating children, from dedicated kale-smoothie drinkers to those who eat only meat and white food (pappy bread, pasta, etc.), and we know that there is no child (and very few adults with the strongest of wills) who can resist a sausage roll dunked in sauce. As the filling for these ones is more than half veg, they fulfil a parent's dual, often mutually incompatible, needs for food that a) they won't feel guilty feeding their children and b) the kids will actually eat.

Make ahead: It is really worth making a big batch of these ahead and freezing them, raw, in containers with layers of baking paper in between. Then they can be whipped out for a quick supper or to cook ahead for kids' lunch boxes with no effort involved. Bake them straight from frozen and just add 15 minutes to the cooking time. If you're not freezing them, they can be made the day ahead and stored, covered, in the fridge before baking.

In a wide, heavy-based frying pan, heat the olive oil over medium–low heat and cook the onion, garlic, capsicum, zucchini and carrot, stirring often, until all the vegetables are soft, even mushy. Continue to cook until the mixture is reduced by half and quite dry. This should take about 20 minutes.

Stir through the fennel, chickpeas, thyme and parsley. Add the salt and taste for seasoning, remembering that the meat still has to go in.

If the vegetable mixture still has discernible chunks, especially if you're really trying to sneak them past suspicious small people, allow it to cool slightly and purée it with a stick blender or in a food processor. Allow to cool to room temperature, then chill in the fridge.

When ready to assemble, mix the vegetable mixture thoroughly with the minced pork or beef in a large mixing bowl. Pluck out a small ball of the mix and fry it in a small, non-stick frying pan to taste for seasoning. Adjust, as you'd like.

If the puff pastry is thick, we roll it out further, so the ratio of pastry to filling isn't too overwhelming and to make more sausage rolls from the filling. (Baking paper on the top and bottom of the pastry makes this job much less stressful.)

You should have squares or rectangles of pastry in front of you. Spoon blobs of filling in a continuous line down the length of the pastry, about 5 cm (2 inches) in from the left-hand side, and smoosh them together with your fingertips to make one long sausage shape (you could also pipe the filling through a bag but it's probably easier not to). Leave a 10 cm (4 inch) space and make another line of filling, and so on, until there's no more filling left. With a sharp knife, cut a line halfway between each line of filling. Using a pastry brush, paint the right-hand exposed pastry of each line with water and roll up each long sausage roll, pressing the pastry gently to seal. Then, depending on the length of the pastry and how long you'd like your sausage rolls, cut them across with a sharp knife and a decisive action. Chill or freeze the sausage rolls until you're ready to cook.

Preheat the oven to 200°C (400°F).

Line a baking tray with baking paper and lay the sausage rolls on top. Brush with a pastry brush dipped in beaten egg. Put in the oven and bake until puffed and golden brown – approximately 25 minutes from fresh and up to 40 minutes from frozen.

Remove from the oven and cool a little before serving with tomato sauce for dunking.

Coconut Curry Lentil Soup

<u>SERVES</u> 4–6   <u>PREP TIME</u> 20 MINUTES   <u>COOKING TIME</u> 45 MINUTES

1 tablespoon peanut oil or other mild-
  flavoured oil
1 large brown onion, chopped
2 garlic cloves, finely chopped
1 x 5 cm (2 inch) piece ginger, grated
pinch of salt
1½ tablespoons tomato paste
  (concentrated purée)
2 teaspoons ground cumin, toasted
2 teaspoons ground coriander, toasted
½ teaspoon ground turmeric
pinch of ground nutmeg
pinch of freshly ground black pepper
pinch of chilli flakes
305 g (10¾ oz/1½ cups) red lentils
1 litre (35 fl oz/4 cups) vegetable stock
1 litre (35 fl oz/4 cups) coconut milk
400 g (14 oz) tinned chopped tomatoes
4 kale stalks, tough stems removed and
  leaves coarsely chopped
1 large handful coriander (cilantro),
  leaves plucked and coarsely chopped
  (reserve some whole leaves to serve)
1 tablespoon lemon juice

TO SERVE
plain yoghurt
coriander (cilantro) leaves

This warming vegan dish is a filling meal in a bowl on its own or could be served over rice as a sort of dal. It's based on a spiced masala of onion, garlic and ginger, with collapsed red lentils and enriched with coconut milk. A few handfuls of chopped kale gives the soup an extra dimension of texture and minerally flavour.

Make ahead: This will keep for up to 3 days, covered, in the fridge or up to 3 months in the freezer. For best results, keep the kale out and add it when reheating so that it retains its brilliant green colour.

Heat the oil in a large saucepan over medium–low heat, add the onion, garlic and ginger with the salt and cook, stirring frequently, until soft and sweet – about 10–15 minutes. Still stirring, add the tomato paste, cumin, ground coriander, turmeric, nutmeg, pepper and chilli flakes.

Turn the lentils through the spiced onions, then cover with the stock, coconut milk and tomatoes. Turn the heat up to high and bring to the boil, then turn down to low and simmer gently for about 25–30 minutes until the lentils are completely cooked and have collapsed into a purée.

At this stage, check the consistency and seasoning of the soup – you may need to add some water to thin it down. The salt level will depend on the stock you've used – add some salt if the soup needs it.

Fold the kale into the soup and continue to simmer until it is just tender. Stir through the chopped coriander. Add the lemon juice and taste again for balance.

Serve, with a swirl of plain yoghurt, scattered with coriander leaves.

Family Beef AND Vegetable Stew

SERVES 4   PREP TIME 20 MINUTES   COOKING TIME 2 HOURS

1 tablespoon olive oil

1 kg (2 lb 4 oz) chuck or blade steak, diced into 4 cm (1½ inch) cubes

1½ teaspoons salt

2 small brown onions, chopped

2 garlic cloves, crushed

2 tablespoons tomato paste (concentrated purée)

250 ml (9 fl oz/1 cup) veal or beef stock (home-made or low/no salt)

400 g (14 oz) tinned chopped tomatoes

2 carrots, sliced into rounds 5 mm (¼ inch) thick

2 celery stalks, cut into 5 mm (¼ inch) slices

300 g (10½ oz) parsnip (or celeriac, sweet potato or other starchy veg), diced into 3 cm (1¼ inch) cubes

3 thyme sprigs, leaves stripped

zest of 1 lemon, finely grated

195 g (7 oz/1½ cups) frozen baby peas

3 rosemary sprigs, leaves plucked and chopped

TO SERVE

mashed or baked potato

This is the sort of dish Sophie would cook up in batches when she had very little children, happy in the knowledge that she'd covered all bases. (Not one but six vegetables! All different colours! No Tiny Teddies!) She'd blitz a bowlful for the baby, mix some with pasta for the toddler and dish up the parents' version with a baked potato and a glass of red so large as to be held in only by its meniscus. Happy times, those early years, but occasionally trying. If you're making this for babies, leave most or all of the salt out.

Make ahead: *The whole stew will benefit from being made ahead and stored, covered, in the fridge for up to 3 days or in the freezer for up to 3 months. Defrost before reheating.*

Heat the oil in a large, heavy-based saucepan or flameproof casserole dish over medium heat and brown the beef in batches, seasoning with 1 teaspoon of the salt as you go. The beef doesn't need to be evenly browned on all sides – it's for added flavour, not to 'seal' the meat. Scoop each batch out with a slotted spoon and set aside.

In the same oil, cook the onions over low heat until tender, then add the garlic and cook until very soft and sweet – about 10 minutes.

Add the tomato paste, veal or beef stock and tomatoes and bring to the boil, scraping up any bits of onion or beef that are stuck to the bottom.

Turn the heat back down to low and return the beef to the pan along with the carrots, celery, parsnip and thyme. Partially cover with a lid and simmer for about 2 hours or until the beef is very tender.

When you're almost ready to serve, stir in the lemon zest, baby peas and rosemary and cook for another 5 minutes until the peas are warmed through.

Taste for seasoning and add the remaining ½ teaspoon of salt if necessary (if you're really making this toddler-friendly you should probably stick to the lower amount).

Serve with mashed or baked potato.

Meatballs with Sweet Tomato Sauce

SERVES 4   PREP TIME 30 MINUTES   COOKING TIME 1 HOUR 5 MINUTES

MEATBALLS

600 g (1 lb 5 oz) minced (ground) pork
   and veal
½ large brown onion, finely chopped
1 plump garlic clove, crushed
60 g (2¼ oz/¼ cup) fresh ricotta
finely grated zest of ½ lemon
2 thyme sprigs, leaves stripped
1 small handful parsley, finely chopped
pinch of freshly grated nutmeg
1 egg, beaten
1 teaspoon salt

TOMATO SAUCE

1 tablespoon olive oil
½ brown onion, finely chopped
1 large garlic clove, crushed
½ teaspoon salt
800 g (1 lb 12 oz) tinned chopped
   tomatoes

TO SERVE

spaghetti (vegetti if you prefer –
   see below) or polenta
grated parmesan cheese
1 small handful basil leaves, torn

Meatballs are the epitome of comfort food in so many cultures – these ones have their roots in Italy and, no matter how many times we've made them, we still find them absolutely delicious, as do all our families. We roast our meatballs rather than fry them, for a lighter result, but feel free to fry yours if you prefer. Just make sure they cook all the way through to the middle.

Make ahead: *The whole dish can be made ahead and stored, covered, in the fridge for up to 3 days or in the freezer for up to 3 months. Defrost before reheating.*

Combine all the meatball ingredients in a large mixing bowl. With a clean or gloved hand, give the mixture a good pounding to develop the proteins, which will help the balls keep their shape and not break apart when cooking. Cover with plastic wrap and keep refrigerated until ready to cook.

Meanwhile, start the tomato sauce by heating the olive oil in a large saucepan over low heat and adding the onion and garlic with the salt. Cook for 5 minutes, stirring, until the onion is sweet and soft but not coloured. Add the tomatoes, turn the heat up to medium and cook, stirring occasionally, for about 15 minutes or until slightly reduced and no longer watery looking. Blitz with a stick blender and taste for seasoning. Keep warm while you prepare the meatballs.

Preheat the oven to 200°C (400°F) and line a baking tray with baking paper. Have a small bowl of water handy for dipping your fingers, which will make the rolling easier and less messy. With a tablespoon or your hands, pluck out spoonfuls of the mixture and roll with wet hands into meatballs about the size of golf balls. Place the balls in neat rows on the baking tray – the recipe should make about 24.

Roast the meatballs in the oven for 30–35 minutes or until golden brown and cooked through. Transfer them from the tray to the tomato sauce.

Simmer the meatballs in the tomato sauce for 5–10 minutes, then serve with spaghetti (or vegetable ribbons – 'vegetti' – if you're so inclined) or polenta, lots of grated parmesan and torn basil leaves.

Tip

If you're avoiding carbs, vegetable spaghetti (aka zucchetti or vegetti) is a satisfying substitute for pasta. Making it is dead simple if you have a spiralizer, but you can also make ribbons out of any vegetable – zucchini (courgette), carrot, sweet potato – with a vegetable peeler. Lightly blanch them in salted boiling water for 30 seconds, drain and toss with the sauce.

Salmon Fish Cakes

SERVES 4 (MAKES 8 GOOD-SIZED FISH CAKES) PREP TIME 20 MINUTES, PLUS 1 HOUR CHILLING IN FRIDGE
COOKING TIME 55 MINUTES

3 teaspoons salt

400 g (14 oz) boneless, skinless salmon
fillet or tinned salmon

400 g (14 oz) potatoes, peeled and cut
into 4 cm (1½ inch) chunks

zest of ½ lemon, finely grated

1 small handful parsley, finely chopped

2 spring onions (scallions), ends
removed and white and pale green
parts finely chopped

2 teaspoons capers, drained and rinsed,
finely chopped

3 tablespoons plain (all-purpose) flour

freshly ground black pepper

2 eggs, beaten

30 g (1 oz/½ cup) panko breadcrumbs

peanut oil or other mild-flavoured oil

TARTARE SAUCE

4 tablespoons good-quality mayonnaise

2 teaspoons chopped cornichons

2 teaspoons chopped capers

2 teaspoons chopped red onion or
French shallot

2 teaspoons flat-leaf parsley, finely
chopped

2 teaspoons tarragon, finely
chopped

a good squeeze of lemon juice

TO SERVE

Tartare Sauce (above)
Mixed Leaf Salad (see page 59)
lemon wedges

Crunchy on the outside, pillowy soft within, fish cakes are perfect home comfort food – but if you serve them with home-made tartare and a mixed leaf salad, they're special enough to serve anybody.

Make ahead: *These can be made and stored, covered, in the fridge for up to 3 days or in the freezer for up to 3 months. Defrost, then cook and turn very gently – they'll be soft after defrosting. It's worth making a few batches at once – once you're on a roll with shaping and crumbing, you might as well keep going.*

Fill a medium saucepan with water and bring to a gentle simmer over medium heat. Add 1 teaspoon of salt then gently add the salmon fillet and poach for 8 minutes. With a slotted spoon, remove the salmon from the water and flake with a fork. Cool to room temperature.

Meanwhile, put the potatoes in a medium saucepan and cover with cold, well-salted water. Bring to the boil, turn down to a simmer and continue to cook until tender when pierced with a fork (about 25–30 minutes). Drain well, then mash with a ricer or potato masher and cool to room temperature.

In a large mixing bowl, combine the salmon, potatoes, lemon zest, parsley, spring onions and capers. The mixture should have chunks of salmon and potato. Mix through ½ teaspoon of the salt, taste and add extra if needed. Chill the mixture, covered, in the fridge for at least 1 hour to firm up.

Prepare four plates: one with plain flour seasoned with salt and pepper, the next with beaten egg, the third with panko breadcrumbs and the fourth to hold the finished fish cakes. With wet hands, take a ball of the fish cake mixture – a bit smaller than a tennis ball, about 100 g (3½ oz) – and flatten it into a disc. Dip in the seasoned flour, then the beaten egg and finally in the panko breadcrumbs. Try to keep one hand for the egg and one for the panko, but don't worry too much. Place the finished fish cakes on a clean plate, using baking paper in between if you need to stack them, and cover with plastic wrap. Refrigerate until ready to cook.

While you wait, gently combine the tartare sauce ingredients in a bowl. Season then taste, adding more salt or lemon if needed, then cover and put in the fridge until needed.

Pour about 1 cm (½ inch) of oil into a deep, heavy pan and place over medium heat. When the oil is hot enough to sizzle a breadcrumb, carefully add as many fish cakes as you can without crowding them. Cook for about 4 minutes or until golden brown on one side, then gently flip with a spatula and cook for a further 4 minutes or until golden brown on the second side. Drain on paper towel, keeping warm while you cook the remaining fish cakes. Serve with the tartare sauce, mixed leaf salad and lemon wedges.

Lion's Head Meatballs

<u>SERVES</u> 4 <u>PREP TIME</u> 25 MINUTES <u>COOKING TIME</u> 40 MINUTES

650 g (1 lb 7 oz) minced (ground) pork

100 g (3½ oz) water chestnuts, drained if tinned, defrosted if frozen, coarsely chopped

2 egg whites

¼ red onion, finely chopped

1 x 5 cm (2 inch) piece ginger, grated

2 garlic cloves, crushed

1 large handful coriander (cilantro), stems and leaves, washed and finely chopped

1¼ teaspoons salt

1 tablespoon cornflour (cornstarch)

3 tablespoons Chinese rice wine

800 ml (28 fl oz) good quality chicken stock (home-made or low/no salt)

3 tablespoons soy sauce (gluten-free if desired)

1 teaspoon white sugar

150 g (5½ oz) bean thread vermicelli (aka glass or mung bean noodles)

½ Chinese cabbage (wong bok), end removed, thinly sliced

TO SERVE

coriander (cilantro) leaves

Sriracha or other chilli sauce

We love soupy, slurpy, noodle-y dishes like this one. The lion's head meatballs have all the satisfaction of dumplings but without the heaviness of the wrappers; to make the dish lighter still, you could swap Shirataki Noodles (see page 27) for the bean thread vermicelli.

Make ahead: The meatballs for this dish can be made ahead of time (any extras make delicious food with drinks as well) and stored in the fridge for up to 3 days or in the freezer for up to 3 months. You could also completely make the whole dish, broth and all, and refrigerate or freeze for the same time. Defrost before reheating.

Preheat the oven to 200°C (400°F).

In a large stainless steel bowl, mix the minced pork, water chestnuts, egg whites, onion, ginger, garlic, coriander, salt, cornflour and 1½ tablespoons of the rice wine. Get your hands stuck in and give the mixture a good slap and pound – it will develop the proteins, which will help the balls stick together.

Fry up a small disc of the mixture to taste for seasoning and adjust accordingly. Roll into biggish meatballs – about the size of a squash ball, about 75 g (2¾ oz) – and lay them in rows on baking trays lined with baking paper. Roast these in the oven for about 30 minutes, then break one apart to make sure it's cooked. Oh dear, you'll have to eat that one now. When the meatballs are all cooked, set them aside in a warm place.

In a large saucepan, heat the stock with the soy sauce, the remaining rice wine and the sugar over medium heat. Taste the broth for flavour and reduce if it needs more intensity, but bear in mind that it should be quite a gentle backdrop to the meatballs. Add the bean thread vermicelli and cabbage to the hot broth till both have softened – this should only take a few minutes.

Serve the meatballs in four deep bowls. Ladle the soup over the top, making sure that the meatballs are coated with cabbage and noodles (we ask you to suspend disbelief and imagine the king of the beasts as a pork meatball with a cabbage and noodle mane). Scatter with a few coriander leaves and serve with some chilli sauce on the side.

Chicken AND Roast Vegetable Pie

SERVES 4 PREP TIME 45 MINUTES–1 HOUR (IF MAKING YOUR OWN PASTRY)
COOKING TIME 1½ HOURS, PLUS 5 MINUTES RESTING

200 g (7 oz) pumpkin (winter squash/
    peeled weight), seeded and diced
    into 3 cm (1¼ inch) cubes
1 large carrot, cut into 1.5 cm (5⁄8 inch)
    slices
1½ teaspoons salt
1½ tablespoons olive oil
1 brown onion, thinly sliced
500 g (1 lb 2 oz) boneless, skinless
    chicken thigh fillets, trimmed of fat
    and cut into bite-sized pieces
1 tablespoon salted butter
1 tablespoon plain (all-purpose) flour,
    plus extra for dusting
200 ml (7 fl oz) full-cream (whole) milk
zest of 1 lemon
1 tablespoon wholegrain mustard
1 tablespoon chopped tarragon
50 g (1¾ oz) baby frozen peas
475 g (1 lb 1 oz) Shortcrust Pastry (see
    page 187 or use store-bought)
olive oil spray
1 egg, beaten

TO SERVE
mashed potato

. . . .

NOTE: If you don't want to use
shortcrust pastry, you can simply make
a top of 250 g (9 oz) puff pastry.

The ultimate family dinner in one: a home-made shortcrust pastry crust chock-full of chunks of free-range chicken and caramelised roast vegetables, in a wholegrain mustard, lemon zest and tarragon sauce. We make our pies with a shortcrust top and bottom but, obviously, it would be easier and much quicker just to whack on a bought puff pastry lid.

Make ahead: The whole pie can be made ahead and refrigerated overnight or frozen for up to 3 months. If you have disposable pie foils, it's worth making a few at a time and freezing one or two for later. You can cook straight from frozen – just apply egg wash and add 15 minutes to the cooking time.

Preheat the oven to 180°C (350°F).

Toss the pumpkin and carrot in ½ teaspoon of the salt and 2 teaspoons of the olive oil. Line a baking tray with baking paper and spread the veggies on top. Roast in the oven for 25–30 minutes or until tender and beginning to brown at the edges. Remove and keep warm, covered, until the rest of the filling is ready.

In a medium, heavy-based frying pan, heat the remaining tablespoon of olive oil and cook the onion with the remaining salt over medium–low heat for about 10–15 minutes until soft, sweet and lightly golden. Add the chicken pieces and cook, flipping and stirring frequently, until they are cooked through and opaque. Keep warm while you make the sauce.

In a medium saucepan, melt the butter over low heat and sprinkle in the flour, stirring vigorously with a wooden spoon. Continue to cook until the flour smells toasty and no longer raw-tasting (about 3–4 minutes), then add the milk gradually, stirring constantly – a whisk works well for this – until it has all been incorporated. Keep stirring over low heat until the béchamel begins to thicken to about the consistency of cream – it should coat the back of a spoon. If there are any lumps in the sauce, blitz with a stick blender. Stir through the lemon zest, mustard and tarragon, then the chicken and onion mixture. Finally fold through the roast vegetables and baby peas and taste the mixture for seasoning. Chill the mixture and refrigerate, covered, until ready to make the pie.

Ideally, you will have split your pastry when you were making it, into two flat rounds, one slightly larger than the other. Flour your rolling pin and your work surface, and roll out the pastry into two rounds to the required size to match a 21 x 25 x 4 cm (8¼ x 10 x 1½ inch) pie tin. The smaller piece will make the pie top. The larger piece needs to fit the bottom and sides of the pie tin. Use baking paper above and below the pastry to make this job less stressful.

Preheat the oven to 180°C (350°F) again.

Spray or brush the pie tin with a little olive oil. Make sure the lip is well oiled – this is the place your pie is most likely to stick. Line the bottom with the larger pastry round and fill with the chicken mixture. Using a little cup of water and your fingertip, wet the pastry rim to help the top stick down, then put the pastry top on. Crimp around the edge of the pie's top with a fork to seal the edge of the pie. Once you have finished, pierce two little holes in the middle of the pie with a sharp knife to let the steam escape in the cooking process.

Brush the pastry lid with the beaten egg and put the pie in the oven for 45 minutes or until golden brown all over. To make sure that the pastry base is cooked, cover the top with foil and cook for another 15 minutes.

If you're cooking a pie with a puff pastry lid only, roll out the pastry to a little larger – about 4 cm (1½ inches) – than your pie dish. Cut a strip of pastry 2 cm (¾ inch) wide and stick it onto the rim of the pie dish with water. Now wet the top of that pastry rim before placing the pastry lid on the rim and crimping as before. Cut two slits in the lid, brush with the egg wash and bake for 25 minutes or until brown and puffed.

Rest the pie for 5 minutes before serving with mashed potato.

Pancetta-wrapped Meatloaf

SERVES 4   PREP TIME 15 MINUTES, PLUS 3 HOURS CHILLING IN FRIDGE
COOKING TIME 1 HOUR, PLUS 10 MINUTES RESTING

1 small brown onion, coarsely chopped

1 carrot, cut into 3 pieces

¼ red capsicum (pepper), seeded and coarsely chopped

1 celery stalk, cut into 3 pieces

2¼ tablespoons olive oil

1 garlic clove, crushed

1½ teaspoons salt

550 g (1 lb 4 oz) minced (ground) pork and veal

1 small handful parsley, leaves and top stems, finely chopped

2 thyme sprigs, leaves stripped and finely chopped

1 egg, beaten

50 g (1¾ oz) breadcrumbs (use rice crumbs or gluten-free breadcrumbs if you'd like)

pinch of freshly grated nutmeg

2 tablespoons tomato paste (concentrated purée)

100 g (3½ oz) pancetta, thinly sliced

TO SERVE

mashed or baked potato

Coleslaw (see page 85)

tomato chutney

We've always loved meatloaf, slightly kitsch and '70s though it is. This one – long since borrowed and adapted from 72 Market Street in Venice, California – is packed with flavour from a base of slowly cooked vegetables. For a pork-free version, use beef and skip the pancetta – it won't be exactly the same but it's still good.

Make ahead: The uncooked meatloaf can be completely made up to 1 day ahead, covered in plastic wrap and refrigerated, or frozen for up to 3 months (defrost before cooking). If you're not using the mixture immediately, it is essential that the vegetable mixture is fridge-cold before mixing with the meat.

Put the onion, carrot, capsicum and celery in the bowl of a food processor and process till evenly chopped, pulsing and using a spatula to scrape down the sides of the bowl.

Heat 2 tablespoons of the olive oil in a large non-stick frying pan and add the vegetable mixture, garlic and 1 teaspoon of the salt. Cook, stirring frequently, for 15 minutes or until the veggies are sweet and soft and most of the moisture has evaporated. Empty into a bowl and leave aside to cool.

In a large mixing bowl, combine the pork and veal with the now cool vegetables, as well as the parsley, thyme, egg, breadcrumbs, nutmeg, the remaining ½ teaspoon of salt and the tomato paste. Mix really well – clean or gloved hands will do the job most thoroughly – until the mixture is uniformly coloured with herbs and vegetables, adding more breadcrumbs if it's too wet. Roll a small ball of the mixture, flatten it, and cook in 1 teaspoon of olive oil in a small, non-stick frying pan over medium to check for seasoning. Adjust if necessary.

Take a 10 x 20 cm (4 x 8 inch)/1 litre (35 fl oz/4 cup) capacity loaf (bar) tin or terrine mould (a plastic takeaway container does the job nicely too) and line it with overlapping strips of pancetta. Fill the tin with the uncooked mixture and pat down well, so that the mix is evenly spread into the corners. Cover with plastic wrap and put in the fridge for at least 3 hours to firm up.

When you're ready to cook, preheat the oven to 180°C (350°F) and line a baking tray with baking paper. Up-end the meatloaf on the baking tray to un-mould it like a sandcastle. If it's proving stubborn, run a knife around the perimeter of the mould – it should slip out easily.

Put the tray in the centre of the oven and cook for 45 minutes. To test if the meatloaf is cooked, insert a skewer or sharp knife into the centre and lightly touch the end to your lip – if it's not piping hot, return it to the oven for a further 5 minutes and test again. Alternatively, use a meat thermometer and check that it reads 70°C (158°F).

After removing from the oven, set aside for 10 minutes before slicing thickly and serving with potato, coleslaw and tomato chutney.

Potager Pie

SERVES 4   PREP TIME 30 MINUTES   COOKING TIME 1½ HOURS

150 g (5½ oz) Puy lentils or tiny
    blue-green lentils
350 ml (12 fl oz) vegetable stock
    (home-made or low/no salt)
2 teaspoons olive oil
½ brown onion, chopped
1 carrot, chopped
1 celery stalk, chopped
1 large garlic clove, crushed
1 teaspoon salt
1 rosemary sprig, leaves plucked
    and chopped
1 thyme sprig, leaves stripped
    and chopped
2 bay leaves
100 g (3½ oz) button mushrooms,
    diced
10 g (¼ oz) dried porcini mushrooms,
    ground to a powder
2 teaspoons tomato paste
    (concentrated purée)
100 ml (3½ fl oz) red wine
2 teaspoons red wine vinegar
200 g (7 oz) tinned chopped tomatoes
1 tablespoon chopped parsley
600 g (1 lb 5 oz) potatoes, diced into
    4 cm (1½ inch) cubes
1 heaped tablespoon salted butter
80 ml (2½ fl oz/⅓ cup) milk
2 tablespoons grated parmesan cheese
150 g (5½ oz) frozen baby peas

We were more than usually pleased with ourselves when we came up with the name of this veggie pie – potager being the French word for a kitchen garden and sounding a little like cottage pie, in which it has its roots. We've converted many a meat-lover with this dish – the lentils, braised in stock with loads of herbs and vegetables, make a satisfyingly meaty alternative and we've upped the umami levels with porcini powder in the base and parmesan in the mash. For this sort of dish, where we want the lentils to stay firm and separate (as opposed to a porridgy dal, for example) we'll always use Puy-style lentils – they're the small, dark blue-green ones. To be true Puy lentils, they must come from a specific region of France, but versions grown in Australia and elsewhere are now available in most supermarkets.

Make ahead: *The whole pie can be assembled and stored, covered, in the fridge for 3 days or in the freezer for 3 months. You can cook the pie from frozen – just add 15 minutes to the cooking time and check that it's heated right through to the middle.*

Put the lentils in a medium saucepan, cover with the vegetable stock, and bring to the boil over medium–high heat. Turn down to a simmer and cook until just tender but still firm – about 20 minutes. Leave in the stock until ready to use.

Heat the oil in a large frying pan over medium heat, then add the onion, carrot, celery, garlic and salt and cook, stirring frequently, until soft and sweet – at least 10 minutes. Add the rosemary, thyme and bay leaves with the button mushrooms and cook till the mushrooms are tender, about 5 minutes. Stir through the porcini powder, tomato paste, red wine and vinegar, and turn the heat up so that the mixture comes to the boil, cooking off some of the liquid. Add the tomatoes and reduce to a simmer.

With a slotted spoon, lift the lentils out of their cooking liquid and add them to the vegetable base. Continue to simmer until the mixture is a good consistency (we're aiming for a similar consistency to traditional cottage pie mince). Taste for seasoning and stir in the chopped parsley. Set aside, covered, while you make the mashed potato topping.

Meanwhile, for the mash, put the potatoes in a medium saucepan and cover with cold, well-salted water. Bring to the boil, turn down to a simmer and continue to cook until tender when pierced with a fork (about 25–30 minutes).

Mash the potatoes in the way you usually would – we like the texture produced by a potato ricer but a masher is fine. Whisk in the butter, milk and half the parmesan and taste for seasoning.

Preheat the oven to 180°C (350°F).

Take a 1.5 litre (52 fl oz/6 cup) capacity ovenproof dish and spread the lentil mixture across the base, then scatter over the baby peas. Cover the peas with the potato topping (the easiest way to do this is to dob large spoonfuls across the dish, then gently spread them with a spatula so that they meet up). Fluff up the potato topping with a fork to create interesting ridges that will brown nicely. Sprinkle with the remaining parmesan.

Put the pie in the oven and cook for 35–45 minutes or until golden on top and heated right through.

Roast Pumpkin, Ricotta AND Sage Lasagne

<u>SERVES 4–6</u>   <u>PREP TIME</u> 25 MINUTES   <u>COOKING TIME</u> 1 HOUR 40 MINUTES, PLUS 10 MINUTES RESTING

1.1 kg (2 lb 7 oz) pumpkin (winter squash), peeled, seeded and chopped into 5 cm (2 inch) pieces
pinch of chilli flakes
3 teaspoons salt
1½ tablespoons olive oil
1 small handful sage, leaves plucked and torn
good grind of black pepper
375 g (13 oz) fresh ricotta (from a deli if possible, not a pre-packaged tub)
pinch of ground nutmeg
1 fat garlic clove, finely chopped
135 g (4¾ oz) parmesan cheese, grated
700 ml (24 fl oz) full-cream (whole) milk, plus 4 tablespoons extra for the pumpkin filling
70 g (2½ oz) salted butter
70 g (2½ oz) plain (all-purpose) flour
9 instant lasagne sheets
75 g (2¾ oz) shelled walnuts, toasted and coarsely chopped
95 g (3¼ oz/⅔ cup) shredded mozzarella cheese

TO SERVE
1 tablespoon walnuts, crushed
rocket (arugula) or radicchio salad

Pumpkin, sage and walnuts are a beautiful combination – the savouriness of the sage and slight bitterness of the walnuts give an edge to the pumpkin's full-bore sweetness.

Make ahead: The whole lasagne can be made ahead of time and kept, covered, in the fridge for up to 3 days or in the freezer for up to 3 months – foil baking trays from the supermarket are perfect for this. Lasagne may be cooked straight from frozen – just add 15 minutes to the cooking time.

Preheat the oven to 180°C (350°F).

Toss the pumpkin with the chilli flakes, 1 teaspoon of the salt and 1 tablespoon of the olive oil. Line a baking tray with baking paper and spread the pumpkin pieces on top. Roast for 30–40 minutes or until soft and browning at the edges. Slide the pumpkin into a stainless steel bowl and allow to cool, then mash roughly with a fork or a potato masher before folding through the torn sage leaves. Taste for seasoning and grind in some black pepper.

In a large mixing bowl, whisk the ricotta with the nutmeg, garlic, a third of the grated parmesan and enough milk to make the mix a spreadable consistency (about 4 tablespoons).

Stir the butter in a medium saucepan over medium–low heat until melted. Stir in the flour and continue to cook, stirring constantly, till the flour smells toasty and is no longer raw-tasting. Slowly drizzle in the 700 ml (24 fl oz) of milk, using a whisk to incorporate it into the flour–butter roux. Keep whisking until all the milk has been added, then continue to cook, stirring constantly until the béchamel has thickened to the consistency of thickish cream. Stir in a third of the parmesan and the remaining 2 teaspoons of salt – taste for seasoning. If your béchamel is lumpy, whizz through it with a stick blender.

Place a 20 x 30 cm (8 x 12 inch) rectangular lasagne dish on the work surface and brush it with the remaining 2 teaspoons of olive oil. Spread 1 heaped tablespoon of the pumpkin mixture on the bottom of the dish to hold the lasagne sheets in place, then place 3 sheets side by side on top of the mix. Divide the rest of the pumpkin mix and the ricotta mix into two equal bowls or tubs (so, four in all). Spread one lot of pumpkin on the lasagne, dob the ricotta mix on top and scatter with walnuts and 1 tablespoonful of shredded mozzarella. Repeat until all the lasagne sheets and filling are finished. Pour the béchamel sauce over the top and scatter with the final third of the grated parmesan.

Bake, uncovered, in the centre of the oven for 50–60 minutes or until it is golden and blistered right across the surface (this will take longer if being cooked straight from the fridge or freezer).

Remove from the oven and allow to stand for 10 minutes before scattering with walnuts and serving with a rocket or radicchio salad.

Pea AND Ham Soup

<u>SERVES 8</u>   <u>PREP TIME</u> 20 MINUTES   <u>COOKING TIME</u> 2 HOURS

2 carrots, chopped
1 large brown onion, chopped
2 garlic cloves, peeled but left whole
2 bay leaves
4 thyme sprigs, leaves stripped
1 smoked ham hock, about 800 g
    (1 lb 12 oz)
400 g (14 oz) split peas, yellow or green
195 g (7 oz/1½ cups) frozen baby peas
    (optional)

TO SERVE
freshly ground black pepper
Sourdough Croutons (below)

This timeless, essential winter soup recipe was inspired by Stephanie Alexander but we've fiddled with the cooking method a little. Rather than combining everything at the start and risking the peas sticking to the bottom of the saucepan, we cook the ham and vegetables together first, so that the ham can impart its smoky porkiness to the cooking broth. Then, after removing the ham, we cook the peas. Give it a go – this method works really well for cooking in large quantities.

Make ahead: *The whole soup can be made ahead and stored, covered, in the fridge for 3 days or in the freezer for 3 months. Defrost before reheating and stir well as you heat, to bring the soup's texture back together.*

Choose a large, heavy-based saucepan big enough to take the ham hock, and add the carrots, onion, garlic, herbs and ham. Cover with 3 litres (105 fl oz) of water and bring to the boil over high heat. Turn the heat down to low and simmer, partially covered, for about 1 hour or until the ham is tender. Skim off any foam that rices to the surface.

Use a pair of tongs to transfer the ham to a plate, leaving the stock and vegetables in the saucepan. Add the split peas, raise the heat to high and bring the stock to the boil, skimming off any foam that rises to the surface. Reduce the heat to low and simmer, stirring occasionally and adding water if necessary, until the peas have completely collapsed (about 45 minutes). Add the baby peas, if using – they'll boost the colour as well as adding a bit of sweetness. Purée with a stick blender and taste for seasoning – hams can vary hugely in saltiness so judge for yourself what the soup needs.

When the ham is cool enough to handle, pull off its skin, which should take most of the fat with it. Trim off any excess fat and shred the ham into small, bite-sized pieces. Discard the bones, gristle and fat, and return the ham pieces to the soup. Taste again and adjust the seasoning if you'd like.

Serve warm with a good grind of black pepper and a handful of sourdough croutons.

Sourdough Croutons

A jar of sourdough croutons will give a crunchy lift to any soup or salad. To make them, trim the crusts off slices of sourdough, then cut into cubes. Pour extra virgin olive oil to a depth of 2 cm (¾ inch) in a heavy frying pan and heat until a dropped crumb sizzles immediately but doesn't burn. Fry your bread cubes until golden brown on all sides, then drain on paper towel. When cool, store in an airtight container. They will keep for up to 1 month.

Minestrone

SERVES 4   PREP TIME 20 MINUTES   COOKING TIME 1½ HOURS

160 g (5½ oz) dried white beans, soaked overnight – or 400 g (14 oz) tinned cooked beans, drained and rinsed
2 teaspoons olive oil
1 large brown onion, chopped
2 carrots, finely diced
3 celery stalks, thinly sliced
4 garlic cloves
3 silverbeet (Swiss chard) stalks, stems and leaves separated and both thinly sliced but kept separate
2 teaspoons salt
400 g (14 oz) Savoy cabbage, core removed, leaves thinly sliced
3 kale stalks, tough stems removed and discarded, leaves coarsely chopped
1 parmesan cheese rind (don't buy this specially but try to remember to keep your rinds for recipes like this)
400 g (14 oz) tinned chopped tomatoes
1 litre (35 fl oz/4 cups) vegetable stock (home-made or low/no salt)
1 tablespoon tomato paste (concentrated purée)
1 large handful parsley, chopped

TO SERVE
extra virgin olive oil
finely grated parmesan cheese
sourdough bread

This soup is based on The River Café's classic recipe where the vegetables cook very slowly in their own juices till they're a delicious, deep, dark mess. Every time we make it, we marvel that such humble, healthy ingredients can be transformed into something so very special.

Make ahead: The whole soup can be made ahead and stored, covered, in the fridge for 3 days or the freezer for 3 months. Defrost before reheating.

Drain the beans, put them in a medium saucepan and cover with fresh water. Bring to the boil over high heat and skim the foam that rises to the surface. Turn the heat down to low and simmer till tender – this will vary according to the age of the dried beans and the length of soaking time but begin checking after 45 minutes. Or you could always open a tin.

In a large saucepan, heat the oil over low heat and add the onion, carrot, celery, garlic and silverbeet stems with the salt. Cook, stirring frequently, until soft and sweet, about 15–20 minutes. Don't rush this job – it's essential to the minestrone's success that this soffritto is cooked long and slowly. Now add the cabbage, half the silverbeet leaves, half the kale and the parmesan rind (the leafy greens will be very bulky at this stage but will cook down). Stir though the tomatoes, stock and tomato paste, partially cover with a lid and cook for about 30 minutes until the cabbage is very tender. Add the cooked white beans and at this stage make a decision about whether the soup needs to have more liquid. We like our minestrone to be as thick as a stew, but add water or vegetable stock if you prefer yours soupier.

Cook for another 10 minutes after adding the beans, then stir in the remaining silverbeet and kale with the parsley. Cook on until the leaves have wilted but are still vibrantly green.

Remove the parmesan rind and serve the soup in wide shallow bowls, drizzled with extra virgin olive oil and scattered with finely grated parmesan, with toasted sourdough on the side.

Salmon, Sweet Potato AND Broccoli Bites

MAKES 20 SMALL BITES – ENOUGH FOR 5–6 LITTLE CHILDREN OR 4 ADULTS   PREP TIME 20 MINUTES
COOKING TIME 40 MINUTES

200 g (7 oz) sweet potato, diced into
    3 cm (1¼ inch) cubes
70 g (2½ oz) broccoli, chopped into
    small florets
320 g (11¼ oz) salmon
1 garlic clove, chopped
zest of ¼ lemon
1 tablespoon dill, chopped
1 egg, beaten
1–2 heaped tablespoons rice flour
1 teaspoon salt
2 tablespoons peanut oil or other mild-
    flavoured oil

TO SERVE
lemon wedges
Tartare Sauce (see page 120) or tomato
    sauce (ketchup)

We wish we'd had this recipe when we had small, fussy people to feed. It's a perfect little package of protein, carbs and veg – and quite delicious enough to feed to large, fussy people, too. Sometimes fishmongers will have cheaper, uneven-sized offcuts of salmon from cutting fillets. As the fish is going to be minced anyway, it makes no difference to this dish so it's worth asking.

Make ahead: *The mixture can be made ahead, rolled into balls and kept, covered, in the fridge for 1 day or in the freezer for up to 3 months. Defrost before cooking.*

Put the sweet potato in a small saucepan and cover with well-salted water. Bring to the boil over high heat and cook for about 20–25 minutes until completely tender. Drain and cool, then cover till needed.

Fill the same saucepan with well-salted water, bring to the boil and add the broccoli. Cook until tender, then drain under a running cold tap, to arrest the cooking and keep the colour.

In a food processor, pulse-chop the sweet potato, broccoli, salmon, garlic, lemon zest, dill, egg, 1 tablespoon of the rice flour and the salt until thoroughly combined. If the mixture still seems a bit wet, add more rice flour. Chill, covered, until ready to use.

Roll a small, flat piece of the mixture and fry in a little of the oil in a non-stick frying pan over high heat for 1 minute each side, taste for seasoning and adjust if necessary.

Before you start rolling the patties, have ready a small bowl or jug of water for dipping your hands in – it will make the job a lot cleaner and easier. Scoop out tablespoons of the salmon mixture and, using wet hands, form into balls about the size of a golf ball, then flatten into patties.

When all the mixture has been rolled, heat the non-stick frying pan over medium heat with a little oil. Pan-fry the patties in batches, adding more oil as necessary, for 2 minutes each side or until they are golden brown and cooked through.

Drain on paper towel and serve with lemon wedges, tartare or tomato sauce, depending on the age and sophistication of the intended diners.

Sang Choi Bau of Pork and Shiitake Mushrooms

SERVES 4–6 AS A STARTER, 3 AS A MAIN COURSE   PREP TIME 20 MINUTES, PLUS 1 HOUR SOAKING
COOKING TIME 15 MINUTES

30 g (1 oz) dried shiitake mushrooms
2 tablespoons Chinese rice wine
1½ tablespoons light soy sauce
1 tablespoon oyster sauce
2 teaspoons rice vinegar
2 teaspoons sugar
1 teaspoon sesame oil
1 tablespoon peanut oil or other mild-
    flavoured oil
1 brown onion, chopped
2 garlic cloves, crushed
1 x 4 cm (1½ inch) piece ginger, grated
2 Chinese sausages (lap cheong), finely
    diced
600 g (1 lb 5 oz) minced (ground) pork
50 g (1¾ oz) water chestnuts, diced
4 spring onions (scallions), ends
    removed, sliced diagonally
1 large handful coriander (cilantro),
    roots removed, stems and leaves
    finely chopped

TO SERVE
lettuce cups
    or
steamed rice or noodles and stir-fried
    Asian greens

· ·

NOTE: Chinese sausage (or lap cheong)
is a sweet, dried sausage, available in
the Asian section of most supermarkets
or from Asian grocers.

Anything wrapped in lettuce is irresistible – it's the cool/warm, crunchy/soft contrast that does it for us. You can serve this as a stir-fry over rice or noodles, with a side dish of Asian greens. Otherwise, wrap spoonfuls in lettuce and serve as a first course or lighter dinner. Non-pork eaters can substitute chicken or quail for the pork – unfortunately, there's no easy substitute for the lap cheong.

Make ahead: You can approach this in two ways as a make-ahead dish. For the best results, you could make the sauce and prep all the separate elements up to 1 day ahead, then cook everything immediately before serving. But for convenience – and if it's a midweek dinner and you're just after something easy and yummy – you can make the mixture in advance, just leaving out the spring onions (scallions) and coriander (cilantro), which can be added when you reheat the pork. We often freeze this, too. The addition of fresh green spring onions and coriander gives the defrosted dish the lift it needs at the end.

Soak the shiitake mushrooms for 1 hour in warm water. Drain, remove and discard the stems, then finely chop the mushrooms. Set aside.

For the sauce, mix the rice wine, soy sauce, oyster sauce, rice vinegar, sugar and sesame oil in a small bowl. Taste and make sure it has a balance you like. Set aside till needed.

Heat a large wok over high heat until smoking. Swirl around the peanut oil and add the onion, garlic and ginger, stir-frying briskly till aromatic, no longer raw but not completely soft. Add the Chinese sausage, continuing to fry over high heat for 1–2 minutes, before adding the pork.

Stir-fry the pork, breaking up any lumps, till it's opaque and starting to brown – at this stage, try to boil off as much excess liquid as you can. Add the shiitake mushrooms and toss through.

Tip in the sauce, stirring vigorously so it coats the pork mixture, then fold through the water chestnuts, spring onions and coriander. Taste again for balance.

Serve with lettuce cups for a first course or light dinner, or make it go further with steamed rice or noodles and stir-fried Asian greens.

SPICE *and* ⭐ FIRE

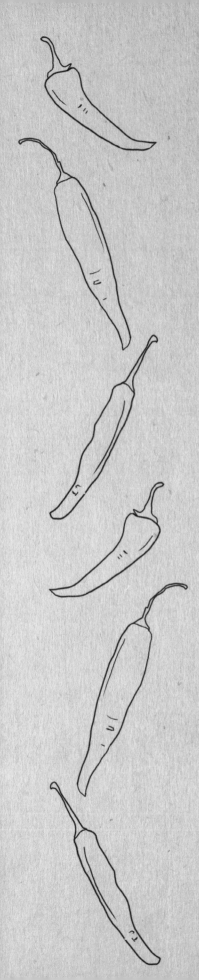

One of the first things we made in a professional capacity (and we use the term loosely) was a curry – a lamb roghan josh, to be exact. If you're cooking ahead of time, curries of all sorts (Indian, Thai, Malaysian, Indonesian, whatever) are a no-brainer because they reheat so well and all their aromatic herbs and spices give them a wonderful complexity. Best of all, the cooking usually takes care of itself while you get on with life.

We both grew up in the Australia of the 1970s, where a curry meant the leftover Sunday roast, diced and cooked with Keen's curry powder with rice, and a breathtaking array of side dishes. We still have early South East Asian cookbooks from the 1980s that suggest substituting lemon zest for lemongrass and milk with coconut essence for coconut milk.

So we're aware of our good fortune now. Every decent-sized supermarket sells coriander with its roots still attached, fresh lemongrass, kaffir lime leaves, whole dried spices and anything else you need to make an authentic-tasting curry. We know, we know – jars of curry pastes are very convenient, but they do make everything taste the same. It's a bit like an okay takeaway but one you wouldn't rave about. It's so easy to make a paste of fresh herbs, fresh spices (ideally freshly ground but at least toasted to bring back their flavour) and basics like onions, garlic and ginger, that will sing with vibrancy and taste nothing like Number 12 from the local Thai or Indian. Plus, making curry pastes is a great use for all those super-powered blenders we bought intending to make green smoothies and which now languish, unloved, alongside the ice-cream machine and popcorn maker.

Most of the dishes in this chapter aren't palate-strippingly hot. With one or two flagged exceptions, they're pitched at a level most people can handle – but you're very welcome to crank the heat up as high as you'd like.

Madras Beef Curry

SERVES 4   PREP TIME 30 MINUTES   COOKING TIME AT LEAST 2 HOURS 15 MINUTES

1 tablespoon peanut oil or other mild-flavoured oil
2 brown onions, chopped
4 garlic cloves, chopped
1 x 3 cm (1¼ inch) piece ginger, grated
1½ teaspoons salt
1 handful curry leaves
1 heaped teaspoon ground turmeric
1 heaped teaspoon ground chilli
1 tablespoon ground coriander, toasted
1½ teaspoons ground cumin, toasted
1 teaspoon tomato paste (concentrated purée)
400 g (14 oz) tinned chopped tomatoes
800 g (1 lb 12 oz) stewing beef, such as shin, chuck or blade, diced into 3 cm (1¼ inch) cubes
375 ml (13 fl oz/1½ cups) coconut milk
1 tablespoon cider vinegar
2 tablespoons desiccated (shredded) coconut
90 g (3¼ oz/1 bunch) coriander (cilantro), leaves only, coarsely chopped, reserve a few whole leaves to garnish

TO SERVE
shaved fresh coconut or toasted desiccated (shredded) coconut
steamed basmati rice or Spiced Rice (right)
Cucumber-Yoghurt Sauce (see page 45)

A beefy crowd-pleaser, full of roast spices, the warmth of chilli, the sour-sweetness of tomato and vinegar and the smooth roundness of coconut milk. Cook the diced beef very gently in a fresh spice paste until it falls apart at the pressure of a fork and finish the curry with toasted coconut and fresh coriander (cilantro) leaves.

Make ahead: *The whole recipe can be made ahead and kept in an airtight container in the fridge for up to 3 days or in the freezer for up to 3 months. Garnish with freshly shaved coconut and fresh coriander leaves before serving.*

Heat the oil over medium heat in a large, heavy-based saucepan and cook the onions, garlic and ginger with a fat pinch of the salt for 10–15 minutes till soft, stirring frequently.

Add the curry leaves, turmeric, chilli, ground coriander, cumin, tomato paste and chopped tomatoes to the onions, and combine. Season the beef with the remaining salt and stir through. Cover with the coconut milk and vinegar and cook till tender. The cooking time will depend very much on the beef – start checking to see if it is tender after 2 hours, but it may well take more than 3 hours, especially if you're using shin.

To finish, stir through the desiccated coconut and chopped coriander.

Serve with shaved fresh coconut or toasted desiccated coconut, steamed basmati rice or spiced rice, and a handful of coriander leaves. A cooling cucumber-yoghurt sauce on the side is always welcome.

Spiced Rice

Bright yellow rice, flecked with whole spices and studded with peas, always looks celebratory and lifts a curry out of the everyday. It's also about as quick to make as plain steamed rice and means you can get away without a vegetable dish (maybe just a raita for good luck). For four people, heat 1 tablespoon oil in a saucepan over medium–low heat and throw in 2 cloves, 1 teaspoon cumin seeds and 1 cinnamon stick and fry till the cumin seeds darken. Add 1 teaspoon salt and ½ teaspoon ground turmeric, then 400 g (14 oz/2 cups) basmati rice, stirring to coat with the spices. Cover with 750 ml (26 fl oz/3 cups) of water, bring to the boil, then add 140 g (5 oz/1 cup) thawed frozen peas, cover the pan tightly with a lid and turn the heat down to the barest simmer for 20 minutes. Take the lid off, fluff up with a fork and remove the cinnamon stick and cloves (if they're easy to find) before serving.

Sweet Potato, Kale AND Chickpea Curry

SERVES 4   PREP TIME 30 MINUTES   COOKING TIME 25 MINUTES

1 tablespoon peanut oil or other mild-flavoured oil
12 curry leaves
1 heaped teaspoon black mustard seeds
1 large brown onion, diced
1 x 3 cm (1¼ inch) piece ginger, grated
3 garlic cloves, crushed
1½ teaspoons salt
1 heaped teaspoon ground coriander, toasted
1 heaped teaspoon ground cumin, toasted
½ teaspoon ground cardamom
¼ teaspoon freshly ground black pepper
¾ teaspoon ground turmeric
pinch of chilli flakes
500 g (1 lb 2 oz) orange sweet potato, diced into 2 cm (¾ inch) cubes
375 ml (13 fl oz/1½ cups) coconut milk
200 ml (7 fl oz) vegetable stock
400 g (14 oz) tinned chickpeas, drained and rinsed
250 g (9 oz/½ bunch) kale, washed, stalks removed, coarsely chopped
juice of ½ lemon

TO SERVE
plain yoghurt
steamed basmati rice
lime wedges
chutney

This curry is a light, beautifully balanced vego dinner, with mineral-rich kale, nutty chickpeas and sweet potato in a spiced coconut-based sauce. It also makes a lovely side dish for a meat-heavy curry such as Lamb Roghan Josh (see page 148) or Lamb Doh Piaza (see page 161).

Make ahead: The whole recipe can be made ahead of time. It will keep in a covered container in the fridge for 3 days or in the freezer for up to 3 months. If you prefer, you can leave the kale out and add it to cook when you reheat the dish, to keep it as green and bright as possible.

Heat the oil in a large, heavy-based saucepan over medium heat. Add the curry leaves and the mustard seeds, stirring, until the seeds start to pop, then add the onion, ginger, garlic and salt. Turn the heat down to low and cook for 10–15 minutes till soft and sweet, stirring occasionally. When soft, stir in the coriander, cumin, cardamom, pepper, turmeric and chilli flakes.

Add the sweet potato to the onion mixture. Cover with the coconut milk and vegetable stock and turn the heat back up to bring the curry to simmering point, then lower the heat again and cook for 10–15 minutes until the sweet potato is just tender. Add the chickpeas, then the kale, and cook for a further 5 minutes. When the kale is wilted, add the lemon juice. Taste for seasoning and balance, and make any adjustments you'd like.

Serve with a swirl of plain yoghurt, steamed basmati rice, lime wedges and chutney.

Butter Chicken

SERVES 4   PREP TIME 20 MINUTES, PLUS AT LEAST 2 HOURS MARINATING   COOKING TIME 35 MINUTES

800 g (1 lb 12 oz) boneless, skinless chicken thigh fillets, trimmed and cut into bite-sized pieces
2½ tablespoons salted butter
2 teaspoons peanut oil or other mild-flavoured oil
½ teaspoon salt
1 large brown onion, diced
¼ teaspoon ground cardamom
1 teaspoon ground cinnamon
½ teaspoon fenugreek seeds, ground
2 bay leaves
1½ teaspoons paprika
50 g (1¾ oz) tomato paste (concentrated purée)
200 ml (7 fl oz) tomato passata (puréed tomatoes)
80 ml (2½ fl oz/⅓ cup) thin (pouring) cream
2 tablespoons almond meal
40 g (1½ oz/¼ cup) unsalted roasted cashew nuts

MARINADE
100 g (3½ oz) plain yoghurt
1 tablespoon lemon juice
1 teaspoon salt
½ teaspoon ground turmeric
2 teaspoons garam masala, toasted
½ teaspoon ground chilli
2 teaspoons ground cumin, toasted
1 x 3 cm (1¼ inch) piece ginger, grated
1 garlic clove, crushed

TO SERVE
steamed basmati rice
Cucumber-Yoghurt Sauce (see page 45)

Whether or not to put this popular British curry house invention on the menu was one of our very first, ahem, differences of opinion (Sophie being a bit of a stickler for authenticity and Katherine being in the I-don't-care-as-long-as-it-tastes-good camp). It was a rare fight that Katherine actually won. Of all the dinners that we make at The Dinner Ladies, this is Katherine's children's number one favourite.

Make ahead: The entire recipe can be made ahead and stored in an airtight container either in the fridge for up to 3 days or in the freezer for up to 3 months. The chicken will benefit from marinating for at least 2 hours or overnight. If you're making ahead of time, leave the cashews out and add towards the end of reheating the dish.

To make the marinade, mix all of the ingredients in a glass or ceramic bowl. Stir through the chicken and set aside in a sealed container in the fridge for at least 2 hours. Overnight is ideal, but any time sitting in the marinade is better than none.

Heat the butter and oil with the salt in a frying pan over low heat. Add the onion and cook, stirring frequently, till soft and sweet – around 10 minutes. Add the cardamom, cinnamon, fenugreek, bay leaves and paprika, and cook for a further 5 minutes, continuing to stir frequently.

Turn the heat up and add the marinated chicken, turning and cooking to seal on all sides and coat with the spiced onions. Turn the heat down and add the tomato paste and tomato passata. Cook slowly, partially covered and stirring occasionally, till the chicken is tender – around 20 minutes.

When the chicken is cooked through, add the cream, almond meal and cashew nuts. Taste for seasoning.

Serve with steamed basmati rice and cucumber-yoghurt sauce.

Thai Chicken Curry with Ginger and Thai Basil

<u>SERVES</u> 4   <u>PREP TIME</u> 30 MINUTES, PLUS 30 MINUTES SOAKING   <u>COOKING TIME</u> 35 MINUTES

1 x 3 cm (1¼ inch) piece ginger, peeled and cut into thin matchsticks

1½ tablespoons coconut oil

1 tablespoon shaved palm sugar (jaggery) or light brown sugar

1½ tablespoons fish sauce

800 g (1 lb 12 oz) boneless, skinless chicken thigh fillets, trimmed and cut into 3 cm (1¼ inch) pieces

8 kaffir lime leaves, spine removed

300 ml (10½ fl oz) coconut milk

130 g (4½ oz/1 cup) frozen baby peas

1 large handful baby English spinach

1 handful Thai basil, leaves plucked

1 long red chilli, seeded and cut into thin matchsticks

CURRY PASTE

1 dried chilli, soaked in hot water, drained and coarsely chopped (reserve the soaking water)

1 x 2 cm (¾ inch) piece ginger, coarsely chopped

2 garlic cloves, coarsely chopped

1 French shallot, coarsely chopped

1 coriander (cilantro) stem, including root, washed carefully and coarsely chopped

zest of 1 lime, finely grated

1 teaspoon shrimp paste

½ teaspoon salt

1 lemongrass stem, white part only, tough outer layer removed, finely chopped

TO SERVE

jasmine rice

This recipe started out as one of David Thompson's, with all his attendant trademark intensity of flavour and authenticity. We've kept the fresh zestiness of the home-made curry paste but made it a bit more midweek-friendly. We use baby peas and English spinach instead of pea eggplants (aubergines) – a bit of an acquired taste – and tone down the chilli heat, though feel free to ramp it back up. This is probably our favourite dish to have in the freezer. Add some rice, and dinner is complete. What bliss.

Make ahead: The whole recipe can be made ahead and stored in an airtight container either in the fridge for up to 3 days or in the freezer for up to 3 months. For maximum vibrancy and freshness, add the peas, red chilli, baby English spinach, Thai basil and some of the lime leaves just before serving.

Soak the ginger matchsticks in warm water for about 30 minutes.

To make the curry paste, blitz all the ingredients in a food processor. If necessary, use a little of the chilli soaking water to help make a fine paste. Make sure the lemongrass is well processed; otherwise, it can be fibrous. Set aside the paste.

Strain the ginger matchsticks. Heat the coconut oil in a large, heavy-based frying pan or wok over medium–high heat. Fry the curry paste till fragrant. Add the palm sugar and fish sauce and stir the curry mixture for about 5 minutes till caramelised, then add the ginger. Turn the chicken pieces through the paste, ensuring each piece is well coated. Add 4 of the lime leaves, crushing them as you go. Cover with the coconut milk, stirring, and turn the heat down to medium. Simmer till the chicken is cooked through. This should take about 20–25 minutes.

When the chicken is cooked, add the peas, spinach, the remaining lime leaves and most of the Thai basil and red chilli, keeping a bit aside for garnish. Taste for sugar and fish sauce, adding more if you think it needs it. Thai flavours should be very punchy, with a balance of sweet, salty, sour and hot.

Serve with jasmine rice and scattered with the reserved Thai basil and red chilli.

Tom Kha Gai

SERVES 4–6   PREP TIME 10 MINUTES   COOKING TIME 1 HOUR

400 ml (14 fl oz) coconut milk
600 ml (21 fl oz) chicken stock
(home-made or low/no salt)
1 x 4 cm (1½ inch) piece galangal, sliced
(see note on page 27)
10 kaffir lime leaves
½ teaspoon salt
300 g (10½ oz) boneless, skinless
chicken thigh fillets, thinly sliced
1 handful oyster mushrooms (or other
available mushrooms if you can't get
oyster)
1½ tablespoons fish sauce
1½ tablespoons lime juice
2 teaspoons shaved palm sugar
(jaggery) or light brown sugar

PASTE
3 coriander (cilantro) stems, washed,
roots cut off, leaves reserved for
garnish
1 lemongrass stem, white part only,
sliced
1 red onion, chopped
2 long green chillies, seeded,
1 chopped, 1 cut into thin matchsticks

TO SERVE
1 long red chilli, cut into thin
matchsticks
2 kaffir lime leaves, cut into thin
matchsticks

Simple to make, everyone's favourite Thai soup is gently spicy, creamy and fragrant, with poached chicken and oyster mushrooms in a coconut base, infused with galangal, lime leaves, lemongrass and coriander. It's a good first course before something coconut-free like the Isaan Barbecued Pork (see page 51) or Thai Marinated Chicken (see page 173). If you're serving it as a main course, you could bulk it up with some cooked rice noodles, making it into a sort of Thai laksa. You're very welcome to use chicken breasts instead of thighs (hey, it's your dinner) but we'd then poach them in the soup only once, just before serving.

Make ahead: *Make the recipe ahead of time and store in an airtight container in the fridge or freeze ahead for 3 months. Add the coriander leaves just before serving.*

To make the paste, blitz all the ingredients in a small food processor. This can be a very rough paste – it will be strained out later.

In a large saucepan over medium heat, bring the coconut milk and chicken stock to a simmer, then add the paste, galangal and 5 of the lime leaves, crushing them as you go to release their flavour. Mix in the salt, turn the heat down to low and simmer for 30 minutes. Strain to remove the herbs and spices.

Bring the soup back up to a low simmer and add the chicken. Poach gently for 20 minutes or until tender and cooked. Add the remaining lime leaves, the chilli matchsticks and the mushrooms and bring them up to heat.

Finish with the fish sauce, lime juice and palm sugar. Taste for the balance of flavours, adding more of any of these if necessary.

Serve in wide bowls, scattered with coriander leaves and strips of chilli and lime leaves.

Lamb Roghan Josh

SERVES 4   PREP TIME 30 MINUTES   COOKING TIME 2 HOURS 15 MINUTES

1 large brown onion, chopped
1 tablespoon peanut oil or other
  mild-flavoured oil
1½ teaspoons salt
8 cardamom pods
½ teaspoon ground turmeric
800 g (1 lb 12 oz) lamb shoulder,
  trimmed and diced into 3 cm
  (1¼ inch) chunks
130 g (4½ oz/½ cup) plain yoghurt
400 g (14 oz) tinned chopped tomatoes
1½ teaspoons garam masala, toasted
1 small handful coriander (cilantro),
  leaves only, chopped

CURRY PASTE
5 garlic cloves, crushed
1 x 5 cm (2 inch) piece ginger, grated
1 teaspoon desiccated (shredded)
  coconut, toasted
1 tablespoon almond meal
1 tablespoon ground coriander, toasted
1 teaspoon ground cumin, toasted
1 teaspoon poppy seeds, toasted
½ teaspoon ground fennel
½ teaspoon ground cardamom
¼ teaspoon ground cloves
¼ teaspoon ground nutmeg
½ teaspoon ground chilli

TO SERVE
steamed basmati rice or Spiced
  Cauliflower Rice (see page 37)
Coriander-Mint Chutney (below)
Cucumber-Yoghurt Sauce (see page 45)
Sweet Potato, Kale and Chickpea Curry
  (see page 143)

The first week we started cooking together, we sent out this famously deep, rich, dark red curry to ten of our friends. Somehow (though it's difficult to fathom why considering how small our operation was), we got our maths wrong and ended up sending a puddle of about one cup of curry to each household. But what a curry! 'F*#%ing awesome' was one response. Clearly size doesn't matter, though we've since brushed up on our maths.

Make ahead: *The whole dish can be made ahead of time and stored in an airtight container in the fridge for 3 days or in the freezer for up to 3 months. Garnish with fresh coriander leaves before serving.*

To make the curry paste, use a small food processer or stick blender to blitz all the ingredients together – you may need to use a little water to get the paste nice and fine.

In a heavy-based saucepan over low heat, fry the onion slowly in the oil with ½ teaspoon of the salt for about 10–15 minutes. When it is soft and sweet, add the cardamom pods and turmeric, then the spice paste.

Season the diced lamb with the remaining 1 teaspoon of salt, then add to the spiced onions, ensuring that the lamb pieces get a good coating all over. Cover with the yoghurt and tomatoes, stir through, then partially cover with a lid and simmer gently till tender – around 2 hours. Stir the curry occasionally and at any time add a little water if it looks like it's going to stick. When it is done, the curry should be deep red, rich and thick.

Finally, stir through the garam masala and the chopped coriander. Taste for seasoning and adjust as you like.

Serve with steamed basmati rice, coriander-mint chutney, cucumber-yoghurt sauce and a vegetable curry like sweet potato, kale and chickpea. Spiced cauliflower rice would be a good accompaniment for carb-avoiders.

Coriander-Mint Chutney

In the bowl of a food processor, blend the leaves of 40 g (1½ oz/½ bunch) mint and 45 g (1½ oz/½ bunch) coriander (cilantro), 1 garlic clove, 1 x 2 cm (¾ inch) piece ginger, ½ teaspoon salt, the juice of ½ lemon and 2 spring onions (scallions). Add seeded green chilli to taste – Sophie would add at least a whole one, Katherine would add the little tip off the end! To make this chutney into a dipping sauce for all sorts of things (Indian spiced meatballs, tandoori chicken pieces, barbecued prawns), add 130 g (4½ oz/½ cup) plain yoghurt (more if you need to tame the chilli).

Vegetable Tagine WITH Olives, Eggplant AND Chickpeas

SERVES 4   PREP TIME 20 MINUTES   COOKING TIME 1 HOUR

400 g (14 oz) pumpkin (winter squash) or sweet potato (peeled weight), diced into 3 cm (1¼ inch) cubes

3 tablespoons olive oil

2 teaspoons salt

1 small eggplant (aubergine), approximately 350 g (12 oz), cut into 4 cm (1½ inch) chunks

1 zucchini (courgette), cut into 3 cm (1¼ inch) chunks

1 large brown onion, chopped

1 red capsicum (pepper), seeded and cut into thick strips

2 garlic cloves, crushed

1 x 3 cm (1¼ inch) piece ginger, grated

3 teaspoons ground coriander, toasted

1½ teaspoons ground cumin, toasted

½ teaspoon ground allspice

½ teaspoon mild paprika

1 heaped teaspoon caraway seeds, toasted and ground

400 g (14 oz) tinned chopped tomatoes

4 long green chillies

2 tablespoons honey

400 g (14 oz) tinned chickpeas, drained and rinsed

50 g (1¾ oz/1 handful) kalamata olives, pitted

TO SERVE
Couscous (see page 159)

1 handful parsley, mint or coriander (cilantro) leaves, chopped

Garlic Yoghurt Sauce (below)

This delicious and slightly unusual vegetable tagine uses roasted rather than steamed vegetables, combined in a lightly spiced tomato-based sauce. There are whole green chillies poached in the sauce (which can be avoided or not, as you see fit) and nuggets of pitted black olives, which give a nice salty counterpoint to the sweet roasted vegetables. This could go well on the side of a meatier dish like the Middle Eastern Lamb with Prunes, Mint and Pistachios (see page 195) or makes a well-rounded vegetarian dish with couscous and a dollop of garlicky yoghurt.

Make ahead: *The whole recipe can be made ahead and stored in an airtight container in the fridge for up to 3 days or in the freezer for up to 3 months. Defrost before reheating gently – the pumpkin or sweet potato will be delicate.*

Preheat the oven to 180°C (350°F). Line two baking trays with baking paper.

Toss the pumpkin in 1 tablespoon of the oil and ¼ teaspoon of the salt, and the eggplant and zucchini in 1 tablespoon of the oil and ¼ teaspoon of the salt and spread over the two trays. Don't overcrowd your trays – the vegetables will stew instead of roast if they are on top of each other. Roast in the oven for around 35 minutes for the pumpkin, and 25 minutes for the eggplant and zucchini till everything is caramelised and cooked through.

Meanwhile, slowly cook the onion, red capsicum, garlic and ginger in the remaining 1 tablespoon of oil and 1 teaspoon of salt in a large saucepan over low heat for 10–15 minutes. When soft and translucent, add the spices and the tomatoes. Add the whole chillies (in one piece, stalk and all), then 400 ml (14 fl oz) of water. Simmer for 30 minutes, then add the honey.

Add the roast vegetables, chickpeas and olives to the spiced broth. Stir together gently, adding more water if it is too thick. Taste for seasoning.

Serve with couscous, chopped herbs and garlic yoghurt sauce.

Garlic Yoghurt Sauce

A dollop of garlic yoghurt sauce is a quick way to liven up kebabs, tagines and koftas – and takes about 5 seconds to make. Combine 260 g (9½ oz/1 cup) Greek-style yoghurt with 1–2 crushed garlic cloves, a good pinch of salt and 1 tablespoon lemon juice. Beat together, taste for balance and adjust. Easy, hey?

VEGETABLE TAGINE WITH OLIVES,
EGGPLANT & CHICKPEAS, *page* 149

RED CURRY OF BEEF
& PEANUTS, *page* 152

Red Curry OF Beef AND Peanuts

SERVES 4   PREP TIME 30 MINUTES   COOKING TIME 2 HOURS 10 MINUTES

1 heaped tablespoon coconut oil

1 tablespoon shaved palm sugar (jaggery) or light brown sugar

1 tablespoon fish sauce

800 g (1 lb 12 oz) beef shin, trimmed and diced into 3 cm (1¼ inch) cubes

8 kaffir lime leaves

400 ml (14 fl oz) coconut milk

50 g (1¾ oz) tinned sliced bamboo shoots, rinsed

3 tablespoons roasted peanuts, coarsely chopped

2 long red chillies, seeded and cut into thin matchsticks

1 large handful Thai basil, leaves plucked

CURRY PASTE

1 star anise, ground

1 teaspoon ground coriander, toasted

1 teaspoon ground cumin, toasted

1 teaspoon ground cinnamon

2–4 dried red chillies, broken up and soaked in hot water (soaking water reserved)

3 garlic cloves, chopped

1 red onion, coarsely chopped

1 lemongrass stem, white part only, outer layers removed, finely chopped

1 x 3 cm (1¼ inch) piece galangal, finely chopped (see note on page 27)

1 coriander (cilantro) stem, including the root

zest of 1 lime

1 teaspoon shrimp paste

1 heaped teaspoon sweet paprika

½ teaspoon salt

TO SERVE

steamed jasmine rice

Green Papaya Salad (opposite)

We know some really excellent cooks who still won't make curry pastes – if this is you (and you know who you are), give it a whirl with this curry. Even the best store-bought pastes have a generic flavour whereas this one is so individual, with its notes of cinnamon and star anise alongside the usual Thai suspects, such as lemongrass and galangal. With a good blender, it should only take a couple of minutes. And you know, if you can't achieve a really fine texture in your paste, a bit of roughness lets people know that you made it yourself. If you're serving this as a one-dish dinner, throw in some lightly blanched snow peas (mangetout) or broccoli florets so that all bases are covered.

Make ahead: *The entire recipe can be made ahead of time and stored in the fridge for up to 3 days or in the freezer for up to 3 months. Garnish with extra crushed roasted peanuts, Thai basil leaves and red chillies just before serving.*

To make the curry paste, use a small food processor or stick blender to blitz all the ingredients together until you have a fine paste. Use a little oil, or some of the chilli soaking water if you need to, so that you can get everything nice and smooth. The more finely you chopped the ingredients to begin with the easier this will be.

Heat a large, heavy-based frying pan or wok with the coconut oil over medium–high heat and fry the curry paste for about 5 minutes till dark and fragrant, stirring constantly.

Add the palm sugar and fish sauce, which will sputter and caramelise, then stir in the beef, coating it all over in the curry paste. Add half the lime leaves, crushing them in your hand as you go, then cover with the coconut milk. Simmer the curry gently until the beef is completely tender, which will take about 2 hours.

When the beef is ready, add the bamboo shoots to the curry with most of the peanuts, the chillies and Thai basil (leaving some of each to scatter on the finished dish). Taste for fish sauce and sugar balance, adding a little of either if you'd like.

Serve with steamed jasmine rice and green papaya salad.

Green Papaya Salad

Crisp, refreshing green papaya salad (or som tum) goes so well with any rich, coconut-based curry as well as being a virtuous Thinner Dinner accompaniment to grilled fish or chicken. You can make and dress it a few hours in advance - re-taste for seasoning just before serving in case excess liquid has diluted the dressing. If you have a food processor with a julienne attachment, it's ready in a couple of minutes; otherwise, you could use a large grater or a mandoline with a julienne blade. Whichever your method, you'll need ½ green papaya (seeded, peeled and julienned - cut into thin matchsticks). Make a dressing by blitzing together 1 garlic clove, 1 seeded long red chilli, 2 tablespoons fish sauce, 2 tablespoons lime juice, 2 teaspoons tamarind purée and 2 tablespoons caster (superfine) sugar. Toss the dressing through the green papaya. You could almost leave it at that - the essentials are the papaya and the dressing - but a true som tum usually also includes cherry tomatoes (quartered), snake (yard-long) beans (chopped), dried shrimp and roasted peanuts, all of them added to the salad and then bruised lightly with a pestle to soften them.

Chicken AND 100 Almonds

SERVES 4   PREP TIME 30 MINUTES   COOKING TIME 55 MINUTES

180 ml (6 fl oz) peanut oil or other mild-
    flavoured oil
2 tablespoons blanched almonds
2 large brown onions, 1 thinly sliced,
    1 chopped
1 x 2 cm (¾ inch) piece ginger, grated
3 garlic cloves, crushed
1½ teaspoons salt
1 tablespoon ground coriander, toasted
1 tablespoons ground cumin, toasted
¾ teaspoon ground turmeric
½ teaspoon ground fennel, toasted
½ teaspoon chilli flakes
250 g (9 oz) tinned chopped tomatoes
90 g (3 oz/1 bunch) coriander (cilantro),
    roots removed and saved for another
    dish, leaves and fine stalks chopped,
    some leaves reserved whole for
    garnish
800 g (1 lb 12 oz) boneless, skinless
    chicken thigh fillets, trimmed and
    diced into 3 cm (1¼ inch) cubes
200 g (7 oz/¾ cup) plain yoghurt
2 tablespoons almond meal
1 teaspoon garam masala, toasted

TO SERVE
poppadoms or steamed basmati rice
Cucumber-Yoghurt Sauce (see page 45)
Fresh Chopped Tomato Salad
    (see page 99)

Katherine's husband once sent her a Valentine card saying 'I love you more than Chicken and 100 Almonds'. It's coming up to twenty years. This is a pretty damn good curry. (That's how Katherine chose to read the message, anyway. Looking at it now, she realises there are other possible interpretations ...) Two lots of almonds – meal and whole – (not quite 100, but who's counting?) darkly fried onions and a slow-cooked spice base make this dish deliciously authentic.

Make ahead: The whole recipe can be made ahead and stored in the fridge for up to 3 days or in the freezer for up to 3 months. Stir in the toasted almonds just before serving and garnish with additional fresh coriander.

Heat the oil in a heavy-based saucepan over medium heat until a piece of bread sizzles immediately when dropped in. Deep-fry first the almonds and then the sliced onion till golden brown. Make sure you don't overcook them – they will taste bitter if they blacken. Spread them out on paper towel to drain. Pour off all but 1 tablespoon of the oil and reserve for the next curry (make a note on it that it was used to cook almonds and onions, just in case of allergies and so you're not tempted to use it in a dessert).

Bring the oil back up to medium heat and cook the chopped onion with the ginger, garlic and a fat pinch of the salt, stirring frequently, until soft and sweet. Don't rush this stage – it should take at least 10 minutes. When this mixture is well cooked, add the ground coriander, cumin, turmeric, fennel, chilli flakes, tomatoes and most of the fresh coriander. Cook for about 20 minutes, stirring occasionally, till the tomato is pulpy.

Season the chicken with the remainder of the salt and add to the spice mixture. Stir through so that it's completely coated. Turn the heat down to low, cover partially with a lid, and simmer for 20 minutes, checking occasionally that the chicken isn't sticking and giving it a stir if it is. When the chicken is just cooked through, stir in the yoghurt, almond meal, fried almonds, garam masala and fried onions (save some of the fried onions for garnish at the table if you like). Taste for seasoning and balance.

Scatter the curry with the reserved coriander leaves and some of the reserved fried onions. Serve with poppadoms or steamed basmati rice, cucumber-yoghurt sauce and a fresh chopped tomato salad.

Chicken Laksa

SERVES 4   PREP TIME 30 MINUTES   COOKING TIME 30 MINUTES

500 g (1 lb 2 oz) boneless, skinless chicken thigh fillets, left whole
700 ml (24 fl oz) chicken stock (home-made or low/no salt)
1 tablespoon peanut oil or other mild-flavoured oil
500 ml (17 fl oz/2 cups) coconut milk
1 tablespoon tamarind purée
1 tablespoon sugar
juice of 1 lime
200 g (7 oz) dried rice noodles (a mixture of fat round ones and vermicelli would be good but whatever's to hand will work)

CURRY PASTE
1 dried chilli
125 ml (4 fl oz/½ cup) boiling water
1 small brown onion, finely chopped
1 x 3 cm (1¼ inch) piece ginger, finely chopped
2 garlic cloves, finely chopped
1 lemongrass stem, white part only, very finely chopped
1 candlenut, chopped
1 heaped teaspoon shrimp paste
1 teaspoon ground turmeric
1 teaspoon ground coriander, toasted
1 teaspoon ground cumin, toasted
1 teaspoon mild paprika
1 teaspoon salt

TO SERVE
bean sprouts
mint leaves
coriander (cilantro) leaves
crisp fried shallots
lime wedges
finely chopped bird's eye chilli

We were cooking laksa in our production kitchen the last time the council came round to conduct a surprise inspection of the premises, and the officer was so distracted by the delightful aromas she almost missed telling us off about the missing air-conditioning vent that we hadn't got round to putting up yet. We make our laksa with chicken Marylands (leg quarters) or thighs; if you'd rather substitute chicken breast or seafood, or a mixture, make the laksa base only and add the chicken or seafood for one final cook only. You can also substitute vegetable stock, tofu and vegetables for a vegetarian version.

Make ahead: *Make a large batch of the paste and store in batches in zip-lock bags in the freezer, so that cooking this up on a time-pressed weeknight in the future will be a doddle. Making a large batch of the paste also makes the job of getting a nice fine paste in a food processor easier. You can make the soup and store it in an airtight container in the fridge for up to 3 days or in the freezer for up to 3 months. Serve with the fresh garnishes at the table.*

To make the curry paste, first soak the dried chilli in the boiling water for about 10 minutes then drain. Using a small food processor or a stick blender, blitz all the ingredients together. Add some of the coconut milk or stock if you need some liquid to get a really smooth paste.

Place the chicken in a saucepan and cover with the stock. Bring just to the boil over medium–high heat, skim off any gunk that rises to the surface, then turn the heat down to low. Partially cover with a lid and simmer till the chicken is cooked through – about 10 minutes. Remove the chicken with tongs, then strain and reserve the stock. Shred the chicken into bite-sized pieces when it is cool enough to handle. Set aside in the fridge.
Heat the oil in a large, heavy-based saucepan over high heat and fry the paste for about 5 minutes till it is well cooked and fragrant, stirring

. . . .

NOTE: Tamarind purée and candlenuts are available at some larger supermarkets and Asian grocers.

Macadamia nuts or Brazil nuts can be substituted for the candlenuts (1 macadamia nut or ½ Brazil nut to replace 1 candlenut). If you can't find tamarind, add some extra lime juice.

constantly. Add the coconut milk and chicken stock and turn the heat down to low. Simmer, stirring occasionally, for 10 minutes, then add the tamarind, sugar and lime juice. Taste for seasoning, and add more salt/tamarind/sugar/lime juice until you have a good salt/sour/sweet flavour balance. Once you are happy with the taste, add the shredded chicken to the soup.

Meanwhile, cook the noodles separately according to the instructions on the packet; drain and keep warm.

Divide the noodles among deep individual serving bowls and ladle the hot laksa over. Put the bean sprouts, mint, coriander, crisp fried shallots, lime wedges and chopped chilli in the middle of the table for people to help themselves, and serve.

Moroccan Chicken with Pumpkin and Preserved Lemon

SERVES 4   PREP TIME 20 MINUTES   COOKING TIME 40 MINUTES

300 g (10½ oz) pumpkin (winter squash), peeled and seeded weight, cut into 4 cm (1½ inch) cubes
1 teaspoon salt, plus a pinch
1½ tablespoons olive oil
1 large brown onion, chopped
2 garlic cloves, crushed
250 g (9 oz/1 cup) tinned chopped tomatoes
¾ teaspoon ground ginger
1½ teaspoons ground cumin, toasted
800 g (1 lb 12 oz) boneless, skinless chicken thigh fillets, trimmed of fat and cut into bite-sized pieces
250 ml (9 fl oz/1 cup) chicken stock
¼ preserved lemon, insides discarded, peel rinsed of salt and cut into thin matchsticks
pinch of saffron threads, soaked in 1 tablespoon hot water

TO SERVE
Couscous (below)
1 small handful coriander (cilantro), washed, leaves plucked

Food and memories ... this dish holds a lot of them. It was one of the very first dishes that we made – back when we were working in the shed in Katherine's backyard. Chopping the pumpkin was one of Denise's first jobs when she started working for us. She didn't like chopping pumpkin much, so very quickly became Head of Everything Else Not to Do With Cooking.

Make ahead: *The whole dish can be made ahead and stored in an airtight container in the fridge for up to 3 days or in the freezer for up to 3 months. Add the fresh coriander just before serving.*

Preheat the oven to 200°C (400°F).

On a baking tray, season the pumpkin with the pinch of salt, toss in 2 teaspoons of the olive oil and roast in the oven for approximately 20 minutes or until cooked through. Set aside.

Heat the remaining tablespoon of olive oil in a frying pan over medium heat and cook the onion and garlic for 10–15 minutes till soft. Add the tomatoes, ginger and cumin, and cook till reduced and pulpy.

Season the chicken with the remaining teaspoon of salt, and stir through the onion and tomato mixture. Add the stock and simmer, partially covered with a lid, stirring occasionally, till the chicken is cooked through, which should take about 20 minutes.

Stir through the preserved lemon and saffron, then very gently fold through the cooked pumpkin. Bring the whole dish back up to heat and serve with couscous, scattered with coriander leaves.

Couscous

To lift your couscous up a notch, use stock instead of water (following the instructions on the packet). After it has cooked, fluff it up with a fork, then stir through any combination of chopped fresh herbs, toasted almonds and pistachios, diced preserved lemon, pomegranate seeds, thinly sliced spring onions (scallions) and currants or barberries. Maybe not all at once, though you could give it a whirl.

Lamb Doh Piaza

SERVES 4   PREP TIME 30 MINUTES   COOKING TIME 2 HOURS 40 MINUTES

100 ml (3½ fl oz) peanut oil or other mild-flavoured oil

800 g (1 lb 12 oz) brown onions, half sliced and half chopped

800 g (1 lb 12 oz) lamb shoulder, trimmed and diced into 3 cm (1¼ inch) cubes

1½ teaspoons salt

2 teaspoons nigella seeds

3 cardamom pods

3 garlic cloves, crushed

1 x 3 cm (1¼ inch) piece ginger, grated

½ teaspoon ground chilli

½ teaspoon mild paprika

1 tablespoon ground coriander, toasted

150 g (5½ oz) plain yoghurt

1½ teaspoons garam masala, toasted

1 large handful coriander (cilantro), leaves and stems chopped, a few leaves reserved for garnish

TO SERVE

basmati rice

Cucumber-Yoghurt Sauce (see page 45)

Doh piaza means 'two onions' and the onions in this deliciously deep, dark curry are used both in the initial curry paste – along with ginger, garlic, yoghurt, coriander and whole spices – and sliced and fried until golden brown and added towards the end of cooking.

Make ahead: The whole recipe can be made ahead of time and stored in an airtight container in the fridge for up to 3 days or in the freezer for up to 3 months. Garnish with fresh coriander and extra fried sliced onions before serving.

Heat the oil in a heavy-based, deep-sided frying pan over medium–high heat. Fry the sliced onions for about 5–10 minutes till dark golden, drain on paper towel and set aside. Save the onion-flavoured oil.

Season the lamb with 1 teaspoon of the salt. In a large, heavy-based saucepan, heat 2 tablespoons of the reserved onion oil over high heat and brown the lamb in batches. Don't overcrowd or the meat will stew rather than brown.

Lower the heat to medium–low. Add a splash more of the onion oil if you need to, then fry the nigella seeds and cardamom pods for about 30 seconds–1 minute before adding the chopped onions, garlic and ginger and the remaining ½ teaspoon of salt. As the onions start to release some juice, use a wooden spoon to scrape up all the brown bits from the bottom of the pan – this will add to the flavour of the dish as well as preventing the curry from sticking and burning later. Cook the onions and garlic gently for about 10–15 minutes till they are soft and sweet.

Add the chilli, paprika and ground coriander to the pan, then the yoghurt and the browned lamb. Partially cover with a lid and cook till completely tender, about 2 hours, stirring occasionally and adding water as needed.

When the lamb is done, stir in the fried onion slices, garam masala and chopped coriander, keeping a few leaves to garnish, along with a few of the fried onions.

Serve with basmati rice and a cucumber-yoghurt sauce.

Kerala Beef Curry

SERVES 4   PREP TIME 30 MINUTES   COOKING TIME AT LEAST 2 HOURS 20 MINUTES

2 teaspoons peanut oil or other mild-flavoured oil
1 large brown onion, sliced
2 teaspoons salt
4 garlic cloves, crushed
1 x 4 cm (1½ inch) piece ginger, grated
2 long green chillies, finely chopped, seeds included
½ teaspoon chilli flakes
1 teaspoon ground coriander, toasted
½ teaspoon freshly ground black pepper
1 teaspoon ground cinnamon
⅓ teaspoon ground cloves
3 teaspoons ground cumin, toasted
½ teaspoon ground turmeric
900 g (2 lb) braising beef, such as chuck, shin or blade, diced into 3 cm (1¼ inch) cubes
1 large handful curry leaves
400 g (14 oz) tinned chopped tomatoes
45 g (1½ oz/½ bunch) coriander (cilantro), leaves only, coarsely chopped, a few leaves reserved for garnish

TO SERVE
basmati rice
Cucumber-Yoghurt Sauce (see page 45)
naan bread
Sweet Potato, Kale and Chickpea Curry (see page 143)

Although we are as one on many things, chilli divides us. For Katherine, it is something to be approached with latex gloves and caution; for Sophie, it is as mother's milk. It's strange, then, that we're both fans of this cheeky little curry from India's pepper capital in the south-west, where beef is the red meat of choice and spice is king. It is flavoured with both fresh green chilli and chilli flakes, as well as curry leaves, cumin, coriander, cinnamon and cloves, and its thick, clingy, tomato-based sauce is delicious with plain rice and/or naan bread.

Make ahead: *The entire recipe can be made ahead of time and stored in an airtight container in the fridge for 3 days or in the freezer for 3 months. Garnish with fresh coriander before serving.*

Heat the oil in a large heavy-based frying pan over medium heat and fry the onions gently with 1 teaspoon of the salt for 10–15 minutes till they are soft and golden. Add the garlic, ginger and green chillies and cook for a further 5 minutes, stirring and scraping the bottom of the pan so nothing sticks.

Lower the heat and add the chilli flakes, ground coriander, pepper, cinnamon, cloves, cumin and turmeric.

Season the beef with the remaining teaspoon of salt and add to the pan, together with the curry leaves. Cover with the tomatoes and stir gently to combine. Partially cover the pan with a lid and simmer till the beef is tender, stirring and adding a little water from time to time if the sauce is getting too thick and sticking. The cooking time will depend very much on the beef – start checking to see if it is tender after 2 hours.

When the beef is done, taste for seasoning and stir through the fresh coriander, saving a few leaves to scatter on top.

Serve with basmati rice, cucumber-yoghurt sauce and naan bread. A vegetable curry like the sweet potato, kale and chickpea curry would work well with this dish, too.

Massaman Chicken Curry

SERVES 4   PREP TIME 25 MINUTES   COOKING TIME 45 MINUTES

250 g (9 oz) kipfler (fingerling) potatoes, chopped into 3 cm (1¼ inch) chunks
8 French shallots
2 tablespoons peanut oil or other mild-flavoured oil
800 g (1 lb 12 oz) boneless, skinless chicken thigh fillets, trimmed and diced into 3 cm (1¼ inch) cubes
200 ml (7 fl oz) coconut milk
2 tablespoons pineapple juice
2 tablespoons tamarind purée
2 teaspoons sugar
1½ tablespoons fish sauce

CURRY PASTE
80 g (2¾ oz) unsalted roasted peanuts
1 small red onion, chopped
1 dried chilli, soaked in hot water, drained and chopped (reserve the soaking liquid)
1 x 2 cm (¾ inch) piece galangal, finely chopped (see note on page 27)
4 garlic cloves, chopped
2 coriander (cilantro) stems, roots included, washed and chopped, a few leaves reserved for garnish
1 lemongrass stem, white part only, tough outer layer removed, thinly sliced
1 tablespoon ground coriander, toasted
1 heaped teaspoon ground cumin, toasted
pinch of ground cloves
pinch of ground cardamom
pinch of ground nutmeg
½ teaspoon ground cinnamon
1 teaspoon salt

TO SERVE
steamed jasmine rice
Green Papaya Salad (see page 153)

A complex Thai curry with hints of the Middle East in its spicing and a deliciously sweet, sour and aromatic coconut sauce.
If you're going to make it ahead of time to freeze, we'd suggest leaving the potatoes out and adding them, cooked, when you're reheating the defrosted dish. Frozen, defrosted potatoes can go really weird and spongy, not always but frequently enough to raise a little spectre of uncertainty. This curry is equally good made with beef, using diced shin or chuck. Obviously, it will take a lot longer than chicken – probably two hours. If you're using beef, add a little coconut cream at the end with the other finishing ingredients to freshen up the coconut flavour.

Make ahead: The whole dish can be made ahead and stored in an airtight container in the fridge for up to 3 days or in the freezer for up to 3 months. Garnish just before serving with fresh coriander and crushed roasted peanuts.

Put the potatoes in a large saucepan, cover them with cold, salted water, bring to the boil and cook till they are just tender – about 10 minutes. Drain and set aside.

To make the curry paste, blitz the peanuts in the bowl of a small food processor till fine. Take out half and set aside. To the remaining half of the peanuts, add the rest of the curry paste ingredients and process till fine. The more finely you've chopped the ingredients first, the easier this job will be, especially with fibrous ingredients like lemongrass and galangal – use a little of the coconut milk or the chilli soaking water if you need some liquid to ensure it blends thoroughly to a smooth paste.

Preheat the oven to 180°C (350°F).

Peel the shallots and place on a baking tray. Toss in a little of the oil and a pinch of salt. Roast in the oven for about 25 minutes till cooked through and golden.

Pour the remaining oil into a large, heavy-based saucepan over medium–high heat and fry the curry paste until it is fragrant. Add the chicken and coat it in the paste. Cover with the coconut milk, turn the heat down to low and simmer, stirring regularly, till the chicken is cooked – about 25 minutes.

When the chicken is cooked through and tender, fold in the potatoes and shallots and bring them up to heat before adding the pineapple juice, tamarind, sugar, fish sauce and remaining ground peanuts. Taste for a balance of flavours – it should be intensely sweet, tangy and creamy. Add more sugar, fish sauce, tamarind or coconut milk if necessary.

Serve with steamed jasmine rice and a green papaya salad. Garnish with the reserved coriander leaves.

Nonya Chicken Curry

SERVES 4 PREP TIME 30 MINUTES COOKING TIME 45 MINUTES

300 g (10½ oz) kipfler (fingerling)
    potatoes, cut into 3 cm (1¼ inch)
    chunks
1 tablespoon peanut oil or other mild-
    flavoured oil
125 g (4½ oz/½ cup) tinned chopped
    tomatoes
800 g (1 lb 12 oz) boneless, skinless
    chicken thighs, trimmed and diced
    into 3 cm (1¼ inch) cubes
1 teaspoon salt
1 handful curry leaves
8 kaffir lime leaves, stems removed, cut
    into very thin matchsticks
200 ml (7 fl oz) coconut milk
2 tablespoons tamarind purée
1 heaped teaspoon shaved palm sugar
    (jaggery) or light brown sugar
juice of ½ lemon

CURRY PASTE
3 teaspoons ground coriander, toasted
2 teaspoons ground cumin, toasted
1 lemongrass stem, white part only,
    tough outer layer removed, thinly
    sliced
1 x 4 cm (1½ inch) piece ginger, grated
1 large red onion, coarsely chopped
3 long green chillies, 2 chopped for
    the paste, 1 cut into thin matchsticks
    and reserved for garnish
1 teaspoon mustard seeds
pinch of ground cloves
pinch of ground turmeric
½ teaspoon salt

TO SERVE
steamed basmati rice
crisp fried shallots
lime wedges
Tomato Sambal (see page 171)

This Malay curry of free-range chicken and waxy kipfler potatoes is wonderfully aromatic, with Indian curry spices as well as more expected South East Asian ingredients like lemongrass and kaffir lime leaves. The sauce should be warmly spicy (but not outrageously hot), with a lick of acidity from the tamarind and tomatoes as well as creaminess from the coconut milk.

Make ahead: *Potatoes don't usually freeze well so if you're making this for the freezer you might want to leave them out and boil them separately while you're defrosting and reheating the curry. They reheat perfectly well from the fridge, though, so the whole recipe can be made ahead of time and stored in an airtight container in the fridge for up to 3 days or in the freezer (minus potatoes) for up to 3 months. Leave the crisp fried shallots, green chilli matchsticks and lime leaves off till you serve.*

Put the potatoes in a large saucepan, cover them with cold, salted water, bring to the boil and cook till they are just tender. This should take about 10 minutes. Drain and set aside when done.

To make the curry paste, in the bowl of a small food processor or using a stick blender, blitz all of the ingredients (only using 2 of the chillies) to a fine paste.

Heat the oil in a large, heavy-based frying pan over medium heat and fry the paste, stirring constantly, till it is fragrant. Add the tomatoes and cook down for about 5 minutes till the mixture is pulpy.

Season the chicken with the teaspoon of salt and add to the pan with the curry leaves and most of the lime leaves, keeping a few slivers for garnish. Cover with the coconut milk, turn down the heat to medium–low and simmer till the chicken is just cooked, which should be about 20 minutes.

Stir the cooked potatoes through the sauce and continue to cook gently for another 5 minutes so that they have time to come up to heat and absorb some of the sauce.

When the chicken is cooked, add the tamarind, palm sugar and lemon juice. Taste for seasoning and sweet/sour balance, adding more salt/tamarind/lemon juice/palm sugar as required.

Serve with steamed basmati rice, scattered with crisp fried shallots, green chilli matchsticks and lime leaves, with lime wedges and tomato sambal on the side.

Chilli Bean Tofu with Ginger and Eggplant

SERVES 4   PREP TIME 15 MINUTES   COOKING TIME 40 MINUTES

750 g (1 lb 10 oz) eggplants (aubergines), diced into 4 cm (1½ inch) cubes (2 medium eggplants)

1 teaspoon salt

2 tablespoons peanut oil or other mild-flavoured oil

1 x 5 cm (2 inch) piece ginger, cut into thin matchsticks

3 garlic cloves, thinly sliced

4 spring onions (scallions), trimmed and sliced into 1 cm (½ inch) slices on the diagonal

2½ tablespoons chilli bean sauce

1½ tablespoons Chinese rice wine

2 tablespoons soy sauce

1 heaped teaspoon white sugar

600 g (1 lb 5 oz) firm tofu, diced into 4 cm (1½ inch) cubes

TO SERVE
steamed jasmine rice

. . . .

NOTE: Both Chinese rice wine and chilli bean sauce are available at Asian grocers and larger supermarkets.

Don't let the name of this dish alarm you – the chilli comes only from the Chinese chilli bean sauce, which is spicy but not mind-blowing. This utterly delicious dish combines the chilli bean sauce with Chinese rice wine, soy sauce, garlic and ginger, coating the pleasantly bland tofu and sweet, diced, roast eggplant. This is a great vegetarian dish and could stand alone with a bowl of rice or would work well as part of a larger Chinese spread.

Make ahead: *The best way to make this dish ahead of time is to make everything up to the tofu, and add that just before serving. If the tofu is included and then frozen, it tends to break apart and look a bit of a mess. Store in a covered container in the fridge for up to 3 days or in the freezer (minus the tofu) for up to 3 months. Garnish with extra spring onions (scallions) before serving.*

Preheat the oven to 180°C (350°F).

Line one or two baking trays (depending on size) with baking paper, toss the eggplant in the salt and 1 tablespoon of the oil and spread out on the tray/s. Roast in the oven for approximately 20 minutes or until cooked through and golden. Set aside.

In a large, heavy-based frying pan or wok, heat the remaining oil over medium–high heat. Throw in the ginger, garlic and half the spring onions, which will sizzle like crazy, so keep moving them about with a wooden spoon or wok tool for a few minutes or until very fragrant. Add the chilli bean sauce, rice wine, soy sauce and sugar and cook for a further few minutes.

Lower the heat and add 125 ml (4 fl oz/½ cup) of water, then stir the eggplant into the sauce and simmer for 5 minutes so that the eggplant sucks up some of the sauce. Gently fold through the tofu and continue to simmer until it's warmed through.

Serve with some steamed jasmine rice, sprinkled with the remaining spring onions.

Keema Mattar, AKA Indian Cottage Pie

SERVES 4   PREP TIME 10 MINUTES   COOKING TIME 30 MINUTES

2 tablespoons peanut oil or other mild-flavoured oil
2 small brown onions, diced
1 x 3 cm (1¼ inch) piece ginger, grated
2 garlic cloves, crushed
2 teaspoons salt
800 g (1 lb 12 oz) minced (ground) beef
1 teaspoon ground turmeric
¾ teaspoon chilli flakes
1 heaped tablespoon garam masala, toasted
400 g (14 oz) plain yoghurt
390 g (13¾ oz/3 cups) frozen baby peas
1 long red chilli, seeded and cut into thin matchsticks
1 large handful coriander (cilantro) leaves, coarsely chopped

TO SERVE
steamed basmati rice
Fresh Mango Chutney (see page 87)
lime wedges

Minced (ground) meat equals comfort in every language – think of British cottage pie, Italian meatballs and American meatloaf, all of them contenders in the food-as-balm-for-body-and-soul stakes. Here it is the turn of the Indian keema mattar, a warm and friendly dish of minced beef, cooked with ginger, yoghurt, garam masala and peas. This has been a Sunday night faithful in Sophie's house for as long as she can remember.

Make ahead: *The entire dish can be made ahead of time and stored in the fridge for up to 3 days or in the freezer for up to 3 months. Garnish with extra fresh coriander and red chilli just before serving.*

Heat the oil in a large, heavy-based saucepan over medium heat. Add the onions, ginger and garlic with 1 teaspoon of the salt and cook for about 10–15 minutes till soft and sweet. Turn up the heat and add the beef, stirring constantly to brown it and break it up. Use a potato masher to break up any recalcitrant lumps of meat. Add the turmeric, chilli flakes and 2 teaspoons of the garam masala. Stir through the yoghurt and simmer, partially covered with a lid, till tender, stirring occasionally. Add the peas and continue cooking for another 5 minutes.

Taste for seasoning, then add the remaining garam masala, the chilli matchsticks and the coriander leaves.

Serve with steamed basmati rice, mango chutney and lime wedges.

Syrian Chicken with Ginger, Lemon and Honey

SERVES 4   PREP TIME 40 MINUTES   COOKING TIME 1 HOUR

2 tablespoons olive oil
1 large brown onion, finely chopped
1½ teaspoons salt
2 garlic cloves, crushed
1 x 7 cm (2¾ inch) piece ginger, cut into thin matchsticks
1½ teaspoons ground cumin, toasted
½ teaspoon cumin seeds, toasted
1 teaspoon ground cinnamon
½ teaspoon ground turmeric
½ teaspoon chilli flakes
300 g (10½ oz) tinned chopped tomatoes
800 g (1 lb 12 oz) boneless, skinless chicken thigh fillets, trimmed and cut into bite-sized pieces
1 large thyme sprig, leaves stripped
300 ml (10½ fl oz) chicken stock (home-made or low/no salt)
3 tablespoons currants
generous pinch of saffron threads
zest and juice of 1 large lemon
1½ tablespoons honey
2 tablespoons chopped coriander (cilantro) leaves

TO SERVE
Couscous (see page 159)
kale or silverbeet (Swiss chard)

We always make this dish in the middle of winter when colds and flus are rampaging their way through our families – the name alone sounds like a health tonic. This delightful Middle Eastern dish is inspired by Karen Martini, using only sweet spices like cinnamon, cumin and saffron, and has a lovely balance of flavours from the lemon, honey, currants and ginger. She uses whole pieces of chicken on the bone for her dish; our take on it uses boneless thigh fillets.

Make ahead: *The whole recipe can be made ahead of time and stored in an airtight container in the fridge for up to 3 days or in the freezer for up to 3 months. Garnish with some additional fresh coriander leaves before serving.*

Heat the oil over medium–low heat in a large, heavy-based saucepan and cook the onion with 1 teaspoon of the salt, stirring occasionally, till it is soft and sweet. This should take 10–15 minutes. Add the garlic and ginger and cook for a further 2 minutes.

Stir the ground cumin, cumin seeds, cinnamon, turmeric and chilli flakes through the onion mixture, add the tomatoes and cook for about 10–15 minutes till slightly reduced and pulpy.

Season the chicken with the remainder of the salt and add to the pan with the thyme, stirring through to coat in the spice and tomato mixture. Pour the stock over the chicken, cover with a slightly ajar lid, turn the heat down to low and simmer for 20 minutes, stirring every so often.

Scatter in the currants and stir the saffron into the hot sauce. Continue to simmer for another 5 minutes or until the chicken is cooked through.

When the chicken is done, add the lemon zest and juice, the honey and the chopped coriander.

Taste for seasoning. Serve with couscous and some dark leafy greens like kale or silverbeet.

Balinese Chicken Curry

SERVES 4   PREP TIME 30 MINUTES   COOKING TIME 30 MINUTES

1 tablespoon peanut oil or other mild-flavoured oil
8 kaffir lime leaves, lightly crushed
800 g (1 lb 12 oz) boneless, skinless chicken thigh fillets, trimmed and cut into bite-sized pieces
1 tablespoon tamarind purée
400 ml (14 fl oz) coconut milk
1 tablespoon kecap manis

CURRY PASTE
2 lemongrass stems
4 candlenuts (you can substitute 4 macadamia or 2 Brazil nuts)
1 x 2 cm (¾ inch) piece ginger, trimmed
2 garlic cloves, crushed
1 x 2 cm (¾ inch) piece galangal, trimmed
1 small red onion, coarsely chopped
½ long green chilli, seeded and coarsely chopped
1 tablespoon ground coriander, toasted
1½ teaspoons ground cumin, toasted
¼ teaspoon freshly ground black pepper
1 tablespoon shaved palm sugar (jaggery) or light brown sugar
1 teaspoon salt

TO SERVE
2 tablespoons crisp fried shallots
coriander (cilantro) leaves, for garnish
steamed basmati rice
Tomato Sambal (opposite)

A lovely gentle curry with plenty of aromatic sauce, this Balinese dish works just as well with fish. Katherine was lucky enough to discover this while on a camping holiday to a remote Barrier Reef island with a bunch of spear fishermen (not everyone's idea of a great time, granted) and just happened to have packed a tub of this curry paste along with her sarongs. You can only imagine how super-organised she felt when she whipped up this curry with the day's catch – and it was delicious!

Make ahead: *This recipe can be made ahead and stored in an airtight container in the fridge for 3 days or in the freezer for 3 months. If you want to use chicken breast or fish, make the sauce ahead of time and just poach the chicken or fish once, in the sauce, for about 5–8 minutes. The crisp fried shallots and some coriander leaves are added as a final garnish just before serving.*

To make the curry paste, cut the lemongrass stems in half crossways. Cut the top half in half again, give them a gentle bash with a mallet (to bruise not pulverise) and set aside, then trim the tough outer layer from the bottom halves and finely chop the white inner part. Place this chopped lemongrass with the candlenuts, ginger, garlic, galangal, onion and green chilli in the bowl of a small food processor or use a stick blender and blitz till very fine. Add the ground coriander, cumin, pepper, palm sugar and salt and blitz again until well combined. You may need to add 1 tablespoon of water while you're doing this to ensure you end up with a fine, even paste.

Heat the oil over medium heat in a heavy-based, deep-sided frying pan or wok and fry the paste, stirring constantly, till it is well cooked and fragrant – about 5 minutes. Add the remaining lemongrass pieces and the lime leaves, and continue to fry for another 2 minutes.

Add the chicken to the pan and stir through until it is all coated in the paste. Add the tamarind and cover with the coconut milk, turn down

NOTES: *NOTES:* Galangal is a rhizome that's often likened to ginger. It's tougher to cut and very perfumed. If you can't find it at the supermarket or an Asian grocer, substitute extra ginger.

Candlenuts, tamarind purée, kecap manis and crisp fried shallots are all available at larger supermarkets and Asian grocers.

the heat to medium–low, and simmer till the chicken is cooked through (about 20 minutes). Stir in the kecap manis, which will add sweetness and colour as well as saltiness – taste the sauce and see whether it needs more salt or tamarind.

Just before serving, garnish with the crisp fried shallots and some coriander leaves.

Serve with steamed basmati rice and tomato sambal on the side.

Tomato Sambal

Along with harissa, tomato sambal is a chilli-lover's fridge essential, so that everyone can customise the heat of dishes, dialling it up or down as they see fit. To make about 400 g (14 oz) of sambal, blitz together 2 long red chillies and 10 bird's eye chillies (seeds in) together with 1 small red onion, 4 garlic cloves, 2 teaspoons shrimp paste, 3 candlenuts (or 3 macadamia nuts), a pinch of salt and 400 g (14 oz) tinned chopped tomatoes. Heat 1 tablespoon peanut oil in a frying pan and cook this mixture over medium heat, stirring frequently, until it's reduced, shiny and pungent. This should take about 15–20 minutes. Cool and store, covered, in the fridge.

Thai Marinated Chicken with *Sweet Chilli Sauce*

SERVES 4   PREP TIME 30 MINUTES, PLUS 3 HOURS–OVERNIGHT MARINATING
COOKING TIME 50 MINUTES, PLUS 10 MINUTES RESTING

1 small chicken, about 1.3 kg (3 lb), split down the back, backbone removed, flattened

MARINADE
2 coriander (cilantro) stems, roots and all, washed carefully and finely chopped
½ teaspoon black peppercorns, ground
4 garlic cloves, crushed
1 tablespoon fish sauce
2 teaspoons shaved palm sugar (jaggery) or light brown sugar
1 tablespoon peanut oil or other mild-flavoured oil

SWEET CHILLI SAUCE
2 coriander (cilantro) roots, finely chopped
2 large garlic cloves, finely chopped
3 long red chillies, seeded (or not, for more heat), finely chopped
80 ml (2½ fl oz/⅓ cup) rice vinegar
75 g (2¾ oz/⅓ cup) white sugar
pinch of salt

TO SERVE
coriander (cilantro) leaves
lime wedges
steamed jasmine rice
Green Papaya Salad (see page 153)

You're very welcome to use store-bought sweet chilli sauce in a bottle for this dish – the marinade for the chicken is simple and delicious on its own – but we're suckers for making things from scratch. Sauces, cheese, bacon, pickles – if a recipe says 'you must start this a day in advance', it's got our name on it. But in this case, making the sauce is dead simple and, as it keeps forever in the fridge, it's worth multiplying the numbers and making a big batch, which you can label in large writing: HOME-MADE SWEET CHILLI SAUCE. You'll feel good every time you see it.

Make ahead: *The sauce can be made ahead of time and will keep for at least 6 weeks. The marinade can be made up to 1 day ahead, and you can then marinate the chicken and keep it in the fridge for up to 2 days or in the freezer for up to 3 months. Defrost frozen chicken before cooking.*

For the marinade, either blitz all the ingredients in a food processor or pound using a mortar and pestle till you have a fine paste. Rub this all over your chicken and set aside in the fridge for a minimum of 3 hours, but preferably overnight.

To make the sweet chilli sauce, mix all the sauce ingredients together in a small saucepan and bring to the boil over medium heat. Boil for about 10 minutes or until the sauce is reduced and syrupy. Cool, then refrigerate in a covered container.

When you're ready to cook the chicken, preheat a barbecue to medium, then turn down to low. Cook the chicken flat and bone side down, with the lid of the barbecue down, for 10 minutes, then pick up gently with tongs and flip the chicken to the flesh side for another 10 minutes. Repeat, so that you have cooked the chicken for a total of 40 minutes. If your barbecue doesn't have a lid, you can improvise with a large stainless steel bowl upturned over the chicken. Take off the heat and rest, covered with foil, for 10 minutes.

Cut the chicken into pieces and serve, piled on a platter, scattered with coriander leaves, with the sweet chilli sauce, lime wedges, steamed jasmine rice and a green papaya salad.

Kung Pao Chicken

SERVES 4   PREP TIME 20 MINUTES   COOKING TIME 25 MINUTES

1 egg white

1 tablespoon cornflour (cornstarch)

800 g (1 lb 12 oz) boneless, skinless chicken thigh fillets, trimmed and cut into bite-sized pieces

2 tablespoons soy sauce

1½ tablespoons chilli bean paste

1½ tablespoons Chinese rice wine

1 tablespoon rice wine vinegar

1 tablespoon sesame oil

1 tablespoon sugar

3 tablespoons peanut oil or other mild-flavoured oil

1 brown onion, sliced

2 garlic cloves, thinly sliced

1 long red chilli, seeded and finely chopped

1 x 5 cm (2 inch) piece ginger, cut into thin matchsticks

1 red capsicum (pepper), seeded and cut into 4 cm (1½ inch) pieces

4 spring onions (scallions), ends removed, sliced into 3 cm (1¼ inch) pieces

TO SERVE

3 tablespoons unsalted roasted peanuts, lightly crushed

steamed jasmine rice

stir-fried or steamed Asian greens

Originally, this was a spicy stir-fry, designed for last-minute cooking. We love the sweet–sour flavours of chilli bean sauce, vinegar, chicken and peanuts so much that we adapted the recipe so that it is a bit saucier (never a bad thing) and able to be reheated.

Make ahead: You can make this recipe ahead and store in an airtight container in the fridge for up to 3 days or in the freezer for 3 months. For maximum freshness, add the capsicum, spring onions and peanuts at the last minute before serving. If you prefer chicken breast, you can use it in this recipe, but don't make it ahead of time – it really doesn't reheat well.

Whisk the egg white and cornflour together with a fork and coat the chicken in this mixture. Set aside in the fridge.

In a small bowl or jug, mix the soy sauce, chilli bean paste, rice wine, vinegar, sesame oil and sugar together to make the sauce.

Heat 2 tablespoons of the peanut oil in a wok over high heat. Stir-fry the chicken till it is just opaque – the cooking will finish later. Don't worry if the cornflour mixture sticks to the wok – this will help thicken the sauce. Set the chicken aside.

Add a bit more oil if you need to, then fry the onion, garlic, chilli and ginger over high heat for a few minutes, stirring constantly. Return the chicken to the pan and pour in the sauce, stirring continuously to lift anything stuck on the bottom of the wok. Turn the heat down and simmer till the chicken is cooked – about 15 minutes. You may need to add some water – about 100 ml (3½ fl oz) – so that nothing sticks, especially if you are making this ahead of time. The extra liquid will help you reheat the dish successfully.

Add the capsicum and spring onions, and stir through till everything is combined and brought up to heat.

Garnish with the peanuts and serve with steamed jasmine rice and stir-fried or steamed Asian greens.

Lamb AND Quince Tagine

SERVES 4   PREP TIME 30 MINUTES   COOKING TIME 3 HOURS

2 quinces, peeled, cored and diced into
    4 cm (1½ inch) cubes
1 lemon, plus extra juice if necessary
2 tablespoons olive oil
650 g (1 lb 7 oz) lamb shoulder, trimmed
    and diced
1 teaspoon salt
2 large brown onions, chopped
¼ teaspoon freshly ground black
    pepper
½ teaspoon ground cumin, toasted
½ teaspoon ground cinnamon
pinch of cayenne pepper
small pinch of saffron threads
½ teaspoon ground ginger
2 teaspoons tomato paste
    (concentrated purée)
300 ml (10½ fl oz) chicken stock
    (home-made or low/no salt)
¾ preserved lemon
2 teaspoons honey
1 handful coriander (cilantro), leaves
    only, coarsely chopped

TO SERVE
Couscous (see page 159)
Vegetable Tagine with Olives, Eggplant
    and Chickpeas (see page 149)
Greek-style yoghurt
Harissa (see page 69)

Quinces are a magical and underused fruit, bitter and tannic (though beautiful) when raw; pink, tender and perfumed when cooked (the longer they cook, the deeper the pink becomes). In this tagine, they're added towards the end of cooking so they retain a bit of sharpness and texture to contrast with the honey-sweet spiced lamb; diced preserved lemon and fresh coriander add another layer of flavour. This tagine can stand alone with rice or couscous for a family midweek supper, but it also makes a fabulous addition to a Moroccan spread for a bigger gathering with a vegetarian tagine, some couscous jazzed up with toasted pistachios, coriander (cilantro) and spring onions (scallions), and bowls of Greek-style yoghurt swirled through with harissa.

Make ahead: *The entire recipe can be made ahead and kept in an airtight container in the fridge for up to 3 days or in the freezer for up to 3 months. Garnish with fresh coriander to serve.*

Put the diced quinces in acidulated water – 1 litre (35 fl oz/4 cups) of water with the juice of 1 lemon – so that the pieces don't brown.

Heat the oil in a large, heavy-based saucepan over high heat. Season the lamb with the salt and brown in batches. Don't overcrowd the pan, or the meat will stew instead of brown.

Lower the heat and, in the same pan and with the same oil, cook the onions slowly for 10–15 minutes till they are soft and sweet. Scrape the bottom of the pan with a wooden spoon to dislodge any brown bits left over from the lamb – it will all add to the dish's flavour.

Add the pepper, cumin, cinnamon, cayenne pepper, saffron and ginger. Stir through the browned lamb and tomato paste, and cover with the chicken stock and 300 ml (10½ fl oz) of water. Partially cover with a lid and simmer gently for about 2 hours, stirring every so often.

Scoop out the middle of the preserved lemon and discard. Rinse and finely dice the peel. Set aside.

When the lamb is just tender, drain the quince, add it to the pan and continue to cook for a further 30 minutes, or until the fruit is pale pink and as tender as a just-cooked apple, but not falling apart.

When everything is cooked, stir through the honey, preserved lemon and most of the coriander and taste. The tagine should be quite sweet, with a punch of salt from the preserved lemon. Adjust with more honey or salt and taste for sweet/sour/salt balance, adding a little bit more honey/lemon juice/salt if you think it needs it.

Serve with couscous, the vegetable tagine with olives, eggplant and chickpeas, and Greek-style yoghurt swirled through with harissa.

Tip

Quinces are only available in autumn and early winter. Out of season, you could substitute 150 g (5½ oz) dried apricots, dates or figs and add whole toasted blanched almonds at the end. The result will be very different but equally delicious.

RIB
Stickers

We have very different approaches to eating. While Sophie emulates the gentle herbivore, grazing most of the day on a variety of greenery, Katherine takes the boa constrictor approach, sating herself to the point of immobility on a passing bison and then lolling about digesting it for the next 10 hours. What Katherine really loves are rib stickers – dishes beloved of skiers, Yorkshire miners or parents of teenage children – the sort of food you know will fill up every corner of a hungry belly.

Rib stickers are comforting, hearty dishes and perfect for cooking ahead. They're mostly cold-weather dishes such as stews and braises, pies and thick soups. They're often made using cheaper cuts of meat so are intended for long, slow cooking to break down fibres and bring out deep, mellow flavours. Without exception, they're dishes that make you inhale deeply, rub your hands together and say, 'Ahhhhh, I'm home'.

While the recipes in this chapter generally cater to just four people, most can be easily adjusted to feed a crowd or to freeze for the future. Cooking in bulk ensures you always have a variety of rib-sticker dinners at the ready. For our tricks and tips on scaling up recipes, see page 9.

Paleo Lasagne

SERVES 4   PREP TIME 30 MINUTES   COOKING TIME 2 HOURS 5 MINUTES, PLUS 10 MINUTES RESTING

1 tablespoon olive oil, plus extra for greasing
1 brown onion, chopped
3 garlic cloves, 2 crushed, 1 left whole
1 teaspoon salt, plus a pinch
500 g (1 lb 2 oz) minced (ground) beef
150 ml (5 fl oz) red wine
350 g (12½ oz) tinned chopped tomatoes
1 heaped teaspoon ground fennel, toasted
1 teaspoon rosemary leaves, chopped
1 thyme sprig, leaves stripped and chopped
500 g (1 lb 2 oz) cauliflower, cut into florets
80 g (2¾ oz/½ cup) unsalted cashew nuts
600 g (1 lb 5 oz) zucchini (courgettes), trimmed and cut into long, thin, wide strips, about 5 mm (¼ inch) thick
1 large handful baby English spinach
2 teaspoons extra virgin olive oil, for drizzling

TO SERVE
2 tablespoons chopped parsley

While we're wary about jumping on health bandwagons, we do like to have fun with our food, so when we heard that you could make a fake 'béchamel' sauce using cauliflower and cashews, we thought it sounded like something for us. And it is a convincing substitute, creamy and delicious. Using zucchini (courgettes) and baby English spinach instead of layers of pasta guarantees a 'lasagne' that leaves you feeling light and healthy but still very satisfied.

Make ahead: The whole dish can be made ahead of time and stored in an airtight container in the fridge for up to 3 days or in the freezer for up to 3 months. Cook straight from frozen, adding 15 minutes to the cooking time.

Heat the olive oil over medium–low heat in a large, heavy-based frying pan and cook the onion and the crushed garlic with a pinch of salt for about 10–15 minutes till soft and sweet. Turn the heat to high, add the beef and 1 teaspoon of salt and cook till it has all changed colour, breaking up any lumps as you go – a potato masher works well for this. Splash in the red wine and bring to the boil, stirring constantly, then drop the heat to low and stir in the tomatoes, fennel, rosemary and thyme. Cover partially with a lid and simmer gently for 1 hour. Taste for seasoning and set aside to cool slightly.

Meanwhile, in well-salted water, boil the cauliflower with the cashews and the whole clove of garlic for about 20 minutes till soft. Drain (reserving some of the cooking water) and process in a food processor till the cauliflower and cashews have formed a fine purée. Taste for seasoning and consistency, adding a little more salt or cooking water till you have a good, fairly stiff 'béchamel' consistency – it should be like thick (double) cream.

Preheat the oven to 180°C (350°F).

To assemble the 'lasagne', take a rectangular baking tray of around 20 x 30 cm (8 x 12 inches)/1.5 litre (52 fl oz/6 cup) capacity and grease it lightly with oil. Start with a single layer of zucchini and a small handful of baby English spinach, then a layer of meat sauce, then another layer of zucchini slices and baby English spinach, and so on till everything is used up. Top with the cauliflower sauce to finish and drizzle with the extra virgin olive oil.

Cook in the oven for 40 minutes, or until the top is well browned and the zucchini slices are tender.

Rest for 10 minutes, sprinkle with chopped parsley and serve.

Cassoulet OF White Beans AND Pork

SERVES 4 PREP TIME 30 MINUTES, PLUS 24 HOURS SOAKING (IF USING DRIED BEANS)
COOKING TIME 3–4 HOURS

800 g (1 lb 12 oz) tinned cannellini
  beans, drained and rinsed, or 300 g
  (10½ oz) dried great northern beans
2 tablespoons olive oil
100 g (3½ oz) pancetta, thick cut and
  diced
400 g (14 oz) piece pork belly, skin off,
  cut into 4 cm (1½ inch) cubes
1½ teaspoons salt
300 g (10½ oz) good quality, pure pork,
  coarse-textured sausages (Toulouse
  or similar)
1 brown onion, diced
2 garlic cloves, finely chopped
300 g (10½ oz) tinned chopped
  tomatoes
1 thyme sprig, leaves stripped and
  chopped
1 rosemary sprig, leaves plucked and
  finely chopped
350 ml (12 fl oz) chicken stock (home-
  made or low/no salt)
100–120 g (3½–4¼ oz/1²/3–2 cups)
  good quality, fresh, soft breadcrumbs
  (about ½ loaf)
1¼ tablespoons salted butter

TO SERVE
salad of bitter leaves like witlof
  (chicory), watercress and/or radicchio

This is a simple version of the famous casserole from the South of France. The first time we made it, it took something like 3 days and involved first making our own goose confit as well as braising a breast of mutton – and do you know what? We actually prefer this version, and not just because it's suited to lazy cooks – though that is, of course, a bonus.

Make ahead: *You can make the whole dish just up to the point before you sprinkle on the breadcrumbs, and store in an airtight container in the fridge for up to 3 days or in the freezer for up to 3 months. Defrost if frozen and transfer into an ovenproof dish, sprinkle with the fresh breadcrumbs and bake for the final 40 minutes.*

If using dried beans, soak them in cold water for 24 hours before using, then drain. Put them in a saucepan, cover with fresh water and simmer gently till the beans are cooked through. This can take from 45 minutes to 2 hours, depending on the age of the beans. Drain and set aside.

Heat 1 tablespoon of the oil in a large, heavy-based flameproof casserole dish over medium heat and fry the pancetta till just golden – don't overdo it. Remove from the heat and set aside. Season the pork with ½ teaspoon of the salt and brown in the same dish. Remove and set aside. Brown the sausages on all sides, then remove and slice thickly on the diagonal.

In the same pan and oil, over low heat, cook the onion and garlic with a pinch of salt for 10–15 minutes, stirring frequently, till soft. Add the pancetta, pork, sausage, tomatoes and herbs. Cover with the stock (you may not need it all). Simmer gently, covered, till the pork is tender, topping up with stock as necessary. This should take about 2 hours. Stir in the beans. There should be quite a bit of sauce – add more stock if necessary.

Preheat the oven to 180°C (350°F).

Spoon the bean and pork mixture into an ovenproof dish (if you're not already using a flameproof casserole dish). Scatter with a thick layer of breadcrumbs, drizzle with the remaining 1 tablespoon of olive oil and cook in the oven for 40 minutes or until the breadcrumbs are golden.

Serve with a salad of bitter leaves such as witlof (chicory), watercress and/or radicchio, which will cut through this dish's richness nicely.

Tip

The simplest way to make a small quantity of breadcrumbs is to pull the inside out of a crusty loaf and rub the bread between your fingers till broken up into chunky crumbs.

Beef AND Guinness Pie

SERVES 6   PREP TIME 1 HOUR
COOKING TIME 3½ HOURS, PLUS 5 MINUTES RESTING

650 g (1 lb 7 oz) braising beef, such as
  chuck, oyster blade or shin, cut into
  4 cm (1½ inch) cubes
1½ teaspoons salt
2 tablespoons olive oil
1 large brown onion, chopped
1 garlic clove, crushed
2 carrots, finely chopped
2 celery stalks, finely chopped
250 ml (9 fl oz/1 cup) Guinness
1½ tablespoons tomato paste
  (concentrated purée)
1 thyme sprig, leaves stripped
2 bay leaves
1 tablespoon Worcestershire sauce
475 g (1 lb 1 oz) Shortcrust Pastry (see
  page 187 or use store-bought)
plain (all-purpose) flour, for dusting
olive oil spray
1 egg, beaten

TO SERVE
mashed potato

. . . .

NOTE: You can also make this with
a puff pastry top only, in which case
you'll need 250 g (9 oz) of butter puff
pastry and should cook the assembled
pie for about 25 minutes.

Pie making is a real labour of love. You can obviously take a short cut with shop-bought pastry, but nothing beats a whole pie made from scratch, and it's a great way to spend a miserable, rainy day. While you're at it, make a few – they freeze beautifully. The container you make and cook your pie in is crucial. If you are making a full crust pie, you should use a metal pie tin – ceramic ones will not transfer heat well enough, and you will end up with a soggy, undercooked bottom crust. We actually find that the best pie dishes are disposable foil trays, if you are able to get your hands on them.

Make ahead: The whole pie can be made ahead of time and stored in the fridge for up to 24 hours – it can keep for longer than this, but fresh pastry starts to develop a mottled look very quickly. If you want to make pies ahead of time, the best option is to assemble and freeze the whole thing. Brush the pie with egg wash and cook straight from frozen, adding an extra 15 minutes to the cooking time. In any case, make the filling ahead of the pastry so you assemble the pie with all the components cold.

Season the beef with 1 teaspoon of the salt. Heat 1 tablespoonful of the oil in a heavy-based saucepan or flameproof casserole dish over high heat, then brown the beef in batches and set aside.

Add a little more oil to the pan if necessary, lower the heat to medium–low and cook the onion, garlic, carrots and celery for 10–15 minutes till soft. Return the beef to the pan, add the Guinness, tomato paste, thyme and bay leaves and cook, partially covered, for 1½–2 hours. Stir and check the liquid level from time to time, adding a splash more liquid if necessary. When the beef is completely fall-apart tender, stir through the Worcestershire sauce and taste for seasoning.

To cool down the filling quickly, put it in a stainless steel bowl and place this in a sink or larger bowl of cold water with ice. Just be careful to keep a good grip on the bowl so you don't empty your filling into the water! Stir it carefully to bring the temperature down. When most of the heat is out, put it in the fridge, covered with a tea towel (dish towel).

Ideally, you will have split your pastry into two flat rounds when you were making it, one slightly larger than the other. Flour your rolling pin and your work surface, and roll out the pastry into two rounds to the required size to match a 21 x 25 x 4 cm (8¼ x 10 x 1½ inch) pie tin. The smaller piece will make the pie top. The larger piece needs to fit the bottom and sides of the pie tin. Use baking paper above and below the pastry to make this job less stressful.

Preheat the oven to 180°C (350°F).

Spray or brush the pie tin with a little olive oil. Make sure the lip is well oiled – this is the place your pie is most likely to stick. Line the bottom with the larger pastry round and fill with the cold beef filling. Using a little cup of water and your fingertip, wet the pastry rim to help the top stick down, then put the pastry top on. Crimp around the edge of the pie's top with a fork to seal the edge of the pie. Once you have finished, pierce two little holes in the middle of the pie with a sharp knife to let the steam escape.

Brush the top of the pie with the beaten egg, then put it in the oven for 45 minutes. Remove from the oven, cover with foil and return to the oven for another 15 minutes to ensure that your pastry bottom is cooked.

Rest the pie for 5 minutes before serving with mashed potato.

BEEF & GUINNESS PIE, *page* 184

Shortcrust Pastry

MAKES 1 X 475 G (1 LB 1 OZ) PORTION (ENOUGH FOR 1 FAMILY-SIZED PIE)
PREP TIME 10 MINUTES, PLUS 30 MINUTES–OVERNIGHT CHILLING   COOKING TIME NONE

250 g (9 oz/1²/3 cups) plain (all-purpose) flour, plus extra for dusting when assembling a pie
125 g (4¹/2 oz) very cold salted butter, diced into cubes
1 teaspoon salt
80–100 ml (2¹/2–3¹/2 fl oz) ice-cold water

We don't know anyone who wouldn't use store-bought pastry in a pinch, but even the best bought pastry is a paltry imitation of the real thing, with its crumbly, melt-in-the-mouth texture and gloriously homely quality. Once you get in the habit of making your own shortcrust pastry, it's pretty simple, especially using a food processor. It's worth getting on a roll and making a few batches at once because it freezes perfectly, can be used for sweet tarts as well as savoury pies and quiches and, importantly, makes you feel like a brilliantly organised culinary genius whenever you pull some out of the freezer.

Make ahead: Pastry needs to be made at least 30 minutes ahead of time so that it can firm up in the fridge before use. It can be refrigerated overnight but not much longer or it can develop an unappealing mottled look. It also freezes very well for up to 3 months; make sure it's thoroughly covered in plastic wrap and then bagged (pastry hates freezer burn).

You can make pastry by hand, but you'll get a better, much faster result using a food processor. The key to a great pastry is to work quickly, and to keep everything as cold as possible at all times. What you are trying to achieve is a stiff dough cut through with little flecks of butter – if the butter melts into the flour, your pastry will be leaden rather than light and flaky.

Pulse-chop the flour, butter and salt in a food processor. Once your mixture looks like breadcrumbs, add ice-cold water down the funnel of the processor while the motor is running, a little at a time, till your dough just starts to come together.

As soon as it looks like it is forming little lumps of dough, stop the food processor. Press some together – if it holds together well, it is ready. Empty it out into a bowl and bring it together quickly with your hands. Add a little flour if it has ended up too sticky, or a little iced water if it has come out too dry. Don't knead it! That is what you do to bread, to develop the gluten, to give you that characteristic chewy consistency. That is the opposite of the flaky quality you are aiming for in pastry. Shape the pastry into a flat disc – make two of slightly uneven size if you'll be making a pie. Cover in plastic wrap. Place in the fridge for at least 30 minutes or overnight. You can also freeze the discs and defrost when you're ready to use, in which case you'll probably need to dust with a bit more plain flour.

Beef Cheek, Red Wine
AND Roast Vegetable Pie

SERVES 6   PREP TIME 1 HOUR   COOKING TIME 4½ HOURS, PLUS 5 MINUTES RESTING

500 g (1 lb 2 oz) beef cheeks (trimmed weight), diced into 3 cm (1¼ inch) cubes

1½ teaspoons salt

2 tablespoons olive oil

1 large brown onion, chopped

1 garlic clove, crushed

250 ml (9 fl oz/1 cup) red wine

2 heaped teaspoons tomato paste (concentrated purée)

250 g (9 oz/1 cup) tinned chopped tomatoes

1 thyme sprig, leaves stripped

2 bay leaves

2 carrots, cut into 2 cm (¾ inch) chunks

200 g (7 oz) Jerusalem artichokes (or parsnip, celeriac or another flavoursome starchy veg), cut into 2 cm (¾ inch) chunks

200 g (7 oz) French shallots, trimmed

475 g (1 lb 1 oz) Shortcrust Pastry (see page 187 or use store-bought)

olive oil spray

1 egg, beaten

TO SERVE
mashed potato
green salad

. . . .

NOTE: You can also make this pie with a puff pastry top only, in which case you'll need 250 g (9 oz) of butter puff pastry and should cook the assembled pie for about 25 minutes.

Slow-cooked beef cheeks and sweet roasted vegetables make a particularly luxurious pie filling but, if cheeks are hard to come by, you could substitute another braising cut, bearing in mind that it probably won't take as long to cook. Again, you're very welcome to substitute store-bought shortcrust pastry – we're not going to coerce anyone into unwilling pastry-making – or make a lid only of puff pastry.

Make ahead: The whole pie can be made ahead of time and stored in the fridge for up to 24 hours – it can keep for longer than this, but fresh pastry starts to develop a mottled look very quickly. If you want to make pies ahead of time, the best option is to assemble and freeze the whole thing. Brush the pie with egg wash and cook straight from frozen, adding an extra 15 minutes to the cooking time. In any case, make the filling ahead of the pastry so you assemble the pie with all the components cold.

Season the beef with 1 teaspoon of the salt. Heat 1 tablespoon of the oil in a heavy-based frying pan or flameproof casserole dish over very high heat, brown the beef in batches and set aside.

Add a little more oil to the pan if necessary, lower the heat to medium-low and cook the onion and garlic for 10–15 minutes till soft. Increase the heat, add the red wine, and let it bubble up to deglaze the pan. Return the beef to the pan and add the tomato paste, tomatoes, thyme and bay leaves. Simmer, partially covered, till the beef is tender, around 3 hours. Stir occasionally and check the liquid level from time to time, adding a little more wine if necessary.

Meanwhile, preheat the oven to 180°C (350°F).

Toss the carrots, Jerusalem artichokes and shallots with the remaining ½ teaspoon of salt and 1 tablespoon of oil to lightly coat and spread around a roasting tin. Roast in the oven for 30–40 minutes, or till cooked through and golden. Set aside when done.

When the beef is tender, stir through the roast veg. Taste for seasoning – you may need a pinch of salt.

To cool down the filling quickly, put it in a stainless steel bowl and place this in a sink or larger bowl of cold water with ice. Just be careful to keep a good grip on the bowl so you don't empty your filling into the water! Stir it carefully to bring the temperature down. When most of the heat is out, put it in the fridge, covered with a tea towel (dish towel).

Ideally, you will have split your pastry when you were making it into two flat rounds, one slightly larger than the other. Flour your rolling pin and your work surface, and roll out the pastry into two rounds to the required size to match a 21 x 25 x 4 cm (8¼ x 10 x 1½ inch) pie tin. The smaller piece will make the pie top. The larger piece needs to fit the bottom and sides of the pie. Use baking paper above and below the pastry to make this job less stressful.

Preheat the oven again at 180°C (350°F).

Spray or brush the pie tin with a little olive oil. Make sure the lip is well oiled – this is the place your pie is most likely to stick. Line the bottom with the larger pastry round and fill with the cold beef filling. Using a little cup of water and your fingertip, wet the pastry rim to help the top stick down, then put the pastry top on. Crimp around the edge of the pie's top with a fork to seal the edge of the pie. Once you have finished, pierce two little holes in the middle of the pie with a sharp knife to let the steam escape.

Brush the top of the pie with the beaten egg, then place it in the oven for 45 minutes. Remove from the oven, cover with foil and return to the oven for another 15 minutes to ensure that your pastry bottom is cooked.

Rest the pie for 5 minutes before serving with mashed potato and a green salad.

Osso Buco WITH Gremolata

SERES 4   PREP TIME 30 MINUTES   COOKING TIME 2½ HOURS

1 kg (2 lb 4 oz) veal osso buco pieces
1½ teaspoons salt
1 tablespoon olive oil
1 brown onion, chopped
2 carrots, diced into 5 mm (¼ inch) cubes
2 celery stalks, trimmed and diced into 5 mm (¼ inch) cubes
1 garlic clove, crushed
150 ml (5 fl oz) white wine
400 g (14 oz) tinned chopped tomatoes
2 teaspoons tomato paste (concentrated purée)
150 ml (5 fl oz) veal or chicken stock (home-made or low/no salt)
2 bay leaves

GREMOLATA
1 handful parsley leaves, finely chopped
zest of ½ lemon, finely chopped
1 garlic clove, finely chopped

TO SERVE
Risotto alla Milanese (below) or polenta, gnocchi or mashed potato

Talk to your butcher to get the right cut of meat. There's a lot of yearling sold as 'osso buco' and the dish won't have its essential sticky deliciousness if you aren't using tender young veal.

Make ahead: The entire dish can be made ahead of time and stored in an airtight container in the fridge for up to 3 days or in the freezer for up to 3 months. The gremolata is best made fresh (earlier the same day is fine) and served with the dish.

Season the veal with 1 teaspoon of the salt. Heat the oil in a large, heavy-based saucepan over high heat, brown your veal pieces, then set aside.

Lower the heat to medium–low and cook the onion, carrots, celery, garlic and ½ teaspoon of salt for 10–15 minutes till soft and sweet. Increase the heat to high and add the wine, letting it bubble up to deglaze the pan. Lower the heat and stir in the tomatoes, tomato paste, stock and bay leaves. Return the veal to the pan and simmer gently till it's tender (about 2 hours). If you prefer, you can cook it in the oven at 150°C (300°F) for around 2 hours. Taste the sauce and make any necessary final adjustments.

To make the gremolata, simply combine the parsley, lemon zest and garlic. Sprinkle the osso buco with the gremolata just before serving.

The traditional accompaniment to osso buco is a risotto alla Milanese but polenta, gnocchi or even mashed potato would all work well, too.

Risotto alla Milanese

Sorry to sound bossy but there's no point in making a risotto alla Milanese without having a really good stock, either home-made or the best you can buy, because risotto is all about the rice and the stock. So, for 220 g (7¾ oz/1 cup) rice (carnaroli or arborio), first sweat down 1 chopped brown onion with 2 tablespoons olive oil and a pinch of salt in a heavy-based saucepan over low heat for 10–15 minutes till soft and sweet, then add your rice, stirring. Have ready 1 litre (35 fl oz/4 cups) hot chicken stock with a good pinch of saffron threads added. Splash 250 ml (9 fl oz/1 cup) white wine over your rice, turn the heat to medium until it comes to the boil, then turn the heat down and add the first ladleful of hot stock, stirring gently but almost continuously. Add stock as each lot is absorbed, until the rice is creamy but still retains its individual grains. Add more stock and vigorously beat in 1–2 tablespoons salted butter and 2 tablespoons grated parmesan cheese. Stand for 5 minutes, covered, before serving with the osso buco, pushing the marrow from the centre of the cooked shins to further enrich the risotto.

Pork Normandy with Apples and Cider Vinegar

<u>SERVES</u> 4   <u>PREP TIME</u> 30 MINUTES   <u>COOKING TIME</u> 2 HOURS 40 MINUTES

2 tablespoons olive oil
800 g (1 lb 12 oz) pork shoulder, diced
   into 3 cm (1¼ inch) cubes
2 teaspoons salt
2 large granny smith apples, peeled,
   cored and diced into 4 cm (1½ inch)
   chunks
1 large brown onion, sliced
200 ml (7 fl oz) apple cider
1 tablespoon apple cider vinegar
300 ml (10½ fl oz) chicken stock
   (home-made or low/no salt)
1 thyme sprig, leaves stripped and
   chopped
1 heaped tablespoon crème fraîche
good grind of black pepper

TO SERVE
salad of frisée (curly chicory) or baby
   English spinach, bacon and croutons
warm baguette

As is the case with so many of the recipes in this chapter, this dish would be perfect on a cold winter's night, with the wind whistling at the door. It's a touch old-fashioned (oh my goodness, it even contains cream!) but dish it up to some friends who have been dining out on massaged kale and pomegranate seeds for a while and watch it get wolfed down.

Make ahead: *The whole dish can be made ahead of time and stored in an airtight container in the fridge for up to 3 days or in the freezer for up to 3 months.*

Heat the oil in a heavy-based saucepan over high heat, season the pork with 1½ teaspoons of the salt and brown it in batches. Don't overcrowd the pan. The caramelisation of the meat will add fantastically to the flavour of the finished dish. Set the pork aside, covered and warm.

Lower the heat to medium and, in the same pan, brown the apples. Again, do these in batches to avoid overcrowding. You don't need to worry about cooking them all the way through. You just want to give them a nice scorched edge. Set them aside, separately from the pork.

Turn the heat down to low and, in the same pan again, cook the onion slowly with the remaining ½ teaspoon of salt for 10–15 minutes till soft and sweet.

Turning the heat back up to high, pour in the apple cider, vinegar and chicken stock and bring the liquid to the boil as you scrape up all the roasty bits at the bottom of the pan. Return the pork to the pan and add the thyme, turn the heat down to a bare simmer and cook gently, partially covered, until the pork is tender, approximately 2 hours. Keep checking the liquid level, stirring from time to time and adding a little more stock and/or cider if necessary to cover the meat. When the pork is nearly done, add the apples and continue to cook until they are tender but not collapsing.

Finally, stir in the crème fraîche and freshly ground black pepper and taste for seasoning.

Serve with green salad leaves like frisée or baby English spinach, with fried strips of streaky bacon and croutons, and chunky slices of warm baguette to mop up the delicious sauce.

Slow-cooked Beef Cheeks in Red Wine

SERVES 4   PREP TIME 30 MINUTES   COOKING TIME 4½ HOURS

800 g (1 lb 12 oz) beef cheeks, trimmed
    of all visible fat and diced into 4 cm
    (1½ inch) cubes
1½ teaspoons salt
2 tablespoons olive oil
1 large brown onion, diced into 5 mm
    (¼ inch) cubes
2 carrots, diced into 5 mm (¼ inch)
    cubes
1 celery stalk, trimmed and thinly sliced
2 garlic cloves, crushed
400 ml (14 fl oz) red wine
130 ml (4½ fl oz) port
130 ml (4½ fl oz) veal stock
    (home-made or low/no salt)
3 teaspoons tomato paste
    (concentrated purée)
2 bay leaves
1 thyme sprig, leaves stripped and
    coarsely chopped
pinch of freshly ground black pepper

TO SERVE
mashed potato
buttered green beans or peas

. . . .

NOTE: You can also make this dish with
whole cheeks, one per person, for a
more formal presentation. However,
they may take up to 5 hours to cook
and it's a bit harder to work out when
the cheeks are ready – insert a knife
to check.

The hardest-working muscles of an animal need the longest time to break down, so when you think about the amount of cud-chewing cattle do, it's not surprising that their cheeks are the slowest of all beef cuts to cook. But the patient cook (or those, like us, who have learned to bite down on our native impatience) will be rewarded with the most luscious beef you can imagine, with a long, deep flavour and unctuous texture. These make winter worthwhile.

Make ahead: The whole dish can be made ahead of time and kept in an airtight container in the fridge for up to 3 days or in the freezer for up to 3 months.

Season the beef cheeks with half the salt. Heat the olive oil in a large heavy-based saucepan or flameproof casserole dish over medium–high heat and brown the beef cubes in batches. Set aside.

Turn the heat down and add the onion, carrots, celery, garlic and the remaining salt. Cook slowly for 10–15 minutes till soft. Turn the heat up to high, add the wine, port and veal stock, and bring to the boil, scraping any bits of beef from the bottom of the pan.

Stir in the tomato paste and turn the temperature right down before returning the beef to the pan with the bay leaves, thyme and a pinch of freshly ground black pepper. Cover with a lid slightly ajar and simmer for a good long time – 4 hours at least – or until the beef is completely tender and almost at the point of falling apart.

Serve with mashed potato and buttered green beans or peas.

Middle Eastern Lamb with *Prunes, Mint* and *Pistachios*

SERVES 4   PREP TIME 20 MINUTES   COOKING TIME 2½ HOURS

400 g (14 oz) pumpkin (winter squash),
  diced into 4 cm (1½ inch) cubes
1½ teaspoons salt
2 tablespoons olive oil
150 g (5½ oz) broad beans
800 g (1 lb 12 oz) lamb shoulder,
  trimmed and diced into 3 cm
  (1¼ inch) cubes
1 large brown onion, chopped
1½ teaspoons ground cumin, toasted
1½ teaspoons ground cinnamon
½ teaspoon ground cardamom
1 dried lime or 1 teaspoon sumac
500 ml (17 fl oz/2 cups) chicken stock
  (home-made or low/no salt)
pinch of saffron threads
100 g (3½ oz) pitted prunes
1 teaspoon honey
40 g (1½ oz/½ bunch) mint, leaves
  plucked and coarsely chopped
1 tablespoon lime juice

TO SERVE
45 g (1½ oz/⅓ cup) pistachio nut
  kernels, coarsely chopped
Couscous (see page 159) or
  steamed rice

. . . .

NOTE: Dried limes are available from
Middle Eastern grocers and add
an intriguing citrus scent to dishes.
They're not meant to be eaten, though,
so fish it out at the end if you're using
one. You can substitute with sumac, a
ground spice with a lemony tang, which
is available in larger supermarkets now.

We've taken a few liberties with this cracker of a recipe from Neil Perry's wonderful book, The Food I Love, adding podded broad beans for extra freshness, dried lime for citrussy emphasis and a crunchy green sprinkle of pistachios.

Make ahead: The whole dish can be made ahead of time and stored in an airtight container in the fridge for up to 3 days or in the freezer for up to 3 months. Leave the final flurry of mint and pistachios to the end.

Preheat the oven to 180°C (350°F).

Season the pumpkin with a fat pinch of the salt, dress with 1 tablespoon of the oil, and roast in the oven for 25 minutes or until golden brown and cooked through.

Meanwhile remove the broad beans from their pods. Put a small saucepan of water over high heat and bring it to the boil. Add the broad beans and cook for 2 minutes. Drain the beans under cold running water. When cool enough to handle, squeeze each bean until it pops out of its skin and set aside.

Season the lamb with 1 teaspoon of the salt. In a heavy-based saucepan or flameproof casserole dish, heat the remaining tablespoon of oil till just smoking and brown the lamb in batches. Don't overcrowd the pan, and be careful not to let the juices burn. Set aside the lamb when it's browned.

Cook the onion in the same saucepan with another pinch of salt for 10–15 minutes till soft and sweet. Add the cumin, cinnamon and cardamom, then stir through the lamb and the dried lime or sumac. Add the chicken stock to cover, leave a lid slightly ajar on the top of the pan, and simmer gently till approaching tenderness (about 1½ hours).

Add the saffron and prunes and cook for a further 30 minutes. Finally, stir in the double-podded broad beans, the pumpkin, honey, most of the mint and the lime juice. Taste for seasoning, adding further salt, honey or lime juice if necessary.

Sprinkle with the chopped pistachios and the remaining mint leaves and serve with couscous or steamed rice.

Braised Beef Brisket
with Maple Bacon Beans

SERVES 4   PREP TIME 30 MINUTES, PLUS 24 HOURS SOAKING (IF USING DRIED BEANS)
COOKING TIME AT LEAST 3 HOURS 20 MINUTES

MAPLE BAKED BEANS

280 g (10 oz) dried great northern beans, or 1.2 kg (2 lb 10 oz) tinned cannellini beans, drained weight approximately 900 g (2 lb)

2 tablespoons olive oil

75 g (2¾ oz) bacon, cut into strips

½ brown onion, diced into 5 mm (¼ inch) cubes

1 carrot, diced into 5 mm (¼ inch) cubes

1 celery stalk, trimmed and diced into 5 mm (¼ inch) cubes

1 garlic clove, crushed

1 teaspoon salt

1 thyme sprig, leaves stripped and chopped

2 bay leaves

2 tablespoons cider vinegar

1 tablespoon red wine

80 ml (2½ fl oz/⅓ cup) maple syrup

200 g (7 oz) tinned chopped tomatoes

1 tablespoon tomato paste (concentrated purée)

1 tablespoon parsley leaves, chopped

pinch of freshly ground black pepper

This is not the prettiest dish you'll ever see but it is damned tasty and if rib-sticking's what you want, this dish will deliver it by the bucketload. The baked beans are worth making batches of on their own – they're so much more delicious than A Well-known Brand's baked beans and make a great breakfast or snack with toasted sourdough. Skip the bacon for a vegetarian/pork-free version.

Make ahead: *Make both components, and store separately in airtight containers in the fridge for up to 3 days. The beans can be reheated on the stovetop or in the microwave, and the brisket either in the microwave, or carefully in the oven, covered in foil, and with some water in the roasting tin to create steam, which will help prevent the brisket from drying out.*

Maple Bacon Beans

If using dried beans, soak them in cold water for 24 hours before you intend to cook them, then drain. Put them in a medium saucepan, cover with fresh water and simmer gently till the beans are tender. This can take from 45 minutes to 2 hours, depending on the age of the beans. Drain again.

Heat the oil in a heavy-based saucepan over medium heat and cook the bacon till golden but not frazzled. Set aside. Lower the heat and add the onion, carrot, celery, garlic and salt, cooking for about 10–15 minutes till soft. Return the bacon to the pan, then add the thyme, bay leaves, vinegar, wine, maple syrup, tomatoes and tomato paste and cook till thick, stirring occasionally – around 30 minutes. When done, stir through the beans and parsley, add a couple of grinds of black pepper and taste for seasoning.

1 kg (2 lb 4 oz) beef brisket (thin end)
1 teaspoon salt
pinch of chilli flakes
1 teaspoon smoked paprika
pinch of freshly ground black pepper
1 teaspoon ground cinnamon
1 teaspoon ground cumin, toasted
1 tablespoon wholegrain mustard
2 teaspoons olive oil
250 ml (9 fl oz/1 cup) water or stock
   (home-made or low/no salt)

TO SERVE
green salad

Braised Beef Brisket

Meanwhile, preheat the oven to 220°C (425°F).

Trim the brisket of excess fat and, in a small bowl, mix together the salt, chilli, paprika, pepper, cinnamon, cumin and mustard, loosened with the oil. Rub all over the piece of brisket, place in a roasting tin and roast in the oven for 20 minutes. Remove from the oven, splash the water or stock around the brisket, and cover with foil. Lower the oven temperature to 140°C (275°F) and cook slowly for at least 3 hours or until the brisket is very tender. This could take up to 5 hours, depending on the thickness of the brisket. Add water to the roasting tin from time to time if necessary to create steam and stop the brisket from drying out.

Remove from the oven and allow to cool until it's not too hot to handle.

To serve, shred the brisket into big hunks, and serve on top of a pile of maple bacon beans with a green salad on the side.

Pork Chops with Fennel, French Shallots and Raisins

SERVES 4   PREP TIME 30 MINUTES   COOKING TIME 2½ HOURS

2 tablespoons olive oil
1 fennel bulb (or 2 baby fennel bulbs), tough outer layer removed and cut into 1 cm (½ inch) thick slices
8 French shallots, trimmed
1 teaspoon salt
4 x 3 cm (1¼ inch) thick pork neck chops, about 250 g (9 oz) each
200 ml (7 fl oz) white wine
500 ml (17 fl oz/2 cups) chicken stock
2 garlic cloves, coarsely chopped
16 sage leaves, chopped, plus extra small whole ones for garnish
50 g (1¾ oz) raisins
2 star anise
1½ teaspoons balsamic vinegar

TO SERVE
mashed potato
silverbeet (Swiss chard) or kale

. . . .

NOTE: Ask your butcher to cut the pork neck chops to the right thickness.

The combination of meltingly tender pork chops, caramelised fennel and shallots, the earthiness of sage and the sweetness of raisins is terribly good. The idea for this recipe originally came from Sean Moran but we've added the fennel, because fennel and pork make such happy bedfellows and we do love an all-in-one dish. Don't be tempted to substitute a leaner cut of pork such as loin chops – you will end up with a dry and disappointing dish.

Make ahead: The whole dish can be made ahead of time. Once you have cooked it, put it in the dish you intend to serve it in, cover and put in the fridge for up to 3 days, then reheat it when you are ready. The dish can be frozen at a pinch but it's not going to do it any particular favours.

Preheat the oven to 150°C (300°F).

Heat the oil in a heavy-based frying pan over high heat, and brown the fennel slices on each side (you may need to do them in batches). Remove and set side. Add the shallots, and do the same with them. The vegetables don't have to be cooked, just coloured.

Salt the pork chops and brown them on each side. Remove the pork chops and set aside. Deglaze the pan with the wine and chicken stock, scraping up any brown bits from the pork or vegetables. Allow the liquid to boil and reduce by a quarter. This should take about 5 minutes.

Take a large, deep roasting tin that will fit all the chops. First, lay the fennel and shallots on the bottom. Add the pork chops, scatter with the garlic, sage and raisins, and tuck the star anise between them. Pour the stock over the top. Cover with a sheet of crumpled foil but don't tuck it in tightly – we still want some browning and roasting to go on, as well as for the sauce to reduce. Cook for about 2 hours or until the pork is completely tender.

Take the dish from the oven and make a decision about the sauce – it may need skimming and/or reducing (pour off into a separate small saucepan and boil rapidly if it does). When you are happy with the consistency of the sauce, add the balsamic vinegar and taste for seasoning and balance. Adjust if you'd like. Just before serving, scatter the small sage leaves over the chops.

Serve with mashed potato and a dark-green leafy vegetable such as silverbeet or kale.

Daube OF Beef

SERVES 4   PREP TIME 30 MINUTES   COOKING TIME 2½ HOURS

1 tablespoon olive oil
1 thickly cut bacon rasher, sliced into
    5 mm (¼ inch) strips
800 g (1 lb 12 oz) braising beef, such as
    chuck or oyster blade, trimmed and
    diced into 4 cm (1½ inch) cubes
1½ teaspoons salt
2 brown onions, chopped
2 carrots, chopped
1 celery stalk, trimmed and chopped
2 garlic cloves, chopped
300 ml (10½ fl oz) red wine
400 g (14 oz) tinned chopped tomatoes
1 tablespoon tomato paste
    (concentrated purée)
300 ml (10½ fl oz) veal stock (home-
    made or low/no salt)
2 long strips of orange zest
1 thyme sprig, leaves stripped and
    coarsely chopped
2 bay leaves

TO SERVE
mashed potato
buttered green beans or a green salad
small handful parsley leaves

This was probably the first dish Sophie ever committed to memory, from the simple fact of cooking it at least once a month through cold English winters in her early twenties. It's based (increasingly loosely now that we look back at the original) on the Elizabeth David recipe from her beautifully written and influential book, French Provincial Cooking, now a collection of stained pages held together with a rubber band.

Make ahead: *As Ms David said, 'The daube is a useful dish for those who have to get a dinner ready when they get home from the office. It can be cooked for 1½ hours the previous evening and finished on the night itself. Provided they have not overcooked to start with, these stews are all the better for a second or third heating up.' Precisely. You can store it in an airtight container in the fridge for up to 3 days or in the freezer for up to 3 months. Leave the parsley out till just before serving.*

Heat the oil in a large, heavy-based saucepan or flameproof casserole dish over medium heat. Gently cook the bacon just to render the fat, without too much browning; lift it out and set aside. Turn the heat up to high, season the beef pieces with 1 teaspoon of the salt and brown them on all sides in batches. Don't overcrowd the pan, and don't move them around too much – you want a good level of caramelisation. Set aside.

Lower the heat, add some more oil to the pan if necessary and cook the onions, carrots, celery, garlic and remaining ½ teaspoon of salt for 10–15 minutes till soft. Increase the heat to high and add the wine, letting it boil as you stir to deglaze the pan. Lower the heat and return the beef and bacon to the pan with the tomatoes, tomato paste, veal stock, orange zest, thyme and bay leaves. Simmer gently till the beef is tender (about 2 hours). If you prefer, you can cook it in the oven for about 2 hours at 130°C (250°F).

When done, taste for seasoning and adjust if necessary.

Serve with mashed potato and buttered green beans or a green salad to follow. Garnish with a few parsley leaves.

Pearl Barley, Italian Sausage AND Vegetable Soup

SERVES 4   PREP TIME 15 MINUTES   COOKING TIME 1 HOUR 15 MINUTES

2 tablespoons olive oil

400 g (14 oz) Italian sausages, mixture squeezed out of their skin and broken up into clumps

2 pancetta slices, diced, about 50 g (1¾ oz)

2 carrots, diced

2 celery stalks, trimmed and diced

1 large brown onion, diced

2 garlic cloves, crushed

pinch of salt

200 ml (7 fl oz) red wine

200 g (7 oz/1 cup) pearl barley (or substitute farro or spelt)

400 g (14 oz) tinned chopped tomatoes

1 teaspoon chopped rosemary leaves

25 g (1 oz/¼ cup) grated parmesan cheese

1 handful parsley, leaves only, roughly chopped

TO SERVE
freshly ground black pepper
crusty bread

. . . .

NOTE: Substitute a slice of streaky bacon instead of the pancetta if you prefer. Farro and spelt are worthy substitutes for the pearl barley.

This favourite meal-in-a-bowl is thick with pearl barley, carrots, onion and celery, with red wine, tomatoes and parmesan providing extra flavour, and nuggets of crumbled and browned Italian pork sausage for substance. A serious cockle-warmer for a chilly winter's day.

Make ahead: The whole dish can be made ahead of time and stored in an airtight container in the fridge for up to 3 days. It also freezes beautifully, so make a big pot and store it in 1 litre (35 fl oz/4 cup) containers in the freezer for up to 3 months. If you are making ahead, add extra parmesan cheese and parsley when you serve. The barley will keep absorbing liquid once you have made the soup, so add a splash more water or stock to reheat.

In a heavy-based saucepan, heat the oil over medium heat and fry the sausage meat to brown it. You don't want to break it up into minced (ground) meat, just nuggets. Remove and set aside.

In the same pan, adding more oil if necessary, fry the pancetta till golden, but not crisp. Remove and set aside. Lower the heat and, in the same pan, cook the carrots, celery, onion and garlic with a pinch of salt till soft – about 10–15 minutes.

Increase the heat to high, add the wine and let it bubble up. Lower the heat and stir through the pearl barley. Add the sausage meat, pancetta, tomatoes and rosemary. Add 800 ml (28 fl oz) of water. Simmer gently for around 45 minutes or until the barley is soft. Add more water as it cooks if necessary – you want to end up with a nice soupy consistency.

When the soup is done, stir through half the parmesan and parsley. Taste for seasoning – the salt levels in sausages are variable – and adjust if necessary.

Sprinkle with the remaining parmesan and parsley, and serve with freshly ground black pepper and crusty bread.

 Tip

If you have any spare parmesan rinds, a thrifty Italian technique is to save them and put them into the soup while it is cooking to add flavour – just remember to take them out at the end.

Beef Stifado

SERVES 4   PREP TIME 30 MINUTES   COOKING TIME 2½ HOURS

800 g (1 lb 12 oz) braising beef, such as chuck, oyster blade or shin, trimmed and diced into 3 cm (1¼ inch) cubes
1½ teaspoons salt
2 tablespoons olive oil
250 g (9 oz) French shallots, trimmed (or use small pickling onions)
1 large brown onion, chopped
2 garlic cloves, crushed
130 ml (4½ fl oz) red wine
1 cinnamon stick
pinch of ground cloves
pinch of ground nutmeg
250 g (9 oz/1 cup) tinned chopped tomatoes
1 heaped tablespoon tomato paste (concentrated purée)
2 teaspoons chopped fresh rosemary
1 tablespoon red wine vinegar

TO SERVE
crusty bread
Greek Salad (see page 23)

Originally, this delicious sweet and sour Greek stew would have been made using wild hare or rabbit. Beef is easier to come by. What makes the dish special is the addition of slow-cooked French shallots or pickling onions and the use of spices that somehow make it taste very authentically Greek.

Make ahead: The whole dish can be made ahead of time and stored, refrigerated, in an airtight container for 3 days or in the freezer for up to 3 months. Defrost before reheating.

Season the beef with 1 teaspoon of the salt. Heat the oil in a heavy-based frying pan over high heat and brown the beef in batches. Don't overcrowd the pan, or your beef will stew instead of brown. And don't skip this step – the caramelisation of the meat makes all the difference to the final flavour. Set aside, covered.

In the same pan over medium heat, fry the shallots, moving them about with a wooden spoon so that they brown on all sides. Add the onion and garlic with the remaining ½ teaspoon of salt and continue to cook till everything is starting to soften (about another 10 minutes), stirring frequently.

Add the wine to the onion mixture, turn the heat up to high and bring to the boil. Let it bubble for a few minutes. Turn the heat down, return the beef to the pan, and add the spices, tomatoes, tomato paste, rosemary and 125 ml (4 fl oz/½ cup) of water. Cook gently till the beef is tender. This will take about 2 hours, but is very dependent on the beef. Stir occasionally throughout the cooking time, and add more water if it looks like the dish is in danger of drying out.

When done, finish with the red wine vinegar. Taste for seasoning – many recipes include sugar in stifado but we find the tomatoes and onions are usually sweet enough on their own.

Serve with crusty bread and a Greek salad on the side.

Coq au Vin

SERVES 4   PREP TIME 30 MINUTES   COOKING TIME 1 HOUR 20 MINUTES

100 g (3½ oz) bacon
1–2 tablespoons olive oil
100 g (3½ oz) button mushrooms
1½ teaspoons salt
8 French shallots, peeled
4 chicken Marylands (leg quarters)
4 garlic cloves, chopped
400 ml (14 fl oz) red wine
400 ml (14 fl oz) chicken stock (home-
    made or low/no salt)
1 tablespoon tomato paste
    (concentrated purée)
2 fresh bay leaves
2 thyme sprigs, leaves stripped, plus
    extra for garnish

TO SERVE
mashed potato
buttered green beans
toasted slivered almonds
1 small handful parsley leaves

This retro favourite of bone-in chicken, cooked slowly in red wine and stock, is as welcome for a midweek family supper as it is for a weekend dinner party. If you prefer to use breasts on the bone, we suggest that you don't make this ahead of time – breasts don't take kindly to reheating, whereas the Marylands should only improve with time, as do we all.

Make ahead: *This can be made ahead of time and stored, covered, in the fridge for up to 3 days or in the freezer for up to 3 months. Garnish with the parsley leaves just before serving.*

Slice the bacon into batons about 5 mm (¼ inch) wide and 3 cm (1¼ inches) long. Heat 1 tablespoon of the oil in a wide flameproof casserole dish over medium heat and cook the bacon till golden but not crisp. Remove and set aside. Season the mushrooms with ½ teaspoon of the salt, add a little more oil if necessary and cook them with the shallots, moving them about frequently, till golden. Separate the shallots and the mushrooms and set aside, covered. Finally, season the chicken with the remaining teaspoon of salt and brown (on both sides) in the same dish over medium heat, adding a little more oil if you need it. Set aside, keeping warm.

Turn the heat down to low and, in the same dish, gently fry the garlic for 1–2 minutes, then add the wine and chicken stock to the pan, turning the heat up to high so that it comes to the boil. Use a wooden spoon to scrape up any brown bits from the bottom of the dish and reduce for 5 minutes, then turn the heat back down to low and stir through the tomato paste.

Preheat the oven to 160°C (315°F).

Arrange the chicken and the shallots in the casserole dish with the reduced wine and stock and add the bay leaves and thyme. Cover with a lid and cook in the oven for 45 minutes, or until the chicken pieces are cooked through.

When the chicken is done, remove the dish from the oven. Take out the chicken pieces and shallots with a slotted spoon and set aside in your serving dish, keeping them warm. Skim off any excess fat from the sauce in the casserole dish. Put the dish on the stovetop over high heat and reduce the sauce till it has thickened – it should be a good saucy consistency. When you think it is ready, taste for seasoning. Add the mushrooms and bacon and bring back up to heat. Pour the sauce over the chicken.

Serve with mashed potato and a nice green vegetable (such as buttered green beans) with toasted slivered almonds. Garnish with parsley leaves and a few extra thyme leaves.

Spanish Meatballs with Chorizo and Chickpeas

SERVES 4   PREP TIME 45 MINUTES, PLUS 24 HOURS SOAKING (IF USING DRIED CHICKPEAS)
COOKING TIME 45 MINUTES–2 HOURS

130 g (4½ oz) dried chickpeas, or 400 g (14 oz) tinned chickpeas, drained and rinsed

MEATBALLS
1 small brown onion, finely chopped
1 garlic clove, finely chopped
1 egg, beaten
325 g (11½ oz) minced (ground) pork (not too lean – buy from a butcher rather than the supermarket if possible)
zest of 1 orange
2 teaspoons slivered almonds, toasted and roughly chopped
½ teaspoon salt
½ teaspoon smoked paprika
½ teaspoon fennel seeds, ground and toasted
pinch of dried oregano
1 teaspoon ground cinnamon

SAUCE
2 tablespoons extra virgin olive oil
160 g (5½ oz) chorizo (about 2 chorizo), sliced at 1 cm (½ inch) intervals
1 small brown onion, finely chopped
1 garlic clove, crushed
1 small carrot, finely chopped
170 ml (5½ fl oz/⅔ cup) red wine
400 g (14 oz) tinned chopped tomatoes
¾ teaspoon smoked paprika
½ teaspoon salt
2 bay leaves

TO SERVE
2 tablespoons chopped parsley
crusty bread
green salad

Please, can we urge you to make these meatballs? The addition of cinnamon, fennel and toasted almonds gives them a delicious difference, and with the chorizo, rich red wine and tomato sauce, the whole package is both comforting and very Spanish.

Make ahead: *The entire dish can be made ahead of time and kept in an airtight container in the fridge for up to 3 days or in the freezer for up to 3 months.*

Soak the dried chickpeas in cold water for 24 hours before you intend to cook them, then drain. Put them in a medium saucepan, cover with fresh water, bring to the boil and simmer till the chickpeas are tender. This will take at least 1 hour and possibly more, depending on their freshness. Drain, then set aside. Skip this entire step if using tinned chickpeas.

To make the meatballs, first preheat the oven to 180°C (350°F) and line a baking tray with baking paper.

In a large mixing bowl, thoroughly combine the ingredients for the meatballs. Get your clean hands in and give the pork mixture a really good pounding. Take a small piece of the mixture – roughly 3 cm (1¼ inches) in diameter – and fry it in a small, non-stick frying pan over medium heat for approximately 2 minutes each side. Taste for seasoning and adjust if necessary.

Using a separate bowl of cold water to dip your hands, roll the pork mixture into balls a bit smaller than a golf ball, and place in rows on the baking tray. Roast in the oven for 25 minutes or till cooked through.

Meanwhile, to make the sauce, heat the olive oil in a large, heavy-based saucepan over medium–high heat and cook the chorizo till golden brown – the fat from the chorizo should render and will flavour and colour the sauce. Lift out with a slotted spoon and set aside.

Turn the heat down to medium–low and add the onion, garlic and carrot. Cook for 10–15 minutes till soft and sweet, stirring frequently, then raise the heat to high as you add the wine. Let it come to the boil, then lower the heat and stir in the tomatoes, paprika, salt and bay leaves. Simmer for around 20–30 minutes, stirring occasionally, until deeper in colour. The tomato should look shiny rather than watery. Remove the bay leaves and purée the sauce with a stick blender. Keep warm.

Add the chickpeas, meatballs and chorizo to the tomato sauce, and bring back to heat.

Sprinkle with parsley and serve with crusty bread and a green salad.

Spiced, Slow-cooked Lamb Shanks

SERVES 4   PREP TIME 25 MINUTES   COOKING TIME 3½ HOURS

1 heaped teaspoon ground coriander, toasted
1 heaped teaspoon ground cumin, toasted
½ teaspoon ground cinnamon
½ teaspoon sweet paprika
1½ teaspoons salt
4 lamb shanks, approximately 350 g (12 oz) each, trimmed and membranes removed
1½ tablespoons olive oil
1 large brown onion, diced
2 carrots, diced into 1 cm (½ inch) pieces
1 large celery stalk, trimmed and diced into 1 cm (½ inch) cubes
2 garlic cloves, crushed
260 ml (9 fl oz) red wine
600 g (1 lb 5 oz) tinned chopped tomatoes
1½ teaspoons balsamic vinegar
1 teaspoon rosemary leaves, chopped
½ teaspoon thyme leaves, chopped

TO SERVE
1 small handful parsley leaves, chopped
mashed potato or soft polenta
English spinach or kale with extra virgin olive oil and garlic

If we were cranky old women (and we rule nothing out for the future), we could have a real whinge about how old-fashioned cuts like shanks used to be so very cheap (good for the dog or the cook's perk) until they were discovered by chefs, when their popularity and prices sky-rocketed. The trouble is, they are so very delicious. We could take or leave a leg of lamb or a backstrap (or loin fillet) but a sticky, shiny, falling-apart shank? Never.

Make ahead: *These will benefit from being made ahead of time and reheated gently in a low-temperature oven, covered with foil. They'll last for 3 days in the fridge or up to 3 months in the freezer. Defrost before reheating.*

Preheat the oven to 150°C (300°F).

Mix together the coriander, cumin, cinnamon, paprika and half the salt. Rub the mixture all over the lamb shanks. Heat the oil over medium–high heat in a large, heavy-based flameproof casserole dish that will fit all the shanks in one layer and brown the shanks all over (tongs are helpful here). Set the shanks aside in a warm place, covered.

Lower the heat to medium–low, add a little more oil if necessary, and cook the onion, carrots, celery and garlic with the remaining ¾ teaspoon of salt till soft. Keep stirring occasionally – cooking this soffritto will take around 10–15 minutes. Increase the heat and add the wine, which will bubble up to deglaze the dish. Stir vigorously. Lower the heat and add the tomatoes, balsamic vinegar, rosemary and thyme. Taste this sauce for seasoning and balance – it will change as it cooks with the shanks but all the elements should be harmonious at this stage.

Return the lamb shanks to the dish, spooning the sauce over so that they are covered. Cover with a lid or foil, place in the oven and cook for 3 hours. Take the dish out every so often and turn the shanks so that they cook evenly. Top up with a little water or stock if the liquid level is too low.

The shanks are ready when the meat is soft and shrinking back from the bone, and the sauce is glossy. Use tongs to lift the shanks out gently and flip them over as you dish them up (the underside is always prettier). Give the sauce a good stir and pour over the shanks.

Sprinkle with the chopped parsley. Serve with mashed potato or soft polenta and some English spinach or kale dressed with olive oil and garlic.

Penne with *Italian Sausage Sauce*

SERVES 4   PREP TIME 15 MINUTES   COOKING TIME 1 HOUR 25 MINUTES

1½ tablespoons olive oil
2 garlic cloves, crushed
pinch of chilli flakes
1 large red onion, diced
pinch of salt
500 g (1 lb 2 oz) pork and fennel sausage mixture (cut sausages down their length and push the mixture out)
150 ml (5 fl oz) red wine
400 g (14 oz) tinned chopped tomatoes
2 bay leaves
2 teaspoons finely chopped rosemary leaves
pinch of ground nutmeg
1½ tablespoons thin (pouring) cream
500 g (1 lb 2 oz) penne

TO SERVE
grated parmesan cheese
handful basil leaves
green salad

In our much-stained and battered copy of The River Café Cookbook, *there are two different versions of this dish, one short and one long. We liked elements of both so have long since amalgamated them into one. It's a big favourite in our houses. We like to think of it as a bolognese with ideas above its station.*

Make ahead: This is an easy dish to make in large quantities, divide into batches and freeze for up to 3 months. You can also make it ahead and store it in an airtight container in the fridge for up to 3 days.

Heat the oil in a large, heavy-based saucepan over medium–low heat and fry the garlic, chilli flakes and onion with a pinch of salt until the onion is soft (about 10–15 minutes). Increase the heat and add the sausage mixture, breaking it up with a wooden spoon and allowing it to brown. Use a potato masher to break up any stubborn lumps. The sausage doesn't have to be completely cooked by this stage, just brown and broken up.

Add the wine to the pan, raise the heat to high and let it come to the boil, then add the tomatoes, bay leaves and rosemary and lower the heat. Simmer gently for about 1 hour, or until the sausage mixture is tender and the sauce is rich and thick. Stir through the nutmeg and cream and taste for seasoning, adding more salt if necessary – we've kept it deliberately low because the salt content of sausages varies. Make any changes you need to at this stage.

About 10 minutes before the sauce is due to be ready, cook the penne according to the packet instructions, drain and toss through the sauce.

Serve with lashings of freshly grated parmesan cheese, a handful of basil leaves and a leafy green salad.

SWEET and EASY

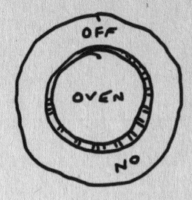

There will be those of you reading this book who are expert bakers and master pâtissiers. This is not the chapter for you – we advise that you find the latest book by Peter Gilmore or Adriano Zumbo instead. Admittedly, Katherine is a little bit that way inclined, with her gingerbread houses and croquembouches and production of outrageously decorated birthday cakes. This is not really the chapter for her either.

This is the chapter for Sophie, and those like her, who are a little challenged in the fine sugar work and co-ordination department and just want to make yummy desserts that don't involve the tempering of chocolate, making of pastry or spinning of caramel.

Sweet things are delightfully unnecessary; bringing out a dessert is a sign that it's a bit of a special occasion. They make us feel like children, they make us happy. All of the desserts we've chosen here are beautifully easy to cook and can either be made well ahead of time – even frozen in some cases – or flung together in a minute with a couple of simple ingredients.

A lot of them are homely, old-fashioned favourites but they work equally well at a dinner party as at the family table. Could there be anyone too sophisticated to feel welcomed and comforted by a crumble, a rice pudding or some brownies, still warm from the oven? If such a snooty beast exists, they won't be getting a second invitation to our place.

Chocolate Pavlova WITH Raspberries

SERVES 8   PREP TIME 30 MINUTES   COOKING TIME 1 HOUR 15 MINUTES

PAVLOVA BASE
6 egg whites
pinch of salt
300 g (10½ oz/1⅓ cups) caster
   (superfine) sugar
2 heaped tablespoons cocoa powder
1 teaspoon balsamic vinegar
50 g (1¾ oz/⅓ cup) good-quality dark
   chocolate, finely chopped, plus
   50 g (1¾ oz/⅓ cup) extra, grated or
   shaved for serving (optional)

TOPPING
500 ml (17 fl oz/2 cups) thin (pouring)
   cream
200 g (7 oz) hazelnut cocoa spread
250 g (9 oz) raspberries

A traditional, fluffy, virginal white pavlova is a fine thing, but we say double the pavlova repertoire, double the fun. The pavlova base (chewy and chocolatey, almost torte-like) is based on a recipe of Nigella's, but where she used plain whipped cream for the topping, we show no such restraint and use a mixture of cream and hazelnut cocoa spread. Oh my.

Make ahead: *The meringue can be made a day ahead and left to cool in the oven overnight. The whipped cream and hazelnut cocoa spread can be made a half day ahead. If you assemble the pavlova early, it will still be delicious but it will lose a bit of its crispness. With the other elements prepared, the assembly only takes moments at the end in any case.*

Preheat the oven to 120°C (235°F) and line a baking tray with baking paper.

Whisk the egg whites in a scrupulously clean, dry stainless steel or glass bowl with the salt till stiff, then gradually rain in the sugar, a little at a time, continuously whisking till the mixture is satiny. Sift in the cocoa powder and stir through the vinegar and dark chocolate.

Pile this meringue mixture onto the baking tray in a 25 cm (10 inch) diameter circle and place in the oven. After 1 hour, turn the oven off but leave the pavlova in the oven to cool and dry out further. We like to make this recipe the night before we need it, then leave the pavlova in the oven overnight after cooking it. Put a shouty note on the oven telling people DO NOT TURN THE OVEN BACK ON UNDER PAIN OF DEATH. This may also prevent you from doing that very thing yourself.

For the topping, whip the cream until soft peaks form. Fold through the hazelnut cocoa spread.

When you're ready to serve, spoon the cream on top of the meringue and dot the raspberries on the cream top – either in concentric circles, or in a haphazard jumble, depending on your artistic bent and level of perfectionism. Finish with a flurry of shaved or grated chocolate, if you wish.

Vanilla Panna Cotta
WITH *Espresso Syrup* AND *Almonds*

SERVES 6   PREP TIME 20 MINUTES, PLUS OVERNIGHT SETTING IN FRIDGE   COOKING TIME 20 MINUTES

NOTE: You will need six dariole moulds or ramekins of about 120 ml (4 fl oz) capacity for this dish.

PANNA COTTA
220 ml (7½ fl oz) full-cream (whole) milk
460 ml (16 fl oz) thin (pouring) cream
75 g (2¾ oz/⅓ cup) caster (superfine) sugar
1 vanilla bean, split lengthways, seeds scraped, both seeds and pod reserved
4 gelatine sheets, about 6.5 g (¼ oz)
pinch of salt

ESPRESSO SYRUP
45 g (1½ oz/½ cup) ground coffee
175 g (6 oz) white sugar
65 g (2¼ oz) dry-roasted almonds

NOTE: Gelatine sheets are increasingly available in supermarkets. They come in different weights and strengths, so it's a good idea to weigh your sheets and try to match the weight given above. If you're using powdered gelatine, use ½ teaspoon for each gelatine sheet and follow the directions on the packet.

Andrew Cibej of Vini in Sydney originally created this recipe. While we have tweaked it a little – his version used ricotta in the panna cotta – we've kept faithful to the wonderful, quite adult combination of bitter-sweet syrup, toasty nuts and creamy panna cotta. We like to make this for Valentine's night dinner.

Make ahead: *Panna cotta must be made at least 6 hours ahead. The syrup can be made up to 1 week ahead. Both should be kept covered in the fridge.*

In a heavy-based saucepan over medium–low heat, combine the milk, cream, sugar, vanilla bean and seeds. Heat till shimmering, just below boiling point, stirring to make sure it doesn't catch. Set aside to cool to about 40°C (104°F), just above blood temperature.

Soften the gelatine in cold water for 5 minutes. Drain, squeezing out the excess water and stir into the panna cotta mixture, making sure that the gelatine has dissolved completely before straining into a jug.

Pour the mixture into six dariole moulds of about 120 ml (4 fl oz) capacity. Cover with plastic wrap and leave in the fridge to set overnight.

To make the espresso syrup, combine the ground coffee with 175 ml (6 fl oz) of water in a plunger and leave to brew for 10 minutes. Plunge and pour the coffee out, then strain it through muslin (cheesecloth). You could also make strong espresso in a coffee machine or with a stovetop espresso maker.

In a heavy-based saucepan, mix the espresso with the sugar and boil vigorously for about 5–10 minutes to reduce until syrupy. Set aside to cool, then refrigerate. If you happen to have over-reduced and have ended up with sticky coffee toffee, fear not – if it hasn't burned, just gently reheat it with 1–2 tablespoons of water to help bring it back to the right syrupy consistency.

Preheat the oven to 180°C (350°F), then toast the nuts in the oven for 5 minutes. Keep a careful eye on them, as nuts burn very easily. Set aside to cool, then crush them roughly using a mortar and pestle, leaving some nuts whole and some broken.

To serve, dip the panna cottas, one at a time, in a bowl of hot water to loosen the edges. The amount of time will depend on the containers you have used – if you have used metal containers, they will loosen in a matter of seconds, but ceramic containers will take longer. Help loosen them by running a knife around the edge if necessary, then turn the panna cottas out onto your serving plates. Spoon a little of the espresso syrup around the edge, strew the broken almonds on top, and serve.

Chocolate Honeycomb Semifreddo

SERVES 8 PREP TIME 20 MINUTES, PLUS AT LEAST 6 HOURS FREEZING COOKING TIME NONE

4 large eggs, separated
1 vanilla bean, split lengthways, seeds
    scraped out, pod reserved for
    another use
100 g (3½ oz) caster (superfine) sugar
500 ml (17 fl oz/2 cups) thin (pouring)
    cream
100 g (3½ oz) chocolate-coated
    honeycomb

. . . .

NOTE: You can stick the reserved
vanilla pod in some caster (superfine)
sugar to make vanilla sugar.

The Europeans have their pralines and nougats – but do any of them really top a chocolate honeycomb bar as the flavouring for a semifreddo? What's brilliant about it is the slight burnt edge of the honeycomb, which stops it from being sickly sweet. Making semifreddo is way easier than making your own ice cream and requires no special equipment. Once you've got the basic recipe down, there is an infinite number of variations. Even plain vanilla, served with berries, can be lovely.

Make ahead: *Semifreddo has to be made ahead. Just remember to get it out to soften 15-30 minutes before you plan to eat it (less on a warm day, more on a cooler day).*

Whisk the egg yolks, vanilla seeds and sugar well till the mixture is pale and thick. In a separate bowl, beat the cream till soft peaks form. In another, scrupulously clean stainless steel or glass bowl, whisk the egg whites till peaks form.

Smash up the honeycomb – you want a mixture of crumbled bits and chunky shards.

Carefully fold the egg yolk mixture and honeycomb into the whipped cream, then add the egg whites and continue to fold gently until everything is well mixed, but trying to keep as much air in your mixture as possible.

Line a 11 x 21 x 6 cm (4¼ x 8¼ x 2½ inch)/1.5 litre (52 fl oz/6 cup) capacity loaf (bar) tin with baking paper or plastic wrap, pour in the mixture, smooth the top with a spatula, cover with plastic wrap and freeze for at least 6 hours.

Semifreddo is usually served in slices, but there is nothing stopping you from scooping this into cones if you'd prefer. Just remember to bring it out of the freezer to let it soften 15–30 minutes before you are going to use it.

VARIATION:
Raspberry, pistachio and nougat make a very pretty semifreddo. Make the basic recipe above, substituting 2 tablespoons honey for 50 g (1¾ oz) of the caster (superfine) sugar. Blitz 200 g (7 oz) hard nougat into small pieces, then fold through the mixture with 100 g (3½ oz/¾ cup) pistachio nut kernels and 100 g (3½ oz) raspberries.

Chocolate, Date AND Almond Torte

SERVES 8–10   PREP TIME 15 MINUTES   COOKING TIME 1 HOUR

250 g (9 oz) blanched almonds

200 g (7 oz) dried pitted dates, chopped into small pieces

200 g (7 oz/1⅓ cups) dark chocolate, chopped into small pieces, plus extra shavings to serve

6 egg whites

pinch of salt

110 g (3¾ oz/½ cup) caster (superfine) sugar

TO SERVE

whipped cream or Vanilla Mascarpone (see page 229)

berries

If you don't already have a version of this most essential cake in your repertoire, here it is – use it wisely. It's a dark, dense and chocolatey little beast – really it's just nuts, chocolate and dried fruit held together by a collapsed meringue. It does very nicely on its own with a mid-afternoon coffee, or as a dessert, smothered in whipped cream with some berries on the side. One of the many beauties of this torte is that it freezes well – make a few at a time and stick a couple in the freezer. The combination of nuts and dried fruit can easily change, depending on what's in the pantry. Chocolate, fig and pecan; chocolate, date and hazelnut – all work beautifully. Obviously the chocolate part is non-negotiable.

Make ahead: *The torte can be made ahead, wrapped tightly in plastic wrap, and kept in the fridge for up to 3 days or in the freezer for up to 3 months. Defrost and allow to come to room temperature before covering with whipped cream.*

Preheat the oven to 180°C (350°F) and line a 24 cm (9½ inch) spring-form cake tin with a circle of baking paper. Grease the sides of the tin.

Scatter the almonds on a baking tray and roast in the oven for 5 minutes till golden. Chop into small pieces.

In a large mixing bowl, mix together the dates, almonds and chocolate.

In a separate clean, dry stainless steel or glass bowl, beat the egg whites with the salt using a hand-held electric beater until soft peaks form. Keep beating while you slowly and gently rain in the sugar until it's all incorporated and the mixture is thick and glossy.

Take a large spoonful of the meringue mixture and stir it fairly vigorously into the dates, almonds and chocolate, then add the rest, folding it in gently but thoroughly, ensuring there aren't any hidden pockets of dry ingredients lurking at the bottom of the bowl.

Spoon the mixture into the prepared cake tin and give it a gentle shake to settle the contents and smooth the surface, then place in the preheated oven for around 40 minutes (start checking at 35 minutes). By the end of the cooking time, the cake should be shrinking away from the side of the tin. Turn the oven off, leave the door ajar, and allow the torte to cool in the oven. Note: tell everyone in the house that you're doing this so that no one else comes along and turns on the oven for another purpose, only to discover the error when the sweet smell of burnt cake starts wafting through the house.

Serve the torte at room temperature, with cold whipped cream or vanilla mascarpone cream on top and blueberries or raspberries on the side. You could also shave some dark chocolate curls over the cream or mascarpone.

Vanilla-scented Baked Rice Pudding with *Rhubarb* and *Strawberry Compote*

SERVES 6–8   PREP TIME 15 MINUTES   COOKING TIME 1 HOUR 5 MINUTES

PUDDING

2 egg yolks (freeze the egg whites for later use)
110 g (3¾ oz/½ cup) caster (superfine) sugar
550 ml (19 fl oz) full-cream (whole) milk
330 ml (11 fl oz) thin (pouring) cream
pinch of ground cinnamon
1 vanilla bean, split lengthways, seeds scraped out and pod reserved
1 strip of orange zest, thinly peeled
120 g (4¼ oz) arborio rice
salted butter, for greasing

COMPOTE

400 g (14 oz/1 bunch) rhubarb, trimmed and chopped into 2 cm (¾ inch) lengths
55 g (2 oz/¼ cup) caster (superfine) sugar
250 g (9 oz/1 punnet) strawberries, hulled and halved

TO SERVE

whipped cream or crème fraîche

Everything about this dessert – its sweet homely scent, gentle creamy texture and wholesome ingredients – harks back to a time when puddings didn't have to whack you over the head with sugar and chocolate to be a family favourite. If you don't like rice pudding because of a traumatic childhood incident, let this version be the one that heals you and makes you whole again.

Make ahead: This really is a brilliant recipe to make ahead in a large amount, then finish later. Simply cook it on the stovetop till the rice is tender but it still has a lot of liquid. At this stage it can be quickly chilled and stored overnight in a covered container in the fridge or frozen in batches. When you are ready to use it, defrost (if frozen) and pour the half-cooked rice pudding into an ovenproof dish, then continue with the last part of cooking. The compote can be made up to 2 weeks ahead and kept, covered, in the fridge. Make it in larger quantities and keep it on hand to jazz up your breakfast muesli (granola) or the weekend's pancakes.

In a small mixing bowl, whisk the egg yolks and sugar until thick, pale and creamy.

Pour the milk and cream into a heavy-based medium saucepan and place over medium–high heat, adding the cinnamon, vanilla seeds and pod and orange zest. When the mixture is almost at boiling point, reduce the heat and simmer very gently for 15 minutes. Allow to cool for 15 minutes.

Strain the cream mixture into another clean medium saucepan and, whisking constantly, pour on the egg yolk and sugar mixture. Add the rice and put the pan over very low heat for about 20–30 minutes, stirring frequently, till the rice is plump and tender but there is still a lot of liquid.

Meanwhile, make the compote by placing the rhubarb and sugar in a medium stainless steel or non-stick saucepan over gentle heat. Cover and cook, checking and stirring frequently, until the rhubarb has started to break down. This should take about 15 minutes. Add the strawberries and continue to cook for another 10 minutes till the mixture starts to thicken. Taste for a pleasing sweet/sharp balance and alter if necessary.

Preheat the oven to 160°C (315°F).

Grease a 1 litre (35 fl oz/4 cup) capacity ovenproof dish, pour the rice pudding into the dish and place in the oven for about 20 minutes or until it is set and golden. If you are cooking it from fridge temperature, add another 10 minutes to the cooking time.

Serve scoops of rice pudding with the warm compote and cold whipped cream or crème fraîche.

Chocolate Strawberry Croquembouche

SERVES 6–8 PREP TIME 45 MINUTES, PLUS 1 HOUR SETTING IN FRIDGE COOKING TIME 6 MINUTES

200 g (7 oz) milk chocolate
4 x 250 g (9 oz) punnets nice strawberries, not too big, with attractive green bits, chilled
200 g (7 oz) dark chocolate
200 g (7 oz) white chocolate

TO SERVE
a rousing 'Happy Birthday'
sparklers

This idea came to Katherine after an attempt at a real croquembouche for a child's birthday went pear-shaped, and she managed to salvage the situation with it. The pressure to deliver a magic birthday can be hell sometimes! We hope this helps you one day.

Make ahead: *This impressive birthday treat should be made ahead of time, and will keep for up to 2 days, uncovered, in the fridge.*

Prepare three baking trays lined with baking paper that will fit in your fridge (and make sure you can fit three trays in your fridge – throw out some spooky old stuff from the back of it or remove a shelf if necessary).

First, break up the milk chocolate, put it in a microwave-safe bowl and melt it. The easiest way to do this is in 20-second bursts in the microwave, stirring in between.

Holding your strawberries by their green tops, dip them into the melted chocolate to coat, then place them on one of your trays. Keep going till you have used a third of your strawberries.

Repeat the process with the dark chocolate, and then the white chocolate. Put everything in the fridge to set for at least 1 hour.

Now, get ready to assemble your tower. Start by creating a circle of strawberries (mix the colours of chocolate up as you wish) as your base layer, inside the rim of your plate, filling the circle in. The rim will help hold your strawberries in place. Work your way up, with smaller sized circles each time. Return your creation to the fridge from time to time to firm it up. This will make it easier to build a high tower. On each new layer, place the higher strawberries in the divets between strawberries on the layer below – this will make your tower stronger. Keep working upwards to build a cone shape.

If you have leftover chocolate, you can use it to pipe 'Happy Birthday xxx' around the base of your croquembouche. You can also drizzle up and down the sides of your creation in an attractively messy way. If you don't have an icing kit, just cut a little hole out of the corner of a zip-lock bag and fill it with warm chocolate to create your icing (piping) bag. If you would like, you could add some silver balls, or any of the many great sparkly cake decorations that you can get in supermarkets now.

Clear a space in your fridge (you will likely have to remove a shelf to accommodate your creation) and keep it in the fridge till you are ready to use it. Alternatively, store things temporarily in an esky with an ice block.

Serve with a rousing Happy Birthday and some sparklers.

Christmas Panna Cotta
WITH *Edible Gold Leaf*

SERVES 10   PREP TIME 20 MINUTES, PLUS 2 NIGHTS SETTING IN FRIDGE   COOKING TIME 10 MINUTES

NOTE: You will need ten dariole moulds or ramekins of about 120 ml (4 fl oz) capacity for this dish.

PANNA COTTA
275 ml (9½ fl oz) full-cream (whole) milk
550 ml (19 fl oz) thin (pouring) cream
110 g (3¾ oz/½ cup) caster (superfine) sugar
1 vanilla bean, split lengthways and seeds scraped (keep both pod and seeds)
tiny pinch of salt
5 gelatine sheets, about 8 g (¼ oz) (see note on page 217)

RASPBERRY JELLY
450 g (1 lb) frozen raspberries
175 g (6 oz) white sugar
2 gelatine sheets, about 3.2 g (¹⁄₁₀ oz)

TO SERVE
edible gold leaf, stars or glitter

We love Christmas pudding and all things traditionally European during the festive season but we are prepared to admit that none of it is well suited to an Australian climate and a post-lunch dip. This light, pretty panna cotta fits the bill for a delightful Southern Hemisphere Christmas pudding – the little touch of bling makes it very festive. If you want something special to dress your cake (and Christmas is a time when we're prepared to go over the top) you can order online from specialist cake decorators. Just google 'edible gold cake decorations' and you'll get a wealth of sparkly choices.

Make ahead: *The raspberry jelly must be made 2 days before serving and allowed to set before topping with the panna cotta layer, which needs 6 hours to set. You can make these up to 3 days ahead of time.*

Start by making the raspberry jelly. Put the raspberries and sugar in a heavy-based saucepan over low heat at first, stirring so they don't catch. Once the raspberries have started to release their juice, you can turn the heat up a little. Cook till the sugar is dissolved and the raspberries have turned into a complete mush. While it is still hot, strain it through a fine metal sieve into a jug, pressing down to get as much liquid out as you can. Set aside to cool slightly. Set out ten dariole moulds or ramekins on a tray.

Soften the gelatine sheets in cold water for 5 minutes, then lift them out of the water, squeezing to drain well, and add them to the raspberry liquid, stirring well to make sure they have dissolved completely. Straight away, pour the liquid into your panna cotta moulds, dividing it equally among them. Cover the tray of jellies with plastic wrap, and put aside to set overnight in the fridge. It is important they are completely set before you move onto the next stage.

Once they are set, make your panna cotta. In a heavy-based saucepan over low heat, combine the milk, cream, sugar, vanilla bean and seeds, and the salt. Heat till shimmering, just below boiling point, stirring to make sure it doesn't catch. Take off the heat and set aside to cool.

Soften the gelatine in cold water for 5 minutes. When the panna cotta mixture is around 40°C (104°F degrees), stir through the drained, softened gelatine – if you don't have a thermometer, you can gauge the temperature by sticking your finger in and making sure it's above blood temperature but not piping hot. When the gelatine has dissolved completely, strain the mixture through a sieve into a jug.

Now comes the only (slightly) tricky part. You need to wait for your panna cotta mixture to cool enough so that it doesn't melt the raspberry jelly, but not so cool that it starts to set (in Australia at Christmas, this is so unlikely to happen so don't concern yourself too much about it) – about 20–27°C (68–81°F). Pour the panna cotta mixture over the raspberry jelly in your moulds, cover again with plastic wrap and place in the fridge to set overnight.

To serve, dip your panna cottas, one at a time, in a bowl of hot water to loosen the edges. The amount of time will depend on the containers you have used – if you have used metal containers, they will loosen in a matter of seconds, but ceramic containers will take a little longer. Don't sit them in the water and leave them, though, or the layers will melt and bleed into one another. Help loosen them by running a knife around the edge if necessary, then turn each panna cotta out onto a dessert plate (place the plate on top of the panna cotta mould, then flip so that the mould is on top of the plate before lifting off). Scatter with your golden decorations.

Merry Christmas.

CHRISTMAS PANNA COTTA WITH
EDIBLE GOLD LEAF, *page* 224

TROPICAL TRIFLE, *page 228*

Tropical Trifle

SERVES 8   PREP TIME 45 MINUTES   COOKING TIME 10 MINUTES

180 g (6½ oz) savoiardi (lady fingers)
2 mangoes (or 4 frozen cheeks if you can't get fresh), flesh puréed in a blender
pulp of 2 passionfruit

VANILLA CUSTARD
3 egg yolks
75 g (2¾ oz/⅓ cup) caster (superfine) sugar
240 ml (8 fl oz) full-cream (whole) milk
240 ml (8 fl oz) thin (pouring) cream
½ vanilla bean, seeds scraped out and both seeds and pod reserved

PASSIONFRUIT-LIME SYRUP
55 g (2 oz/¼ cup) white sugar
juice of 1 lime (reserve the zest for the mascarpone cream), strained
juice of 2 large passionfruit, seeds strained out
2½ tablespoons white rum (optional)

MASCARPONE CREAM
400 ml (14 fl oz) thin (pouring) cream
200 g (7 oz) mascarpone
65 g (2¼ oz) caster (superfine) sugar
zest of 1 lime

TO SERVE
55 g (2 oz/⅓ cup) macadamia nuts, roasted and lightly crushed
pulp of 2 passionfruit
edible gold stars (optional) or 1 extra mango, thinly sliced

For a fully born and bred Australian, Sophie has quite an excessive number of Englishmen in the family, all hankering for a bit of trifle at Christmas – but there are those in the family who would rather a pavlova. We came up with this very tropical, patriotically green and gold version as a sort of happy midway point between trifle and pavlova and adorned it with festive edible gold stars (like the ones on page 226). It's now a Christmas essential but delicious any time – maybe leave off the gold stars for every day. And if you really want to go troppo, you can splash some white rum into the passionfruit-lime syrup.

Make ahead: *All the separate components can be made 3 days ahead of time and refrigerated. The whole trifle should be assembled the day ahead. Cover with the macadamia nuts and passionfruit pulp just before serving.*

To make the custard, whisk the egg yolks with the sugar in a mixing bowl till combined.

Heat the milk, cream and vanilla bean and seeds over medium–low heat in a medium saucepan. When it is almost coming to a simmer (the surface of the mixture should be just shimmering), strain it into a fresh saucepan and allow to cool for 10 minutes. Whisking constantly, add the egg yolk and sugar mixture and set over low heat. Cook very gently, stirring with a wooden spoon, until the custard has thickened enough to coat the back of the spoon – if you have a thermometer, the temperature your mixture should reach is 82°C (180°F). Don't overheat the mixture or it will scramble. Set aside to cool, stirring every so often to prevent a skin forming, then cover and refrigerate.

To make the syrup, boil the sugar and 60 ml (2 fl oz/¼ cup) of water in a small saucepan over high heat for a few minutes till lightly syrupy (a few minutes). Set aside, cool, then add the strained lime juice, passionfruit juice and white rum (if using). Refrigerate in an airtight container.

To make the mascarpone cream, beat the cream and mascarpone together till soft peaks form. Fold through the sugar and lime zest, and set aside, covered, in the fridge.

Now you are ready to assemble your tropical trifle, the day before you plan to eat it.

NOTE: To make this recipe easier, you can skip the Vanilla Custard section and use store-bought custard – but real custard is not difficult to make and is heavenly.

Take out your prettiest glass bowl with a capacity of at least 2 litres (70 fl oz/8 cups). Pour the passionfruit-lime syrup into a shallow bowl and dip the biscuits quickly into it – you want them moistened but not soggy. Use them to line the bottom of your bowl. Spread the mango purée over the biscuits, spoon on the passionfruit pulp, then pour over the vanilla custard. Top everything with the mascarpone cream.

Just before serving, scatter with macadamia nuts and drizzle with passionfruit pulp. Add edible gold stars if the occasion demands them or extra mango slices if not.

Vanilla Mascarpone

Vanilla mascarpone makes an elegant substitute for whipped cream alongside or as a component of many desserts. Its big advantage for us is that it's able to be made well ahead of time – 1–2 days before – unlike whipped cream, which will become weepy. For a vanilla mascarpone that will jazz up a bowl of fruit or berries, whip 200 ml (7 fl oz) thin (pouring) cream with 100 g (3½ oz) mascarpone till soft peaks form, then stir through 2 tablespoons caster (superfine) sugar (you can adjust this according to your taste) and the scraped out seeds from ½ vanilla bean or ½ teaspoon good-quality natural vanilla extract.

Marmalade *and* Chocolate Bread *and* Butter Pudding

SERVES 6–8   PREP TIME 20 MINUTES, PLUS 1 HOUR–OVERNIGHT CHILLING IN FRIDGE
COOKING TIME 30 MINUTES, PLUS 5 MINUTES RESTING

70 g (2½ oz) salted butter, softened
8 good quality white bread slices,
    about 400 g (14 oz) in total
85 g (3 oz/¼ cup) marmalade
3 large eggs
180 g (6½ oz) caster (superfine) sugar
450 ml (15½ fl oz) full-cream (whole)
    milk
1 teaspoon natural vanilla extract
2 big tablespoons golden syrup
2 tablespoons chopped good quality
    dark chocolate
1 tablespoon light brown sugar

TO SERVE
icing (confectioners') sugar, for dusting
whipped cream or ice cream

Oh, we do love a theme and this pudding is infinitely versatile theme-wise. We do a hot cross bun version for Easter, we've substituted panettone at Christmas, and at other times of the year we've used plain old white bread with a couple of handfuls of dried cherries, blueberries or sultanas (golden raisins) to make up for its lack of fruitiness. Orange and chocolate are, of course, a classic partnership and they do all sorts of good things in this pudding, with its crunchy, sugared top, fluffy interior and toffee base.

Make ahead: *The whole dish can be assembled (but not cooked) up to 1 day in advance and stored, covered, in the fridge.*

Grease a 2 litre (70 fl oz/8 cup) capacity ceramic ovenproof dish or shallow pudding basin with 1 tablespoon of the butter. Butter the slices of bread, then spread the marmalade on top and cut into triangles.

Crack the eggs and whisk them with the caster sugar until thick, foamy and pale, then gradually whisk in the milk and vanilla extract.

Drizzle the bottoms and sides of the dish with golden syrup. Cover the base with some marmalade bread slices (marmalade side up), scatter with chocolate and repeat until you've used all the bread and chocolate.

Carefully, a little at a time, pour on the egg and milk mixture, letting it soak into the bread, then sprinkle the top with brown sugar. Allow to stand in the fridge for at least 1 hour or overnight.

Preheat the oven to 175°C (340°F).

Bake the pudding in the middle of the oven for about 25–30 minutes or until crusty and golden on top and just set in the middle. Test the pudding with a skewer to make sure the insides are like set custard rather than raw egg – times will vary depending on whether you've used a flatter, wider dish or a bowl-shaped basin. The pudding will puff up dramatically, but then collapse back down as it cools.

Allow the pudding to cool and set for 5 minutes, dust with icing sugar and serve with whipped cream or ice cream.

Tip

For a richer pudding, simply swap half the milk for cream – use 225 ml (7½ fl oz) thin (pouring) cream and 225 ml (7½ fl oz) full-cream (whole) milk.

Marbled Choc Fudge
AND *Raspberry Brownies*

MAKES 12 BROWNIES   PREP TIME 30 MINUTES   COOKING TIME 35 MINUTES

DARK CHOCOLATE MIX
140 g (5 oz) salted butter
120 g (4¼ oz) dark chocolate (70%
   cocoa minimum), broken into pieces
2 eggs
175 g (6 oz) caster (superfine) sugar
100 g (3½ oz/⅔ cup) plain
   (all-purpose) flour
pinch of salt

CREAM CHEESE MIX
250 g (9 oz) cream cheese
100 g (3½ oz) caster (superfine) sugar
1 egg
1 teaspoon natural vanilla extract
100 g (3½ oz) frozen raspberries

TO SERVE
berries
ice cream

We'd been making the Union Square Café's marbled chocolate and cream cheese brownies for a while when we had the happy thought of adding raspberries – genius! The sharp sweet tang of the berries cuts through the fudgy richness of the brownie, as well as giving the whole dessert a pleasantly retro Neapolitan twist. We make this in trays and cut them into square brownies but you could make them in individual, buttered, cocoa-dusted ramekins for a dinner party and serve them, unmoulded, with ice cream.

Make ahead: *You can make the mixure ahead of time and freeze it in its baking tray, then cook it when you are ready to use it. If cooking from frozen, add another 10 minutes to the cooking time. Or you can make a large batch, cook half and freeze the other half to cook later. Once you have cooked them, the brownies keep very well in an airtight container for up to 3 days.*

Preheat the oven to 150°C (300°F) and line a 22 cm (8½ inch) square cake tin (or thereabouts) with baking paper.

First, make your dark chocolate mix. In a small saucepan over low heat, melt the butter without allowing it to brown. Take off the heat and add the chocolate, stirring occasionally, until it has melted and the mixture is smooth. Set aside to cool.

In a medium mixing bowl, whisk the eggs with the sugar, then, checking first that it's not too hot, mix in the butter and chocolate mixture. Sift in the flour and the salt, and stir through. Don't overbeat at this stage. Set this mixture aside.

To make the cream cheese mixture, in a separate bowl or using a standmixer, beat the cream cheese and sugar together till creamy and lump-free. Add the egg and vanilla extract and continue to beat until everything is smooth.

With a large spoon, place alternate blobs of the dark chocolate and white cream cheese mixture in the tin, and dot with raspberries. Using a fork, poke the raspberries under the surface and swirl the mixture to create a marbled pattern. Don't over-swirl or you will lose the separate colours.

Bake in the preheated oven for 25–30 minutes, depending on how cakey or fudgy you like your brownies. If you are cooking from frozen, add another 10 minutes to the cooking time. Ovens are very variable, so keep an eye on the brownies towards the end of the cooking time.

Serve in squares as is for afternoon tea or with fresh berries and ice cream for dessert.

Oranges in Liqueur Syrup

SERVES 8   PREP TIME 25 MINUTES, PLUS AT LEAST 3 HOURS CHILLING   COOKING TIME 5 MINUTES

3 kg (6 lb 10 oz) oranges
100 ml (3½ fl oz) orange liqueur
100 g (3½ oz) caster (superfine) sugar

TO SERVE
45 g (1½ oz/⅓ cup) slivered almonds,
   toasted
dark chocolate

Katherine includes this recipe for her aunt – a big bowl of these very refreshing and very sunny oranges was always a feature of her summer gatherings on the farm. It's a light, refreshing dessert, but the addition of toasted slivered almonds and dark chocolate curls makes it an easy and elegant way to end a dinner.

Make ahead: *The whole dish should be made at least 3 hours ahead to let the flavours infuse, and will keep well in an airtight container in the fridge for a few days.*

Squeeze 2 of the oranges, then strain the juice. In a saucepan over medium heat, bring the juice, orange liqueur and sugar to the boil, then simmer for 5 minutes, or till syrupy. Take off the heat and let the liquid cool.

Now, it's time to prepare the oranges. Use a small, sharp knife to cut the top and bottom off each orange, then cut the peel off the outside so that you are left with a small orange orb. Holding each orange in your cupped hand, carefully cut out the segments, working your way around the whole orange. You want to end up with orange segments minus any skin or pith. If this all seems too hard, you can cut the peeled oranges across into circle-shaped slices.

When you have prepared all your oranges, place them in your serving bowl or platter and pour over the syrup – don't worry if it has thickened a bit as it has cooled – the juice from the orange segments will dissolve it very quickly. Cover with plastic wrap and refrigerate till needed.

Scatter with toasted slivered almonds and curls of chocolate (use a vegetable peeler to peel curls from a block of chocolate) and serve.

No Time Instant Desserts

We've often found ourselves in the position of having to magic up a dessert out of nowhere. Though a block of decent chocolate and/or dried fruit can go a long way, so many men (sorry, people) still seem to have that awkward, after-dinner, dessert-shaped hole to fill. But with a bit of forethought and a well-stocked freezer and pantry, any of these can be created in 5 minutes.

Ice-Cream Sandwiches

Ice-cream sandwiches can be as tastefully restrained or over the top as the combinations of biscuit and ice cream you choose: shortbread biscuits with berry sorbet, chocolate biscuits with cookies and cream ice cream, choc-chip cookies with peanut butter ice cream ... Bigger biscuits are easier to sandwich, while an array of different flavoured, smaller ones looks cuter. You need to soften the ice cream a bit so that it can be spooned onto the bottom layer of biscuit. Press down with the top biscuit and neaten around the edges with the flat of a knife. Pop each sandwich back into the freezer as you go, until you're ready to serve.

Hazelnut Affogato

This is insanely simple and delicious, as long as you have hazelnuts and hazelnut liqueur in the pantry. Make a shot of coffee for each of your guests. Spoon a scoop of vanilla ice cream into however many shatter-proof tumblers or cups you need. Pour 2 tablespoons of hazelnut liqueur over the top, followed by the hot espresso and sprinkle with roasted, skinned, crushed hazelnuts.

Sparkling Slushy

A sparkling slushy makes a refreshing end to a summer dinner. If you're making it for kids as well, you can substitute lemonade for the sparkling wine. You'll need a couple of different bought sorbets (or our Instant Cheat's Sorbet, see page 241) and a bottle of sparkling wine. Spoon a scoopful each of two sorts of sorbet (strawberry and lemon, raspberry and peach, passionfruit and mango – whatever tickles your fancy) into tumblers or glass bowls. Top with sparkling wine (or lemonade) and serve, with spoons.

➤ *CONTINUED ON PAGE 236*

No Time Instant Desserts

« CONTINUED FROM PAGE 235

Fine Apple Tart

This is tremendously easy, yet delicious. First, preheat the oven to 180°C (350°F). Peel, core and thinly slice 3 granny smith apples. Put a square sheet of puff pastry on a baking tray lined with baking paper, then cover it with the apple slices – go all the way to the edges, and don't overload the centre. Sprinkle with 55 g (2 oz/¼ cup) caster (superfine) sugar, and cook in the oven for 25 minutes. Serve with crème fraîche.

Vanilla Mascarpone Berry Tart

Preheat the oven to 180°C (350°F). Line a baking tray with baking paper. Put a sheet of butter puff pastry on it, then cover with another sheet of baking paper, then top with another baking tray. Cook for 15 minutes till the pastry is golden, but sort of compressed and flat. Let it cool, then spread with Vanilla Mascarpone (see page 229). You'll need to make it with 150 ml (5 fl oz) thin (pouring) cream and 75 g (2¾ oz) mascarpone plus 125–250 g (4½–9 oz) raspberries, blueberries or strawberries (single or mixed) scattered on top. Sprinkle the whole lot generously with icing (confectioners') sugar before cutting into squares and serving. You can also aim for a sort of mille-feuille effect by cutting the cooked pastry into equal rectangles, spreading with the mascarpone cream and berries as before and sandwiching with another rectangle of pastry. Dust the top with more icing sugar and serve with extra berries.

Eton Mess

We'd never go to the trouble of making meringues just to smash them up for Eton mess – store-bought ones are just fine for this. Please, not the ones with hundreds and thousands though. So, your basic ingredients are smashed meringues, whipped cream, strawberry halves and strawberry purée. To make the purée, simply cook down 250 g (9 oz/1 punnet) strawberries with 55 g (2 oz/¼ cup) caster (superfine) sugar in a medium saucepan over medium heat, allow to cool slightly, then blitz in a blender. Presentation-wise we like using glass tumblers and a scattering of toasted flaked almonds on top (it makes it look like you've put in more effort than you actually have). In the tumblers, layer up the meringue, cream, purée and strawberries and, using a spoon, ripple them all together (alternatively, mix it all in a big bowl, and plonk it into the glasses or bowls). Top with the toasted flaked almonds. This is an impossible recipe to stuff up. No matter what ratios of cream to meringue to fruit you use, it will always be delicious and everyone loves it.

Roast Stone Fruit WITH Amaretti Biscuits

This is the fallback dessert of our dear friend Lisa, who always manages to whip up a little something, even in the dodgiest of holiday kitchens. She often substitutes coconut macaroons for the amaretti. You'll need half as many pieces of fruit (peaches or nectarines, ideally free-stone) as there are people to feed (so, half a piece each) with a couple extra for good luck, some unsalted butter and a packet of amaretti biscuits. Preheat the oven to 180°C (350°F). Halve and stone the fruit and arrange in an ovenproof dish. Shake the amaretti biscuits out into a plastic bag and bash with a rolling pin till the pieces are crushed but still chunky. Dot the fruit generously with butter and scatter with the crushed biscuits. Put in the oven for 20–25 minutes or until it all looks crisp and golden, with sticky, oozy juices. Serve with crème fraîche or ice cream.

Brown-sugar Barbecued Fruit

The one essential for this is a clean barbecue hotplate – hand that job to someone else while you prepare your fruit of choice. You can also cook this in a large non-stick frying pan if you don't have an obliging barbecue cleaner. This is a summery dessert for us so we'd choose something like mangoes (skin on cheeks, cross-hatched) or pineapple (chunky sticks sliced lengthways from the top to the bottom of the fruit) or, in late summer, ripe figs (cut in half). Press the cut side of the fruit into brown sugar and then place it on an oiled barbecue hotplate over medium heat until the brown sugar begins to bubble and caramelise. (The pineapple will need this done on all sides.) Serve with lime wedges and vanilla ice cream.

Oven Smores

This version of the American campfire classic is a bit of fun, and involves nothing more complicated than making a marshmallow sandwich of digestive biscuits. Preheat the oven to 200°C (400°F) and line a baking tray with baking paper. On 1 digestive biscuit, place 5 marshmallows in a circle and fill the middle with milk chocolate chips. Put your second digestive on top, then put the whole thing in the oven for 3–4 minutes, or till the marshmallows have toasted on the outside and are just starting to ooze. Oven smores are super sticky and messy, so make sure you serve them outside to kids, and nowhere near any good carpet or furniture.

Chocolate Mint Honey Pots

SERVES 6   PREP TIME 5 MINUTES, PLUS OVERNIGHT CHILLING   COOKING TIME 5 MINUTES

200 g (7 oz) dark chocolate (70% cocoa
   minimum), broken into pieces
1 teaspoon peppermint extract
300 ml (10½ fl oz) thin (pouring) cream
2 tablespoons honey
1 large egg

TO SERVE
whipped cream
shards of peppermint chocolate crisp

These are the simplest things in the world to make, avoiding all the stress of chocolate mousse and without any possibility of the chocolate catching or splitting. While you can make plain chocolate pots, you can also add any number of different flavours. You'll need six serving pots of around 120 ml (4 fl oz) capacity – if you don't have small ramekins, you can use espresso cups.

Make ahead: The pots have to be made at least 1 day ahead of time to set, and will keep for up to 3 days, covered, in the fridge.

In a food processor, blitz your chocolate with the peppermint extract till it is completely pulverised. Leave in the food processor.

Heat the cream in a small saucepan over medium heat to just below boiling point, then with the motor running on the food processor, pour the cream and the honey down the funnel. Continue to blend for 30 seconds. Crack the egg down the funnel, then continue to blend for another minute.

Pour your chocolate mixture into six serving pots, and leave in the fridge to set, at least overnight.

To serve, top with whipped cream and a few shards of peppermint chocolate crisp.

VARIATIONS:
For coffee chocolate pots, add 2 teaspoons good quality instant coffee powder to the chocolate mix (instead of the peppermint extract) and 1 tablespoon coffee liqueur to the whipped cream. Serve with the whipped cream and some sifted cocoa powder on top.

For chilli chocolate pots, add ¼ teaspoon chilli powder and ½ teaspoon ground cinnamon to the chocolate mix (instead of the peppermint extract). Serve with the whipped cream and some finely diced red chilli on top.

Spiced Winter Compote

SERVES 8   PREP TIME 5 MINUTES   COOKING TIME 40 MINUTES

3 Earl Grey tea bags
150 g (5½ oz) raw sugar
1 cinnamon stick
1 x 1 cm (½ inch) piece ginger, cut into
   thin matchsticks
2 star anise
6 whole cloves
1 vanilla bean, split lengthways
2 strips of orange zest
2 strips of lemon zest
6 black peppercorns
600 g (1 lb 5 oz) mixed dried fruit
   (apricots, prunes, figs, peaches,
   pears – any large pieces cut in half)
juice of ½ lemon

TO SERVE
toasted brioche and crème fraîche
or
Greek-style yoghurt and toasted flaked
   almonds
or
good-quality vanilla ice cream

Banish any thoughts of hospital stewed prunes from your mind – this mixture of dried fruit steeped in an Earl Grey syrup and spiced with vanilla, cinnamon and cloves is luscious. Though better paired with crème fraîche and a liqueur muscat than bran flakes, any leftovers would be out of this world with porridge, and even more delicious with brioche French toast.

Make ahead: *This whole recipe can be made well in advance and kept, covered, in the fridge for up to 3 weeks. It gets a bit stiff and toffee-ish in the fridge so warm gently before serving.*

Bring water to the boil in a kettle and measure out 700 ml (24 fl oz) into a medium saucepan. Add the Earl Grey tea bags and allow to steep for 5 minutes. Remove the tea bags and discard.

Add the sugar, cinnamon stick, ginger, star anise, cloves, vanilla bean, orange and lemon zest and black peppercorns to the tea and bring to the boil over high heat. If you would rather not have the whole spices in the compote at the end, you can tie them up in a piece of muslin (cheesecloth) and infuse the tea syrup that way.

Stir the dried fruit into the syrup, reduce the heat to low and simmer gently for a further 20 minutes, stirring regularly. Add the lemon juice and taste for balance. Remove from the heat, discard the spice bundle (if used) and allow the compote to cool before refrigerating until needed. If you haven't used a spice bundle, try and fish out the star anise and the peppercorns before the compote cools – the star anise, in particular, is not very nice to bite into later.

Serve warm with slices of toasted brioche and crème fraîche, or Greek-style yoghurt and toasted flaked almonds, or simply a good-quality vanilla ice cream.

Instant Cheat's Ice Cream AND Sorbet

SERVES 4   PREP TIME 10 MINUTES   COOKING TIME NONE

250 g (9 oz) frozen mango, berries or other fruit
100 g (3½ oz) icing (confectioners') sugar
125 ml (4 fl oz/½ cup) cream (if making ice cream) or 2 egg whites (if making sorbet)

This recipe is almost embarrassing to write down, it's so mind-bogglingly easy. You can vary the fruit according to whatever you can find in the supermarket freezer or freeze your own cut-up fruit if there's a glut when it's in season. Both the ice cream and sorbet are best eaten within 3 hours of making them – which you're unlikely to find too onerous a task, especially with friendly helpers.

Make ahead: *The ice cream and sorbet can be eaten instantly but will benefit from a few hours in the freezer. If they're in for much longer, they may become icy – a fault you can always remedy by bringing them out to soften or giving them another blitz in the food processor or blender. If you're making these for kids, freeze in smaller containers so you can soften individual portions quickly.*

Throw the fruit and sugar into a blender or food processor and begin to pulse-chop until you have small pieces. Continue to blitz until the fruit looks granular and icy.

Scrape down the side of the bowl, add the cream or egg whites and continue to blitz until your ice cream or sorbet looks smooth and creamy. You may need to scrape down the side of the bowl again once or twice. And that's it.

Spoon into a 500 ml (17 fl oz/2 cup) capacity container and pop in the freezer to firm up a bit more till it's needed.

Banana Ice Cream

You can also make instant ice cream with just 1 ingredient: frozen old bananas. Take your blackest, most unloved bananas, peel them and freeze them. Then cut them into slices and blitz as above – you must have faith because it goes through a stage of looking slimy and repellent before magically coming good. Bananas are so sweet they don't need added sugar and they are naturally creamy without the addition of cream or egg whites. If this ice cream is too ridiculously virtuous, stir in some chocolate chips or unsalted roasted peanuts, or both.

Sticky Date Pudding

SERVES 8   PREP TIME 30 MINUTES, PLUS 30 MINUTES SOAKING   COOKING TIME 40 MINUTES

PUDDING MIX
200 g (7 oz) pitted dates
65 g (2¼ oz) salted butter, at room
   temperature
175 g (6 oz) caster (superfine) sugar
2 eggs
1 teaspoon natural vanilla extract
175 g (6 oz) self-raising flour

TOFFEE SAUCE
275 g (9¾ oz) light brown sugar
160 ml (5¼ fl oz) thin (pouring) cream
160 g (5½ oz) salted butter
1 teaspoon natural vanilla extract

TO SERVE
cream, ice cream or crème fraîche

To hell with the diet. Once in a while you just need the greatest comfort pudding ever devised: a simple, homely sponge, studded with dates, with an insanely rich, sticky toffee sauce. The second cook – when you pour the toffee sauce over the pudding and reheat it till it's bubbling and caramelised – is where the magic really happens.

Make ahead: This recipe works very well when made ahead. You can either cook it ahead of time and reheat it with the sauce at the time of serving, or make up the pudding mix and freeze it, cooking it from frozen later (add 10 minutes to the cooking time but keep an eye on it). The sticky toffee sauce keeps for ages (1 week at least) and can also be frozen. Don't be tempted to keep the pudding mix in the fridge and cook it later – the raising agent is fine in the freezer, but doesn't survive the fridge.

Preheat the oven to 180°C (350°F).

To make the pudding, boil 350 ml (12 fl oz) of water and pour it over the dates. Leave for 30 minutes to soften. Whizz with a stick blender, but not to a total purée – it is nice to have some date pieces flecked through the pudding. Let the mixture cool to room temperature.

Cream the butter and sugar in the bowl of a standmixer till pale and fluffy. Add the eggs, one at a time, continuing to beat the mix. Add the vanilla extract. Slow down the mixer, then add the flour and the date mixture, alternating between the two. You will end up with quite a runny mixture.

Lightly spray or grease a square tin with a capacity of around 1 litre (35 fl oz/4 cups).

Pour the batter into the tin and cook in the oven for 25 minutes or until a skewer or knife inserted into the middle comes out clean. If you have made the mix ahead and are cooking it from frozen, add 10 minutes to the cooking time.

To make the toffee sauce, mix all the ingredients in a heavy-based saucepan and simmer for at least 5 minutes, till all the sugar is dissolved and you have a good syrupy consistency.

Pour a few spoonfuls of the toffee sauce over the cooked pudding, cover it with foil and return to the oven for a few minutes (if you're reheating the pudding from cold, you'll need more like 10–15 minutes), until the sauce is starting to soak into the pudding and bubble around the edges.

Cut into squares and serve with cream, ice cream or crème fraîche.

Coconut Panna Cotta
WITH *Lime, Pineapple* AND *Mint*

SERVES 6   PREP TIME 20 MINUTES, PLUS OVERNIGHT SETTING IN FRIDGE   COOKING TIME 10 MINUTES

- -

NOTE: You'll need six dariole moulds or ramekins of 120 ml (4 fl oz) capacity for this – some shops sell them specifically as 'panna cotta moulds'.

PANNA COTTA
270 ml (9½ fl oz) coconut cream
250 ml (9 fl oz/1 cup) thin (pouring) cream
50 g (1¾ oz) caster (superfine) sugar
pinch of salt
4 kaffir lime leaves
3 gelatine sheets, 4.8 g (⅙ oz) gelatine (see note on page 217)

LIME SYRUP
100 g (3½ oz) white sugar
zest and juice of 2 plump limes

TO SERVE
150 g (5½ oz) pineapple, diced into 1 cm (½ inch) cubes
2 tablespoons thinly sliced mint leaves

- -

NOTES: When in season, diced mango makes a lovely substitute for the pineapple.

This makes a brilliant, foolproof end to a dinner party with Asian flavours and tastes much more complex than its simple ingredients would suggest.

Katherine was prejudiced against panna cotta for many years. On one of her first dates with her now husband he failed to show till very late – held up by something important at work, he claimed. She was sitting, sad and lonely, eating a panna cotta, when he eventually turned up. After that, for many years, she was unable to look at panna cotta, let alone cook one. It was only when Sophie made this version for her that she finally recovered from her aversion.

Make ahead: *Panna cotta must be made ahead of time in order to set, so it is a perfect dinner party dessert. Make the panna cottas and the lime syrup up to 3 days ahead.*

In a heavy-based saucepan over medium–low heat, combine the coconut cream, cream, caster sugar, a tiny pinch of salt and the kaffir lime leaves, crushing the leaves as you go. Heat till shimmering, just below boiling point, stirring to make sure it doesn't catch. Set aside to cool.

Soften the gelatine in cold water for 5 minutes, then drain, squeezing out any excess water. When the coconut mixture is around 40°C (104°F) – warmer than blood temperature but not scalding hot – stir through the gelatine thoroughly, making sure it has dissolved completely. Strain the mixture into a jug to ensure easy pouring into moulds.

Pour the mixture equally into six dariole moulds or ramekins of 120 ml (4 fl oz) capacity. Cover the containers with plastic wrap and leave in the fridge to set overnight.

To make the lime syrup, heat the white sugar with 100 ml (3½ fl oz) of water over medium heat in a very small saucepan and boil till it is lightly syrupy – about 5 minutes. Combine with the lime zest and juice, and cool in the fridge in a covered container.

To serve, dip your panna cottas, one at a time, in a bowl of hot water to loosen the edges. The amount of time will depend on the containers you have used – if you have used metal containers, they will loosen in a matter of seconds, but ceramic containers will take longer. Help loosen them by running a knife around the edge if necessary, then turn the panna cotta out onto your individual plates by placing the plate on top of the mould, then flipping to up-end so the panna cotta is on top of the plate before removing the mould. Spoon a little of the lime syrup around the edge, and surround with the diced pineapple and mint leaves.

Hazelnut Tiramisu

SERVES 6   PREP TIME 20 MINUTES, PLUS 6 HOURS CHILLING   COOKING TIME NONE

2 tablespoons ground coffee
80 ml (2½ fl oz/⅓ cup) hazelnut syrup
  (or substitute hazelnut liqueur)
150 ml (5 fl oz) thin (pouring) cream
150 g (5½ oz) mascarpone
1 tablespoon caster (superfine) sugar
175 g (6 oz) savoiardi (lady fingers)
1 teaspoon cocoa powder, sifted

TO SERVE
30 g (1 oz) Roasted and Skinned
  Hazelnuts (below), roughly broken up

· ·

NOTE: Hazelnut syrup is available online from a few speciality suppliers or you can buy it from a couple of the popular coffee shop chains.

We were playing around with the idea of a hazelnut liqueur tiramisu (this drink being one of our many guilty pleasures) and then discovered that Nigella had beaten us to it. As the booze doesn't cook out in this recipe, some of you may prefer our G-rated version using hazelnut syrup – but feel free to swap it back to the hard stuff if you'd like. The other mildly brilliant innovation with our tiramisu is that we use mascarpone lightened with whipped cream rather than beaten egg white. It makes it a bit quicker to prepare as well as safe for anyone concerned about eating raw eggs.

Make ahead: The whole dish has to be assembled at least 6 hours ahead to set firmly but you can make it up to 2 days ahead and leave it, covered, in the fridge. Tiramisu also freezes well. We'd leave off the hazelnuts and cocoa and sprinkle them on the dish after defrosting.

Make 125 ml (4 fl oz/½ cup) of strong espresso coffee whichever way you like – with a machine, plunger or on the stovetop. Mix 3 tablespoons of the hazelnut syrup with the coffee and set aside, covered.

In a medium mixing bowl, beat the cream and mascarpone together till it forms firm peaks. Gently fold through the remaining 1 tablespoon of hazelnut syrup and the sugar.

Use a deep-sided serving dish about 15 x 20 cm (6 x 8 inches). Take as many savoiardi biscuits as will fit in one layer and dunk each one into the hazelnut coffee so that it's coated but not soggy. Lay the biscuits side by side in the dish, then spread with half of the mascarpone cream. Put another layer of dunked biscuits on top, then smooth on another layer of the mascarpone cream. Dust the whole thing with sifted cocoa powder, and refrigerate for at least 6 hours.

Scatter with the crushed hazelnuts just before serving.

Roasted AND Skinned Hazelnuts

For some reason hazelnuts are usually only available with skins on. To remove them, simply roast the nuts, which also gives them a toasty, intensely nutty flavour. Preheat the oven to 180°C (350°F), spread the hazelnuts on a baking tray, and roast for 5 minutes. Immediately tip onto a clean tea towel (dish towel) and rub vigorously – if you wait too long, the skins will attach themselves to the nuts again. The skins should come off all over your nice clean tea towel (slightly annoying) but your hazelnuts will be skin-free!

A Handful of Crumbles

Basic Crumble Topping

75 g (2¾ oz/½ cup) self-raising flour
100 g (3½ oz/½ cup lightly packed) light brown sugar
pinch of salt
50 g (1¾ oz) cold salted butter, diced into 1 cm (½ inch) cubes
50 g (1¾ oz/½ cup) rolled (porridge) oats

<u>MAKES</u> 1 X 275 G (9¾ OZ) QUANTITY   <u>PREP TIME</u> 10 MINUTES
<u>COOKING TIME</u> NONE

The combination of warm, slightly tart fruit and crunchy, biscuity crumble is universally loved – and how about those bits where the fruit's juices have bubbled up around the edges of the topping and gone jammy and toffee-ish? Oh, stop it right now. With a few different crumble recipes up your sleeve, you'll never be at a loss for a fail-safe, make-ahead dessert at any time of the year – we've often used frozen fruit when there's been nothing else available and it's been just fine.

Make ahead: Both the fruit filling and the topping can be made ahead and will keep for 3 days in the fridge or up to 3 months in the freezer. Just keep the filling and topping in separate tubs till you are ready to fill your ovenproof dish for baking.

In a small bowl, combine the flour, brown sugar and salt. Rub the butter into the mix with your fingertips till the mixture resembles clumpy breadcrumbs. Stir through the rolled oats.

Set aside in a covered container in the fridge.

Strawberry AND Rhubarb Crumble

1 quantity Basic Crumble Topping (above)
45 g (1½ oz/⅓ cup) slivered almonds, toasted
400 g (14 oz/1 large bunch) rhubarb, trimmed and chopped
100 g (3½ oz) caster (superfine) sugar
400 g (14 oz) strawberries, hulled, halved if large

TO SERVE
cream or ice cream

<u>SERVES</u> 6   <u>PREP TIME</u> 20 MINUTES
<u>COOKING TIME</u> 45 MINUTES, PLUS 10 MINUTES RESTING

Preheat the oven to 180°C (350°F).

Combine the basic crumble topping with the almonds and set aside.

Place the rhubarb and sugar in a heavy-based saucepan and cook gently over low heat for about 15 minutes till the rhubarb is completely soft. Add the strawberries and bring everything up to heat. Pour your filling into a greased ovenproof dish of about 1.5 litres (52 fl oz/6 cups) capacity. Scatter the topping over your filling to cover.

Cook in the oven for 25–30 minutes till the topping is golden brown and the filling is bubbling up round the edges. Remove from the oven and allow to rest for 10 minutes before serving with cream or ice cream.

⟫ *CONTINUED ON PAGE 248*

A Few Crumbles

« CONTINUED FROM PAGE 247

Pear AND Almond Crumble

1 quantity Basic Crumble Topping (see page 247)
½ teaspoon ground cinnamon
45 g (1½ oz/⅓ cup) slivered almonds, toasted
1 kg (2 lb 4 oz) pears, peeled, cored and quartered
50 g (1¾ oz) light brown sugar

TO SERVE
cream or ice cream

SERVES 6   PREP TIME 20 MINUTES
COOKING TIME 45 MINUTES–1 HOUR, PLUS 10 MINUTES RESTING

Preheat the oven to 180°C (350°F) and line a baking tray with baking paper.
  Combine the basic crumble topping with the cinnamon and almonds and set aside.
  Turn the pears through the brown sugar and place on the baking tray. Roast in the oven for 15–30 minutes, turning once, till golden and soft. The cooking time will depend very much on the ripeness of the pears. When done, put them into a greased ovenproof dish with a capacity of about 1.5 litres (52 fl oz/6 cups) and top the pears with the crumble.
  Cook in the oven for 25–30 minutes till golden and bubbling around the edges. Rest for 10 minutes before serving with cream or ice cream.

VARIATION:
Make a pear, blueberry and almond version by reducing the quantity of pears to 800 g (1 lb 12 oz) and adding 200 g (7 oz) blueberries (fresh or frozen). When the cooked pears are transferred from the baking tray to the ovenproof dish, add the blueberries before topping with the crumble and returning to the oven.

Plum AND Hazelnut Crumble

1 quantity Basic Crumble Topping (see page 247)
40 g (1½ oz) Roasted and Skinned Hazelnuts (see page 245), lightly crushed
1 teaspoon ground cinnamon
1.2 kg (2 lb 10 oz) plums (whatever variety is best at the time), seeded and quartered
30 g (1 oz) caster (superfine) sugar (you may need more, depending on the sweetness of the plums)
1 teaspoon natural vanilla extract

TO SERVE
cream or ice cream

SERVES 6   PREP TIME 20 MINUTES
COOKING TIME 45 MINUTES, PLUS 10 MINUTES RESTING

Preheat the oven to 180°C (350°F).
  Combine the basic crumble topping with the hazelnuts and cinnamon and set aside.
  In a heavy-based saucepan over medium heat, cook the plums with the sugar and vanilla extract until the plums are beginning to collapse. This should take about 10–15 minutes. Plums vary enormously in tartness, so taste and add more sugar if necessary. Dish up into a greased ovenproof dish with a capacity of about 1.5 litres (52 fl oz/6 cups). Top the plum mixture with the crumble.
  Cook in the oven for 25–30 minutes till the top is golden and the filling is bubbling up around the edges. Remove from the oven and rest for 10 minutes before serving with cream or ice cream.

Apricot, Raspberry and Coconut Crumble

1 quantity Basic Crumble Topping (see page 247)

35 g (1¼ oz/⅓ cup) flaked almonds

30 g (1 oz/⅓ cup) desiccated (shredded) coconut

900 g (2 lb) apricots, seeded and halved

50 g (1¾ oz) light brown sugar

150 g (5½ oz) raspberries (frozen are fine)

TO SERVE
cream or ice cream

SERVES 6   PREP TIME 20 MINUTES
COOKING TIME 55 MINUTES, PLUS 10 MINUTES RESTING

Preheat the oven to 180°C (350°F) and line a baking tray with baking paper.

Combine the basic crumble topping with the almonds and coconut and set aside.

Place the apricots, cut side up, on the tray and sprinkle with the sugar. Cook in the oven till they are golden brown (about 25 minutes).

Transfer the apricots into a greased ovenproof dish with a capacity of around 1.5 litres (52 fl oz/6 cups) and scatter on the raspberries, stirring gently to mix together, then top with the crumble.

Cook in the oven for 25–30 minutes till the top is golden and the filling is bubbling around the edges. Remove from the oven and allow to rest for 10 minutes before serving with cream or ice cream.

Apple, Blackberry and Walnut Crumble

1 quantity Basic Crumble Topping (see page 247)

½ teaspoon ground cinnamon

30 g (1 oz/¼ cup) chopped walnuts

800 g (1 lb 12 oz) granny smith apples, peeled, cored and cut into 3 cm (1¼ inch) chunks

50 g (1¾ oz) light brown sugar

200 g (7 oz) blackberries

TO SERVE
cream or ice cream

SERVES 6   PREP TIME 20 MINUTES
COOKING TIME 45 MINUTES, PLUS 10 MINUTES RESTING

Preheat the oven to 180°C (350°F).

Combine the basic crumble topping with the cinnamon and walnuts and set aside.

In a heavy-based saucepan over low heat, cook the apples with the brown sugar for about 10–15 minutes till the apples begin to soften. Remove the pan from the heat, mix through the blackberries, then put the whole lot into a greased ovenproof dish with a capacity of around 1.5 litres (52 fl oz/6 cups). Top the fruit mixture with the crumble.

Cook in the oven for 25–30 minutes till golden and bubbling. Remove from the oven and allow to rest for 10 minutes before serving with cream or ice cream.

Index

Page numbers in *italics* refer to photographs.

affogato, hazelnut 235
almonds
    almond and pear crumble 248
    almond, chocolate and date torte 219
    chicken and 100 almonds *154*, 155
    oranges in liqueur syrup 233
    pork picadillo 86
    Spanish meatballs with chorizo and chickpeas *206*, 207
    strawberry and rhubarb crumble *246*, 247
    super foods salad *24*, *25*
    vanilla panna cotta with espresso syrup and almonds *216*, 217
amaretti biscuits with roasted stone fruit 237
apples
    apple and beetroot relish 19
    apple, blackberry and walnut crumble 249
    apple sauce and fennel and cabbage slaw with porchetta panini *79*, 80–1
    apple tart 236
    pork Normandy with apples and cider vinegar 192
apricot, raspberry and coconut crumble 249
asparagus and broccolini with sesame prawn stir-fry *14*, *15*
avocados, in guacamole 99

bacon
    braised beef brisket with maple bacon beans 196–7
    daube of beef *200*, 201
baked rice pudding with rhubarb and strawberry compote *220*, 221
Balinese chicken curry 170–1
banana ice cream 241
barbecue sauce 85, 89
barramundi fillets with coriander, lemongrass and nahm jim *48*, *49*
basil, in Thai chicken curry with ginger 145
beans
    borlotti bean and freekeh soup 47
    braised beef brisket with maple bacon beans 196–7
    cassoulet of white beans and pork *182*, 183
    minestrone 133
    three bean chilli *97*, 98–9
beef and veal
    beef and green papaya with tamarind dressing *39*, 40–1
    beef and guiness pie 184–5, *186*
    beef and vegetable stew 118
    beef cheeks in red wine 193
    beef cheek, red wine and roast vegetable pie 188–9
    beef stifado 204
    braised beef brisket with maple bacon beans 196–7
    cottage pie *102*, 103
    daube of beef *200*, 201
    dinner ladies lasagne 110–11, *112*
    Indian cottage pie 166
    Kerala beef curry 162
    Korean marinated skirt steak with ginger dipping sauce 33
    Madras beef curry *140*, 141
    meatballs with sweet tomato sauce 119
    osso buco *190*, 191
    paleo lasagne *180*, 181
    pancetta-wrapped meatloaf *126*, 127
    red curry of beef and peanuts *151*, 152
    skirt steak chimichurri 32
    teriyaki beef with sesame pickled vegetables 26
    Texas beef brisket *88*, 89
beetroot and apple relish 19
berries
    berry tart with vanilla mascarpone 236
    instant cheat's and sorbet 241
biscuits, in ice-cream sandwiches 235
black turtle beans, three bean chilli *97*, 98–9
blackberry, apple and walnut crumble 249
blood orange sauce 77
blueberries, in vanilla mascarpone berry tart 236
borlotti beans *see* beans
bread and butter pudding, chocolate and marmalade *230*, 231
bresaola salad with shaved fennel and cabbage *34*, 35
broccoli, salmon and sweet potato bites , 135
broccolini and asparagus with sesame prawn stir-fry *14*, *15*
brownies, marbled choc fudge and raspberry 232
bucatini all'Amatriciana 106
burgers, chickpea and coriander *44*, 45
butter chicken 144

cabbage
    bresaola salad with shaved fennel and cabbage *34*, 35
    cabbage and fennel slaw and apple sauce with porchetta panini *79*, 80–1
    coleslaw 85
    lion's head meatballs *122*, 123
    minestrone 133
    rainbow slaw 95
    Vietnamese chicken salad *28*, 29
cake, chocolate, date and almond 219
candlenuts
    Balinese chicken curry 170–1
    chicken laksa 156–7
cannellini beans *see* beans
capers, in salmon fish cakes 120–1
capsicums
    Asian herb salad with teriyaki salmon *30*, 31
    chickpea and coriander burgers *44*, 45
    fattoush 75
    Greek salad 23
    harissa 69
    kung pao chicken *174*, 175
    pancetta-wrapped meatloaf *126*, 127
    roast vegetable lasagne 90–1
    sausage rolls with sneaky veg *113*, 114–15
    vegetable tagine with olives, eggplant and chickpeas 149, *150*
carrots
    beef and green papaya with tamarind dressing *39*, 40–1
    beef and guiness pie 184–5, *186*
    beef and vegetable stew 118
    beef cheeks in red wine 193
    beef cheek, red wine and roast vegetable pie 188–9
    braised beef brisket with maple bacon beans 196–7
    carrot and lentil 46
    chicken noodle soup *108*, 109
    coleslaw 85
    cottage pie *102*, 103
    daube of beef *200*, 201
    dinner ladies lasagne 110–11, *112*
    duck ragu *70*, 71
    freekeh and borlotti bean soup 47
    minestrone 133
    osso buco *190*, 191
    pea and ham soup 132
    pearl barley, Italian sausage and vegetable soup *202*, 203
    potager pie 128–9
    rainbow slaw 95
    roast vegetable and chicken pie 124–5
    sausage rolls with sneaky veg *113*, 114–15
    sesame pickled vegetables with teriyaki beef 26
    Spanish meatballs with chorizo and chickpeas *206*, 207
    Vietnamese chicken salad *28*, 29
cashews
    butter chicken 144
    paleo lasagne *180*, 181
cassoulet of white beans and pork *182*, 183
cauliflower
    paleo lasagne *180*, 181
    spiced cauliflower rice 37
celery
    beef and guiness pie 184–5, *186*
    beef and vegetable stew 118
    beef cheeks in red wine 193
    braised beef brisket with maple bacon beans 196–7
    chicken noodle soup *108*, 109
    dinner ladies lasagne 110–11, *112*
    duck ragu *70*, 71
    freekeh and borlotti bean soup 47
    minestrone 133
    osso buco *190*, 191
    pancetta-wrapped meatloaf *126*, 127
    pearl barley, Italian sausage and vegetable soup *202*, 203
    potager pie 128–9
    spiced lamb shanks *208*, 209
char siu pork *104*, 105
cheese
    bresaola salad with shaved fennel and cabbage *34*, 35
    dinner ladies lasagne 110–11, *112*
    eggplant parmigiana 72
    Greek salad 23
    marbled choc fudge and raspberry brownies 232
    meatballs with sweet tomato sauce 119
    pearl barley, Italian sausage and vegetable soup *202*, 203
    potager pie 128–9
    potato gratin 59
    ricotta, roast pumpkin and sage lasagne *130*, 131
    ricotta, spinach and feta filo pie *21*, 22–3
    roast vegetable lasagne 90–1
chermoula chicken *74*, 75
cherries

pickled cherries 77
Wimmera grain salad *92, 93*

chicken
    Balinese chicken curry 170–1
    brined and roasted citrus chicken 58–9, *60*
    butter chicken 144
    chermoula chicken *74, 75*
    chicken and 100 almonds *154, 155*
    chicken and roast vegetable pie 124–5
    chicken, chorizo and olive empanadas *61*, 62–3
    chicken laksa 156–7
    chicken noodle soup *108, 109*
    chicken pho *42, 43*
    chicken strips 87
    coq au vin 205
    huli huli chicken wings *82, 83*
    kung pao chicken *174, 175*
    Massaman chicken curry 163
    Mediterranean chicken with fennel and green olives *54, 55*
    Moroccan chicken with pumpkin and preserved lemon *158*, 159
    Nonya chicken curry *164, 165*
    prosciutto-wrapped chicken and pistachio terrine 18–19, *20*
    Syrian chicken with ginger, lemon and honey *168, 169*
    Thai chicken curry with ginger and Thai basil 145
    Thai marinated chicken with sweet chilli sauce *172, 173*
    tom kha gai *146, 147*
    Vietnamese chicken salad *28, 29*

chickpeas
    chickpea and coriander burgers *44, 45*
    chickpea, sweet potato and kale curry *142, 143*
    chickpeas and spinach with snapper curry 36–7, *38*
    hummus 69
    sausage rolls with sneaky veg *113*, 114–15
    Spanish meatballs with chickpeas and chorizo *206, 207*
    vegetable tagine with olives, eggplant and chickpeas 149, *150*

chillies
    chilli bean tofu with ginger and eggplant 165
    guacamole 99
    harissa 69
    Isaan barbecued pork with chilli dipping sauce *50, 51*
    japapeño and coriander salsa 63
    Kerala beef curry 162
    Thai marinated chicken with sweet chilli sauce *172, 173*
    three bean chilli *97*, 98–9
    tom yam goong 27
    tomato sambal 171
chimichurri marinade 32
Chinese cabbage, in Vietnamese chicken salad *28, 29*
Chinese sausages, in sang choi bau of pork and shiitake mushrooms *136, 137*

chocolate
    chocolate and marmalade bread and butter pudding *230, 231*
    chocolate, date and almond torte 219
    chocolate honeycomb semifreddo 218
    chocolate mint honey pots *238, 239*
    chocolate pavlova with raspberries *214, 215*
    chocolate strawberry croquembouche *222, 223*
    marbled choc fudge and raspberry brownies 232
    oven smores 237

chorizo
    chorizo, chicken and olive empanadas *61*, 62–3
    Spanish meatballs with chorizo and chickpeas *206, 207*
Christmas panna cotta with edible gold leaf 224–5, *226*
chutneys 87, 148
cider vinegar and apple with pork Normandy 192
citrus chicken, brined and roasted 58–9, *60*

coconut
    Balinese chicken curry 170–1
    carrot and lentil soup 46
    chicken laksa 156–7
    chickpea, sweet potato and kale curry *142, 143*
    coconut, apricot and raspberry crumble 249
    coconut curry lentil soup *116, 117*
    coconut panna cotta with lime, pineapple and mint 244
    Madras beef curry *140*, 141
    Massaman chicken curry 163
    Nonya chicken curry *164, 165*
    red curry of beef and peanuts *151*, 152
    snapper curry with chickpeas and spinach 36–7, *38*
    Thai chicken curry with ginger and Thai basil 145
    tom kha gai *146, 147*

coffee
    hazelnut affogato 235
    hazelnut tiramisu 245
    vanilla panna cotta with espresso syrup and almonds *216, 217*
coleslaw 85
coq au vin 205

coriander
    chicken and 100 almonds *154, 155*
    coriander and chickpea burgers *44, 45*
    coriander and japapeño salsa 63
    coriander and lemongrass barramundi fillets with nahm jim *48, 49*
    coriander-mint chutney 148
cottage pie *102*, 103
    Indian (keema mattar) 166
couscous 159

cream
    baked rice pudding with strawberry and rhubarb compote *220, 221*
    butter chicken 144
    chocolate mint honey pots *238, 239*
    Christmas panna cotta with edible gold leaf 224–5, *226*
    coconut panna cotta with lime, pineapple and mint 244
    Eton mess 236
    horseradish dill cream with gravlax *64, 65*
    instant cheat's ice cream and sorbet 241
    tropical trifle *227*, 228–9
    vanilla panna cotta with espresso syrup and almonds *216, 217*
croquembouche, chocolate and strawberry *222, 223*
crumbles *246*, 247–9

cucumbers
    Asian herb salad with teriyaki salmon *30, 31*
    cucumber-yoghurt sauce 45
    fattoush 75
    Greek salad 23
    sesame pickled vegetables with teriyaki beef 26
cumquats, spiced 77
currants, in pork picadillo 86

curries 36–7, *38*, *116*, 117, 139–77

dates
    date, chocolate and almond torte 219
    sticky date pudding *242, 243*
daube of beef *200, 201*
dill horseradish cream with gravlax *64, 65*
dinner ladies lasagne 110–11, *112*
doh piaza *160, 161*

duck
    duck confit 76–7, *78*
    duck ragu *70*, 71

edamame *24, 25*

eggplants
    chilli bean tofu with ginger and eggplant 165
    eggplant parmigiana 72
    roast vegetable lasagne 90–1
    vegetable tagine with olives, eggplant and chickpeas 149, *150*
empanadas, chicken, chorizo and olive *61*, 62–3
Eton mess 236

fattoush 75

fennel
    bresaola salad with shaved fennel and cabbage *34, 35*
    fennel and cabbage slaw and apple sauce with porchetta panini *79*, 80–1
    fennel and green olives with Mediterranean chicken *54, 55*
    fish pie 107
    pork chops with fennel, French shallots and raisins *198*, 199
feta *see* cheese
filo pie, spinach, ricotta and feta *21*, 22–3

fish
    coriander and lemongrass barramundi fillets with nahm jim *48, 49*
    fish pie 107
    home-cured gravlax with horseradish dill cream *64, 65*
    salmon fish cakes 120–1
    salmon, sweet potato and broccoli bites *134*, 135
    snapper curry with chickpeas and spinach 36–7, *38*
    teriyaki salmon with Asian herb salad *30, 31*
food safety 8
freekeh and borlotti bean soup 47

fruit
    barbecued 237
    spiced winter compote 240

galangal 27, 163

garlic
    garlic and yoghurt sauce 149
    hummus 69

ginger
    chilli bean tofu with ginger and eggplant 165
    Korean marinated skirt steak with ginger dipping sauce 33
    Syrian chicken with ginger, lemon and honey *168, 169*
    Thai chicken curry with ginger and Thai basil 145
    twice-cooked masterstock pork belly 94–5, *96*
gold leaf, with Christmas panna cotta 224–5, *226*

grain salad *92, 93*
gravlax with horseradish dill cream *64, 65*
great northern beans, mapled, with braised beef brisket 196–7
Greek salad 23
green papaya *see* papaya
guacamole 99
guiness and beef pie 184–5, *186*

ham and pea soup 132
harissa 69
hazelnuts
    hazelnut affogato 235
    hazelnut and plum crumble 249
    hazelnut tiramisu 245
herb-marinated butterflied leg of lamb 73
honey
    honey mint chocolate pots *238, 239*
    Syrian chicken with honey, ginger and lemon *168*, 169
honeycomb chocolate semifreddo 218
horseradish dill cream with gravlax *64, 65*
huli huli chicken wings *82, 83*
hummus 69

ice cream 235, 241
Indian cottage pie 166
Isaan barbecued pork with chilli dipping sauce *50*, 51
Italian freekeh and borlotti bean soup 47
Italian sausages
    Italian sausage, pearl barley and vegetable soup *202*, 203
    penne with Italian sausage sauce *210*, 211

japapeño and coriander salsa 63
Jerusalem artichokes, in beef cheek, red wine and roast vegetable pie 188–9

kale
    coconut curry lentil soup *116*, 117
    kale, sweet potato and chickpea curry *142*, 143
    minestrone 133
keema mattar 166
Kerala beef curry 162
koftas, lamb *56, 57*
Korean marinated skirt steak with ginger dipping sauce 33
kung pao chicken *174*, 175

laksa, chicken 156–7
lamb
    butterflied leg of lamb shawarma *66*, 67–8
    herb-marinated butterflied leg of lamb 73
    lamb and quince tagine 176–7
    lamb doh piaza *160*, 161
    lamb koftas *56, 57*
    Middle Eastern lamb with prunes, mint and pistachios *194*, 195
    roghan josh 148
    spiced lamb shanks *208, 209*
lasagne *see* pasta
leeks

chicken noodle soup *108*, 109
freekeh and borlotti bean soup 47
lemongrass
    lemongrass and coriander barramundi fillets with nahm jim *48, 49*
    tom yam goong 27
lemons
    brined and roasted citrus chicken 58–9, *60*
    hummus 69
    lamb and quince tagine 176–7
    Moroccan chicken with pumpkin and preserved lemon *158*, 159
    Syrian chicken with lemon, ginger and honey *168*, 169
    tabouleh 69
lentils
    coconut curry lentil soup *116*, 117
    lentil and carrot soup 46
    potager pie 128–9
    Wimmera grain salad *92, 93*
lettuce
    lettuce and mint with pea soup *16*, 17
    sang choi bau of pork and shiitake mushrooms *136*, 137
lime, pineapple and mint with coconut panna cotta 244
lion's head meatballs *122, 123*
liqueur syrup, oranges in 233

macadamias, in tropical trifle *227*, 228–9
Madras beef curry *140*, 141
mangoes
    barbecued 237
    instant cheat's ice cream and sorbet 241
    mango chutney 87
    tropical trifle *227*, 228–9
mapled bacon beans with braised beef brisket 196–7
marmalade and chocolate bread and butter pudding *230*, 231
marshmallow, in oven smores 237
mascarpone
    hazelnut tiramisu 245
    tropical trifle *227*, 228–9
    vanilla mascarpone 229
    vanilla mascarpone berry tart 236
Massaman chicken curry 163
mayonnaise, in tartare sauce 121
meatballs
    lion's head meatballs *122, 123*
    meatballs with sweet tomato sauce 119
    Spanish meatballs with chorizo and chickpeas *206*, 207
Mediterranean chicken with fennel and green olives *54*, 55
meringue, in Eton mess 236
Middle Eastern lamb with prunes, mint and pistachios *194*, 195
minestrone 133
mint
    coconut panna cotta with lime, pineapple and mint 244
    fattoush 75
    Middle Eastern lamb with mint, prunes and pistachios *194*, 195
    mint and lettuce with pea soup *16*, 17
    mint chocolate honey pots *238, 239*
    mint-coriander chutney 148
    tabouleh 69

mixed leaf salad 59
Moroccan chicken with pumpkin and preserved lemon *158*, 159
mozzarella *see* cheese
mushrooms
    coq au vin 205
    potager pie 128–9
    sang choi bau of pork and shiitake mushrooms *136*, 137
    sesame prawn stir-fry with asparagus and broccolini *14, 15*
    tom kha gai *146*, 147
    tom yam goong 27

nahm jim with coriander and lemongrass barramundi fillets *48*, 49
nectarines, roasted, with amaretti biscuits 237
Nonya chicken curry *164*, 165
noodles
    chicken laksa 156–7
    chicken noodle soup *108*, 109
    shirataki noodles 27

oats, in crumbles 247
olives
    Greek salad 23
    green olives and fennel with Mediterranean chicken *54*, 55
    olive, chicken and chorizo empanadas *61*, 62–3
    roast vegetable lasagne 90–1
    vegetable tagine with olives, eggplant and chickpeas *149, 150*
onions, in lamb doh piaza *160*, 161
oranges
    blood orange sauce 77
    brined and roasted citrus chicken 58–9, *60*
    in liqueur syrup 233
osso buco *190*, 191
oven smores 237

paleo lasagne *180*, 181
pancetta
    bucatini all'Amatriciana 106
    cassoulet of white beans and pork *182*, 183
    pancetta-wrapped meatloaf *126*, 127
    pearl barley, Italian sausage and vegetable soup *202*, 203
panini, with porchetta, cabbage and fennel slaw, and apple sauce *79*, 80–1
panna cotta
    Christmas panna cotta with edible gold leaf 224–5, *226*
    coconut panna cotta with lime, pineapple and mint 244
    panna cotta with espresso syrup and almonds *216*, 217
papaya
    green papaya and beef with tamarind dressing *39*, 40–1
    green papaya salad 153
parmesan *see* cheese
parmigiana, eggplant 72
parsley
    fattoush 75
    tabouleh 69
parsnips, in beef and vegetable stew 118
passionfruit, in tropical trifle *227*, 228–9
pasta
    bucatini all'Amatriciana 106

chicken noodle soup *108*, 109

dinner ladies lasagne 110–11, *112*

with duck ragu *70*, 71

paleo lasagne *180*, 181

penne with Italian sausage sauce *210*, 211

roast pumpkin, ricotta and sage lasagne *130*, 131

roast vegetable lasagne 90–1

pastry, shortcrust *186*, 187

pavlova, chocolate, with raspberries *214*, 215

peaches, roasted, with amaretti buscuits 237

peanuts

beef and green papaya with tamarind dressing *39*, 40–1

kung pao chicken *174*, 175

Massaman chicken curry 163

red curry of beef and peanuts *151*, 152

Vietnamese chicken salad *28*, 29

pear and almond crumble 248

pearl barley

grain salad *92*, 93

pearl barley, Italian sausage and vegetable soup *202*, 203

peas

beef and vegetable stew 118

cottage pie *102*, 103

Indian cottage pie 166

pea and ham soup 132

pea soup with lettuce and mint *16*, 17

potager pie 128–9

roast vegetable and chicken pie 124–5

Thai chicken curry with ginger and Thai basil 145

penne with Italian sausage sauce *210*, 211

pepitas, in Wimmera grain salad *92*, 93

pho, chicken *42*, 43

pickles

pickled cherries 77

pickled vegetables with teriyaki beef 26

pies

beef and guiness pie 184–5, *186*

beef cheek, red wine and roast vegetable pie 188–9

chicken and roast vegetable pie 124–5

cottage pie *102*, 103

feta, spinach and ricotta filo pie *21*, 22–3

fish pie 107

potager pie 128–9

pineapple

barbecued 237

coconut panna cotta with lime, pineapple and mint 244

pineapple juice, in huli huli chicken wings *82*, 83

pistachios

Middle Eastern lamb with pistachios, prunes and mint *194*, 195

prosciutto-wrapped chicken and pistachio terrine 18–19, *20*

pitta, in fattoush 75

plum and hazelnut crumble 249

pomegranate seeds, in Wimmera grain salad *92*, 93

porchetta panini with cabbage and fennel slaw and apple sauce *79*, 80–1

pork

cassoulet of white beans and pork *182*, 183

char siu pork *104*, 105

dinner ladies lasagne 110–11, *112*

Isaan barbecued pork with chilli dipping sauce *50*, 51

lion's head meatballs *122*, 123

meatballs with sweet sauce 119

pancetta-wrapped meatloaf *126*, 127

porchetta panini with cabbage and fennel slaw and apple sauce *79*, 80–1

pork chops with fennel, French shallots and raisins *198*, 199

pork Normandy with apples and cider vinegar 192

pork picadillo 86

pulled pork in barbecue sauce *84*, 85

sang choi bau of pork and shiitake mushrooms *136*, 137

sausage rolls with sneaky veg *113*, 114–15

Spanish meatballs with chorizo and chickpeas *206*, 207

twice-cooked masterstock pork belly 94–5, *96*

potager pie 128–9

potatoes

cottage pie *102*, 103

fish pie 107

Massaman chicken curry 163

Nonya chicken curry *164*, 165

potager pie 128–9

potato gratin 59

roast duck fat potatoes 77

salmon fish cakes 120–1

squashed potatoes 73

prawns

sesame prawn stir-fry with asparagus and broccolini *14*, *15*

tom yam goong 27

prosciutto-wrapped chicken and pistachio terrine 18–19, *20*

prunes, mint and pistachios with lamb *194*, 195

puff pastry, in sausage rolls with sneaky veg *113*, 114–15

pumpkin

Middle Eastern lamb with prunes, mint and pistachios *194*, 195

Moroccan chicken with pumpkin and preserved lemon *158*, 159

roast pumpkin, ricotta and sage lasagne *130*, 131

roast vegetable and chicken pie 124–5

vegetable tagine with olives, eggplant and chickpeas 149, *150*

quince and lamb tagine 176–7

quinoa, in super foods salad *24*, *25*

radishes

fattoush 75

sesame pickled vegetables with teriyaki beef 26

rainbow slaw 95

raisins, French shallots and fennel with pork chops *198*, 199

raspberries

with chocolate pavlova *214*, 215

Christmas panna cotta with edible gold leaf 224–5, *226*

marbled choc fudge and raspberry brownies 232

raspberry, apricot and coconut crumble 249

vanilla mascarpone berry tart 236

red bean curd, in char siu pork *104*, 105

relish, beetroot and apple 19

rhubarb

baked rice pudding with rhubarb and strawberry compote *220*, 221

rhubarb and strawberry crumble *246*, 247

rice

risotto alla Milanese 191

spiced rice 141

vanilla-scented baked rice pudding with rhubarb and strawberry compote *220*, 221

rice noodles, in chicken pho *42*, 43

ricotta *see* cheese

risotto alla Milanese 191

roghan josh 148

sage, roast pumpkin and ricotta lasagne *130*, 131

salads

Asian herb salad with teriyaki salmon *30*, 31

bresaola salad with shaved fennel and cabbage *34*, 35

Greek salad 23

green papaya salad 153

mixed leaf salad 59

super foods salad *24*, *25*

Vietnamese chicken salad *28*, 29

Wimmera grain salad *92*, 93

salmon

home-cured gravlax with horseradish dill cream *64*, 65

salmon fish cakes 120–1

salmon, sweet potato and broccoli bites *134*, 135

teriyaki salmon with Asian herb salad *30*, 31

salsa *see* sauces

sambal, tomato 171

sang choi bau of pork and shiitake mushrooms *136*, 137

sauces

apple sauce 80–1

barbecue sauce (1) 85

barbecue sauce (2) 89

blood orange sauce 77

chilli dipping sauce 51

chimichurri marinade 33

coriander and japapeño 63

cucumber-yoghurt sauce 45

garlic and yoghurt 149

ginger dipping sauce 33

sweet tomato sauce 119

tartare sauce 121

toffee sauce 243

sausage rolls with sneaky veg *113*, 114–15

savoiardi

hazelnut tiramisu 245

tropical trifle *227*, 228–9

semifreddo, chocolate honeycomb 218

sesame

sesame pickled vegetables with teriyaki beef 26

sesame prawn stir-fry with asparagus and broccolini *14*, *15*

Vietnamese chicken salad *28*, 29

shallots

beef cheek, red wine and roast vegetable pie 188–9

beef stifado 204

coq au vin 205

Massaman chicken curry 163

pea soup with lettuce and mint *16*, 17

pork chops with fennel, French shallots and raisins *198*, 199

shirataki noodles 27

shortcrust pastry *186*, 187

silverbeet, in minestrone 133

slaw *see* cabbage
slushies 235
snapper curry with chickpeas and spinach 36–7, *38*
snow peas, in Asian herb salad with teriyaki salmon *30*, 31
sorbet, instant cheat's 241
soups
    carrot and lentil 46
    chicken noodle soup *108*, 109
    chicken pho *42*, 43
    coconut curry lentil soup *116*, 117
    Italian freekeh and borlotti bean 47
    minestrone 133
    pea and ham soup 132
    pea soup with lettuce and mint *16*, 17
    pearl barley, Italian sausage and vegetable soup *202*, 203
    tom kha gai *146*, 147
    tom yam goong 27
soy sauce, in masterstock pork belly 94–5, *96*
Spanish meatballs with chorizo and chickpeas *206*, 207
sparkling slushies 235
spiced rice 141
spiced winter compote 240
spinach
    Asian herb salad with teriyaki salmon *30*, 31
    chicken noodle soup *108*, 109
    paleo lasagne *180*, 181
    spinach and chickpeas with snapper curry 36–7, *38*
    spinach, ricotta and feta filo pie *21*, 22–3
    super foods salad *24*, 25
    Thai chicken curry with ginger and Thai basil 145
split peas, in pea and ham soup 132
squashed potatoes 73
Sri Lankan snapper curry with chickpeas and spinach 36–7, *38*
stew, beef and vegetable 118
sticky date pudding *242*, 243
stir-fry, sesame prawn, with asparagus and broccolini *14*, 15
stone fruit, roasted, with amaretti biscuits 237
strawberries
    baked rice pudding with strawberry and rhubarb compote *220*, 221
    Eton mess 236
    strawberry and rhubarb crumble *246*, 247
    strawberry chocolate croquembouche *222*, 223
    vanilla mascarpone berry tart 236
sunflower seeds, in Wimmera grain salad *92*, 93
super foods salad *24*, 25
sweet potatoes
    super foods salad *24*, 25
    sweet potato, kale and chickpea curry *142*, 143
    sweet potato, salmon and broccoli bites *134*, 135
Syrian chicken with ginger, lemon and honey *168*, 169

tabouleh 69
tagines
    lamb and quince 176–7
    vegetable, with olives, eggplant and chickpeas 149, *150*
tahini, in hummus 69
tamarind dressing, with beef and green papaya *39*, 40–1
tartare sauce 121

tatsoi
    Asian herb salad with teriyaki salmon *30*, 31
    beef and green papaya with tamarind dressing *39*, 40–1
teriyaki beef with sesame pickled vegetables 26
teriyaki salmon with Asian herb salad *30*, 31
terrine, prosciutto-wrapped chicken and pistachio 18–19, *20*
Texas beef brisket *88*, 89
Thai chicken curry with ginger and Thai basil 145
Thai marinated chicken with sweet chilli sauce *172*, 173
three bean chilli *97*, 98–9
tiramisu, hazelnut 245
toffee sauce 243
tofu, chilli bean, with ginger and eggplant 165
tom kha gai *146*, 147
tom yam goong 27
tomato sauce, in huli huli chicken wings *82*, 83
tomatoes
    beef and vegetable stew 118
    beef cheek, red wine and roast vegetable pie 188–9
    beef stifado 204
    braised beef brisket with maple bacon beans 196–7
    bucatini all'Amatriciana 106
    butter chicken 144
    coconut curry lentil soup *116*, 117
    daube of beef *200*, 201
    dinner ladies lasagne 110–11, *112*
    duck ragu *70*, 71
    eggplant parmigiana 72
    Greek salad 23
    Kerala beef curry 162
    Madras beef curry *140*, 141
    meatballs with sweet tomato sauce 119
    minestrone 133
    Moroccan chicken with pumpkin and preserved lemon *158*, 159
    Nonya chicken curry *164*, 165
    osso buco *190*, 191
    paleo lasagne *180*, 181
    pearl barley, Italian sausage and vegetable soup *202*, 203
    penne with Italian sausage sauce *210*, 211
    pork picadillo 86
    potager pie 128–9
    roast vegetable lasagne 90–1
    roghan josh 148
    snapper curry with chickpeas and spinach 36–7, *38*
    Spanish meatballs with chorizo and chickpeas *206*, 207
    spiced lamb shanks *208*, 209
    tabouleh 69
    three bean chilli *97*, 98–9
    tomato chopped salad 99
    tomato sambal 171
    vegetable tagine with olives, eggplant and chickpeas 149, *150*
trifle, tropical *227*, 228–9

vanilla
    chocolate honeycomb semifreddo 218
    Christmas panna cotta with edible gold leaf 224–5, *226*
    tropical trifle *227*, 228–9

    vanilla mascarpone 229
    vanilla mascarpone berry tart 236
    vanilla panna cotta with espresso syrup and almonds *216*, 217
    vanilla-scented baked rice pudding with rhubarb and strawberry compote *220*, 221
veal *see* beef and veal
vegetable spaghetti 119
vegetables, mixed
    roast vegetable and chicken pie 124–5
    roast vegetable lasagne 90–1
    roast vegetable, red wine and beef cheek pie 188–9
    sesame pickled vegetables with teriyaki beef 26
    vegetable and beef stew 118
    vegetable, pearl barley and Italian sausage soup *202*, 203
    vegetable tagine with olives, eggplant and chickpeas 149, *150*
vegetti 119
vermicelli, in lion's head meatballs *122*, 123

walnut, blackberry and apple crumble 249
water chestnuts
    lion's head meatballs *122*, 123
    sang choi bau of pork and shiitake mushrooms *136*, 137
Wimmera grain salad *92*, 93
wine
    beef cheeks in red wine 193
    beef stifado 204
    bucatini all'Amatriciana 106
    coq au vin 205
    cottage pie *102*, 103
    daube of beef *200*, 201
    dinner ladies lasagne 110–11, *112*
    osso buco *190*, 191
    paleo lasagne *180*, 181
    penne with Italian sausage sauce *210*, 211
    pork chops with fennel, French shallots and raisins *198*, 199
    red wine, beef cheek and roast vegetable pie 188–9
    Spanish meatballs with chorizo and chickpeas *206*, 207
    spiced lamb shanks *208*, 209

yoghurt
    butter chicken 144
    chicken strips 87
    Indian cottage pie 166
    roghan josh 148
    yoghurt and garlic sauce 149
    yoghurt-cucumber sauce 45

zucchetti 119
zucchinis
    paleo lasagne *180*, 181
    sausage rolls with sneaky veg *113*, 114–15
    vegetable tagine with olives, eggplant and chickpeas 149, *150*

Acknowledgements

Our heartfelt thanks to our lovely publisher, Jane Morrow, who listened to us throughout the editorial process but then gently dissuaded us from our wackier ideas. You made the whole thing a pleasure and we've ended up with a much better book because of you. And to Sue Hines, Murdoch's publishing director, who first talked to us about writing this book, thank you.

We were thrilled to be in the capable, stylish hands of photographer Ben Dearnley and stylist, Vanessa Austin, who did a miraculous job in transforming our food into beautiful images. Really great coffee too, Ben.

Thanks also to Susie Ashworth, our editor, for her sensitivity in cutting back our occasional verbosity and for saving us from any embarrassing mistakes. And to design manager Megan Pigott, editorial managers Barbara McClenahan and Katie Bosher, who looked after everything so professionally and so well. Aileen Lord and Dan Peterson, thank you so much for your fabulous work on the design of (respectively) the book and its cover – we love them both.

We're so happy to have a chance to publicly thank Shen Wei, our amazing kitchen manager and Josh Guild, our no less wonderful head chef, both of whom kept things afloat when we were away testing recipes and shooting photographs and both of whom we rely on and value enormously. And our other key people who have been part of the Dinner Ladies family for so long and who always go above and beyond their briefs: Denise, Rosti, Wilson and Raj – you are all stars. We can't name everyone else who contributes so much at the Dinner Ladies but we know who you are and appreciate all your hard work.

We mustn't forget to thank our dear friends and family who helped us with recipe-testing: Judy Lance, Fiona Waller, Sarah Lance, Jenny Moulder, Joss Best, Ness Koltai, Sam Wong and Lisa Smyth. Lovely work, ladies.

Probably our final thanks has to go to our long-suffering children – Finn, Willow, Moby and Iggy (Katherine's) and Fred, Rosy and Joe (Sophie's) – and to our husbands, Perry and Tom. For the past eight years they have chomped (mostly without complaint) through various experiments (both successful and less so), excess kitchen stock and a lot of strange, unlabelled packets of mystery meat in sauce. We know that you'd sometimes prefer just to eat a grilled chop – maybe that day will come now that the book is finished. We love you.

Published in 2016 by Murdoch Books, an imprint of Allen & Unwin

Murdoch Books Australia
83 Alexander Street
Crows Nest NSW 2065
Phone: +61 (0) 2 8425 0100
Fax: +61 (0) 2 9906 2218
murdochbooks.com.au
info@murdochbooks.com.au

Murdoch Books UK
Ormond House
26–27 Boswell Street
London WC1N 3JZ
Phone: +44 (0) 20 8785 5995
murdochbooks.co.uk
info@murdochbooks.co.uk

For Corporate Orders & Custom Publishing, contact our Business Development Team at
salesenquiries@murdochbooks.com.au.

Publisher: Jane Morrow
Editorial Managers: Barbara McClenahan and Katie Bosher
Design Manager: Megan Pigott
Project Editor: Susie Ashworth
Cover Designer: Dan Peterson, Northwood Green
Internal Designer: Aileen Lord
Photographer: Ben Dearnley
Stylist: Vanessa Austin
Production Manager: Alexandra Gonzalez

A cataloguing-in-publication entry is available from the catalogue of the National Library of Australia
at nla.gov.au.

ISBN 978 1 74336 585 4 Australia
ISBN 978 1 74336 605 9 UK

A catalogue record for this book is available from the British Library.

Colour reproduction by Splitting Image Colour Studio Pty Ltd, Clayton, Victoria

Printed by 1010 Printing International Limited, China

· ·

IMPORTANT: Those who might be at risk from the effects of salmonella poisoning (the elderly, pregnant
women, young children and those suffering from immune deficiency diseases) should consult their
doctor with any concerns about eating raw eggs.

OVEN GUIDE: You may find cooking times vary depending on the oven you are using. For fan-forced
ovens, as a general rule, set the oven temperature to 20°C (35°F) lower than indicated in the recipe.

MEASURES GUIDE: We have used 20 ml (4 teaspoon) tablespoon measures. If you are using a 15 ml
(3 teaspoon) tablespoon add an extra teaspoon of the ingredient for each tablespoon specified.